Children Reading Picturebooks

Children Reading Pictures has made a huge impact on teachers, scholars and students all over the world. The original edition of this book described the fascinating range of children's responses to contemporary picturebooks, which proved that they are sophisticated readers of visual texts and are able to make sense of complex images on literal, visual and metaphorical levels. Through this research, the authors found that children are able to understand different viewpoints, analyse moods, messages and emotions, and articulate personal responses to picturebooks – even when they struggle with the written word.

The study of picturebooks and children's responses to them has increased dramatically in the 12 years since the first edition was published. Fully revised with a review of the most recent theories and critical work related to picturebooks and meaning-making, this new edition demonstrates how vital visual literacy is to children's understanding and development. The second edition:

- Includes three new case studies that address social issues, special needs and metafiction
- Summarises key finding from research with culturally diverse children
- Draws upon new research on response to digital picturebooks
- Provides guidelines for those contemplating research on response to picturebooks

This book is essential reading for undergraduate and postgraduate students of children's literature as well as providing important reading for Primary and Early Years teachers, literacy co-ordinators and all those interested in picturebooks.

Evelyn Arizpe is Senior Lecturer at the School of Education, University of Glasgow, UK.

Morag Styles is Emeritus Professor and Fellow of Homerton College, Cambridge. She recently retired from the University of Cambridge, Faculty of Education, UK.

Children Reading Picturebooks

Interpreting visual texts

Second edition

Evelyn Arizpe and
Morag Styles with a new
chapter by Margaret Mackey

With contributions from
Helen Bromley, Kathy Coulthard
and Kate Noble

Routledge
Taylor & Francis Group

LONDON AND NEW YORK

This edition published 2016
by Routledge
2 Park Square, Milton Park, Abingdon, Oxon OX14 4RN

and by Routledge
711 Third Avenue, New York, NY 10017

Routledge is an imprint of the Taylor & Francis Group, an informa business

First edition published 2002 by Routledge

British Library Cataloguing-in-Publication Data
A catalogue record for this book is available from the British Library

Library of Congress Cataloging in Publication Data
Arizpe, Evelyn, 1965-
Children reading picturebooks : interpreting visual texts / Evelyn Arizpe and Morag Styles. — Second edition.
pages cm
Includes bibliographical references and index.
1. Visual learning. 2. Pictures in education. 3. Children—Books and reading. I. Styles, Morag. II. Title.
LB1067.5.A75 2016
371.33'5—dc23
2015021310

ISBN: 978-1-138-01407-7 (hbk)
ISBN: 978-1-138-01408-4 (pbk)
ISBN: 978-1-315-68391-1 (ebk)

Typeset in Sabon
by Swales & Willis Ltd, Exeter, Devon, UK
Printed and bound by CPI Group (UK) Ltd, Croydon, CR0 4YY

This book is dedicated to our dear friend and colleague, Helen Bromley, who was part of the research team and wrote Chapter 5. Helen was an inspirational teacher and researcher who devoted her professional life to children's literacy and literature. She touched the lives of all who knew her.

Contents

viii   Contents

PART II
Theoretical perspectives and new research on
children responding to picturebooks

121

Illustrations

Plate section

Figures

Table

Contributors

Evelyn Arizpe is a Senior Lecturer at the School of Education, University of Glasgow, where she coordinates the MEd Programme in Children's Literature and Literacies. She has taught and published widely in the areas of literacy and children's literature and presented conference papers and keynote addresses at major international conferences. Evelyn has worked on a number of studies related to picturebooks and response, involving both children and adolescents; the most recent was the international research project *Visual Journeys through Wordless Narratives* (Arizpe, E., Colomer, T. and Martínez-Roldán, C. Bloomsbury Academic, 2014) on the responses of immigrant children to Shaun Tan's wordless narrative, *The Arrival*. Her research team won the 2013 BERA Award for University/School research collaboration for the Esmée Fairbairn Foundation funded project *Journeys from Images to Words*. She has recently co-edited, with Vivienne Smith, *Children as Readers in Children's Literature* (Routledge, 2015).

Helen Bromley taught in primary schools for many years, latterly as Deputy Headteacher, before becoming an advisory teacher, then tutor for the Centre for Language in Primary Education. She went on to work as a popular freelance consultant, running courses in literacy, oracy and media texts throughout the UK. Her publications include *Book Based Reading Games* (2001) and chapters in *Talking Pictures* (Watson and Styles 1997), *Small Screens* (Buckingham 2002) and *Pikachu's Global Adventure: Making Sense of the Rise and Fall of Pokemon* (Tobin 2002). She wrote for journals such as *Reading* and *The Cambridge Journal of Education*. This book is dedicated to Helen who died on 5 November 2013. She is greatly missed.

Kathy Coulthard was an advisor for ethnic minority achievement in the London borough of Enfield, having previously been a primary teacher and advisor for English and Assessment. Kathy spent several years as Senior School Development Officer in Westminster prior to retirement. She is author of *Scaffolding Learning in the Multilingual Classroom* (1998) and has contributed to journals such as *English in Education* and *Language Matters*. She was a much respected and popular speaker on teaching and learning in multilingual classrooms and other literacy matters.

Kate Noble (formerly Rabey) took a first class degree from Cambridge in Art and Early Years Education in 1998, then spent three years as a classroom teacher. She was one of the organisers of the exhibition, Picture This!: Picturebook Art

at the Millennium at the Fitzwilliam Museum (2000) and co-author of the cata-
logue which accompanied it. She gained an excellent Ph.D. with her thesis, *Picture
Thinking: The Development of Visual Literacy in Young Children*. Kate has
contributed chapters to *Talking Beyond the Page: Reading and Responding to
Picturebooks* (Evans, 2009), *The Cambridge Guide to Children's Books in English*
(Watson, 2002) and *Teaching Through Texts* (Anderson and Styles, 2001). She
has worked as a researcher for Young Cultural Creators Project, based at the
Tate Gallery, London and has led learning programme evaluation studies across
the University of Cambridge Museums. Kate now works as Education Officer at
the Fitzwilliam Museum, Cambridge where she oversees the schools programme
which works with over 16000 school children every year. She leads a training
programme for teachers and trainees which encourages creative approaches to
teaching and learning from objects and pictures.

Margaret Mackey is Professor Emerita of the School of Library and Information
Studies at the University of Alberta in Edmonton, Canada. She publishes widely
on the subject of literacies both old and new, and has a book forthcoming
on her own childhood literacies in print and all the other media of the 1950s
(working title: *Auto-bibliography*, to be published by the University of Alberta
Press in 2016).

Morag Styles retired in 2014 as Professor of Children's Poetry at the Faculty of
Education, Cambridge, and is an Emeritus Fellow of Homerton College. She is
the author of numerous books and articles including, *From the Garden to the
Street: 300 Years of Poetry for Children* (1998); co-author (with Evelyn Arizpe)
of *Reading Lessons from the Eighteenth Century: Mothers, Children and Texts*
(2006); co-editor of *Poetry and Childhood* (2009); co-author (Martin Salisbury
was lead author) of *Children's Picturebooks: The Art of Visual Storytelling* (2012)
which won UKLA best academic book of the year, 2013; and *Teaching Caribbean
Poetry* (2013). She curated (with Michael Rosen) an exhibition on the history of
children's poetry for the British Library in 2009. She is director of the Caribbean
Poetry Project, a collaboration with The University of the West Indies.

Preface

The first edition of this book described the fascinating results of a two-year study of children's responses to contemporary picturebooks carried out by Evelyn Arizpe and Morag Styles around the millennium with a team of gifted researchers, each of whom contributed a chapter. Children of primary school age, from a range of backgrounds, read and discussed picturebooks by award-winning artists Anthony Browne and Satoshi Kitamura, and then made their own drawings in response to the books. The authors found that many children were sophisticated readers of visual texts, able to understand different viewpoints, analyse moods, messages and emotions, and articulate personal responses to picturebooks – even when they struggled with the written word. With colour as well as black and white illustrations, the book demonstrated how important visual literacy was to children's understanding and development.

The reactions of teachers, scholars and students from many parts of the world have been extremely positive, so fifteen years on from their original study, the authors decided that a second edition was worthwhile. As well as providing new research on children's responses to picturebooks, the authors have updated theory and practice in the field since 2003 and invited their esteemed colleague and friend, Margaret Mackey, to contribute a chapter about digital picturebooks.

Acknowledgements

The authors wish to thank Polly Dunbar and Walker Books for generously allowing us to reproduce a number of pages from *Penguin,* including those with Danny Wilkinson's drawn and written responses to the book. The authors are also grateful to the following for permission to reproduce material: illustrations from *Zoo* by Anthony Browne, published by Jonathan Cape (Artwork © Anthony Browne), reproduced by permission of The Random House Group Ltd; illustrations and text from *Lily Takes a Walk* by Satoshi Kitamura, reprinted by permission of Catnip Publishing; illustrations from *The Tunnel,* copyright © 1989 Anthony Browne, reproduced by permission of Walker Books Ltd; illustrations from *Penguin,* copyright © 2007 Polly Dunbar, reproduced by permission of Walker Books Ltd, London SE11 5HJ www. walker.co.uk; illustrations from *The Three Pigs* by David Wiesner, copyright © 2001 by David Wiesner, reprinted by permission of Clarion Books, an imprint of Houghton Mifflin Harcourt Publishing Company (for all of them, all rights reserved).

We would like to thank our editors, Rebecca Hogg, at Routledge, and especially Alison Foyle for encouraging us to produce this new edition. Finally, many thanks to Emma McGilp who, among other things, made sure that all the references are correct!

Introduction

Reasons for a second edition of
Children Reading Pictures

This book is about how children respond to and interpret picturebooks rather than a study of the picturebook itself, though naturally scholarly work on the subject has informed our research. In our original study, we felt the need to introduce readers to some of the background to picturebooks as a genre and gave a brief account of the most relevant theories that had contributed to our understanding of these texts as aesthetic objects. However, there has been so much scholarship in this field before and since 2003 that we are assuming our readers do not need such a digest. [1]

The first edition of *Children Reading Pictures* began as follows: 'There have been surprisingly few systematic attempts to ask children about their reading of pictorial text . . . ', which was true at the time of writing but is no longer the case. One of the points we were making was that although there had been plenty of critical literature on picturebooks, few scholars had shown much interest in the main audience for this genre and what they had to say about these texts. Despite the fact that we were living in a highly complex visual world, with children increasingly surrounded by images, few educators had considered the implications for communication and learning. In fact, Kress and van Leeuwen (1996) bemoan 'the staggering inability on all our parts to talk and think in any way seriously about what is actually communicated by means of images and visual design' (p. 16).

A lot has changed since 2003 and we are delighted to report that interest in what happens when children interact with visual texts has taken off in exciting ways with new research, edited volumes and doctoral theses[2] devoted to the subject, although our study still remains the largest to date. We alert readers to some of the best recent research in English in Chapters 9, 10, 11 in Part 2, which contains most of our new material. Chapter 9 revises the theoretical chapter in the first edition where we considered what visual literacy can offer our understanding of picturebook reading. In this new version, we look at visual literacy again but we have fine-tuned our focus in order to examine theories, frameworks and approaches that are more closely linked to responses to picturebooks. Chapter 10 provides an overview of the many studies on response and we highlight those which we believe have the most potential to illuminate meaning-making from picturebooks. Chapter 11 provides three new mini case studies of children aged from 5 to 9 responding to picturebooks by Maurice Sendak, Polly Dunbar and David Wiesner, while Chapter 12 considers the use of picturebook apps. In Chapter 13, we reflect on findings emerging from this field overall, including implications for pedagogy, and provide some guidelines for doing research in this area. Chapters 1–8 comprise Part 1, which is devoted to the outcomes of our original study, and in the opening chapter we provide a slightly updated methodology that guided our approach. We have also added fuller Appendices and Bibliography.

Limitations of our original research

There are many things we still like about our original research, including the fact that we offered a template for future scholars and teachers to use, adapt and improve. We are still proud of the discerning responses offered by the children in our study, including their drawings, which provided us with hitherto unknown insights into what young readers were thinking. We were pleased with the positive international response our book received and its translation into other languages. However, with hindsight we also noted some flaws. Some of the most glaring deficiencies were that: we used a limited number of books, including two by the same author, instead of widening our range of illustrators; we were casual about materials used for the drawings, which varied from group to group; we probably asked too many ambitious questions in interviews.

However, one significant critic, Perry Nodelman (2010), has also taken us to task for something we had not thought a weakness of our study (and of other studies in the field) – namely making inferences about how children in general respond to picturebooks given that 'individuals all respond differently to texts'. While we acknowledge his point about the uniqueness of individual response to literature and that suggestions about how more than one individual child responds to a picturebook need to be tentative, there is no reason why we cannot note trends and commonalities in these responses just as other empirical studies in the humanities do.

Our main thrust, which Nodelman recognised, was to challenge commonly held views about the limitations of what children can comprehend at a particular age, but he suggested that this was because we were what he calls 'optimistic' about the creative capacities of children. By believing it we make it so through our choices, our actions, and our encouraging responses to the children. Indeed, we suggested as much in the six-page postscript to our original book and, in any case, for any shortcomings in our approach it is surely better that our understanding of picturebooks includes the voices and drawings of its prime audience.

Why a second edition?

Writing a second edition of a book is almost as hard work as producing the original since you have to write all the new material while honing and improving the prototype as well as deliberating what should be cut. So why did we think it was necessary to revisit our study? First of all, both authors have probably enjoyed more positive feedback from this volume than any of their other work, and this interest has come from many parts of the world. We felt that although our original research was still relevant, we now had access to more information which we would like to share. Second, we have already mentioned the relatively large number of research studies and publications produced in this field since 2003 and it seemed a worthwhile activity to draw readers' attention to their range and variety. Some scholars have taken off in lively new directions and opened up the field in original ways. Third, the number of exceptional picturebooks published in the last ten years has been quite extraordinary and, combined with an awareness of the quality and variety of illustration outside the UK and USA, made us even more enthusiastic about the possibilities that they offer for understanding how children make meaning from picturebooks. Finally, the authors have continued working in this field, accompanied by more than a decade's worth of students, and we simply now have at our disposal so much more evidence of how children interpret picturebooks. Although we can only share a small sample of this evidence, we hope there is enough to excite teachers, scholars and students to probe ever more deeply into what happens when a child engages with a worthwhile picturebook.

When we began doing our research for what became *Children Reading Pictures* in 1999, we didn't dream of picturebook apps and all the many varieties of digital visual texts available now. Clearly these interactive forms have a permanent place in the range of ways children will encounter visual texts in the future – and the possibilities seem limitless. Indeed, all the jokes about adults faced with a new piece of technology needing to consult their children to make them work are ever more true. Neither of the authors felt we had the expertise to write knowledgeably about children's responses to the digital variety of picturebooks so we recruited Margaret Mackey, a foremost scholar in this emerging field. The authors are extremely grateful for her generosity in providing such excellent material for this book. As you will read in Chapter 12, she appraises some of the best and worst of picturebook apps and provides us with valuable evidence of how even very young children quickly learn to manipulate and enjoy these devices.

Even so, the authors and Margaret Mackey all agree that the traditional picture-book is here to stay. It is the perfect size for an adult and child to read together, offering 'the drama of the turning page' (Bader 1976: 1). It is easy to handle and look backwards as well as forwards, offering the aesthetic delight of beautiful and arresting illustrations printed on good quality paper. And just as animation has taken its place alongside paper books (indeed it is often through Disney that classic children's literature is first encountered), picturebook apps may well become the primary exposure to literature of early childhood. However, as Lane Smith amusingly highlights in *It's a Book* (2011), without the internet, batteries or electricity, picturebooks offer something no other medium can quite match. We hope this book provides sound evidence for that statement.

Notes

1 For anyone reading this book without being familiar with critical literature on picturebooks, may we recommend the following: Doonan (1992), Nodelman (1988), Lewis (2001), Nikolajeva and Scott (2001), Salisbury (2007), Salisbury and Styles (2012), Sipe and Pantaleo (2008), Styles and Bearne (2003), Arizpe, Farrell and McAdam (2013), Kümmerling-Meibauer (2014), Painter, Martin and Unsworth (2013); for those with a more educational interest, please see also Sipe (2008), Arizpe (2009), Graham (1990), Meek (1988), Watson and Styles (1996).

2 As doctoral theses mostly remain unpublished, we provide a list in the Appendices of those we have read and valued which can be requested through university libraries.

Part 1

The original empirical research on children responding to picturebooks

Chapter 1

Research design, methodology and underpinning theory

> To read the artist's picture is to mobilise our memories and our experience of the visible world and to test his image through tentative projections. . . . It is not the 'innocent eye', however, that can achieve this match but only the inquiring mind that knows how to probe the ambiguities of vision.
>
> (Gombrich 1962: 264)

The great art critic, Ernst Gombrich, draws our attention to the 'inquiring mind' that is required to understand and analyse the visual world. This book shows that even very young children have inquiring minds and that picturebooks are the vehicles that can 'probe the ambiguities of vision'.

The aims of the original study

The principal aim of our original research was to investigate how multimodal texts were interpreted by children, to explore the potential of visual literacy and to find out more about the skills children needed to deal with visual texts. Some of the questions we set ourselves had not been asked before of readers aged 4–11. When confronted with complex picturebooks, how did children make sense of narrative? What were the specific skills that young readers brought to interpreting visual texts? How did they perceive the relationship between word and image? How could they best articulate their response? Did the reading background of the children affect their viewing? What part did visual texts such as films and other media play in their ability to analyse pictures? What did children's own drawings reveal about their perception of a picturebook? What did complex picturebooks teach them about looking? How did talking about a book in depth, with their peers and with adults, affect their responses? What was the relationship between thinking and seeing?

Research design

The research design was based on the conclusions of a pilot study during which our research instruments were refined. The basic structure was as follows: we worked in seven primary schools serving varied catchment areas, interviewing two boys and two girls per class from three different classes per school, one of which was early years (4–6), one lower primary (7–9) and one upper primary (9–11). This meant we worked closely with twelve children of varying ages in each school, usually requiring three whole-day visits as well as preliminary conferences with teachers. We also identified two further children from each age group in case of illness; these children were not interviewed but they were invited to take part in semi-structured group interviews. We revisited one-third of the sample several months after the initial interviews. We used three picturebooks overall but only one with any given group of children.

The picturebooks

We spent some time trialling a range of picturebooks by contemporary artists to find examples of multi-layered texts which would appeal equally to children aged 4–11; this proved no easy task. However multilayered and inviting the picturebook, so many were discarded as they simply would not straddle the wide age group. In the end we settled on *Zoo* and *The Tunnel* by Anthony Browne and *Lily Takes a Walk* by Satoshi Kitamura, all highly rated examples of picturebook art with appeal to both younger and older children according to our pilot study and ideal for in-depth discussion. Each picturebook was to be used in at least two schools to allow for comparison: *The Tunnel* was read in three of the seven schools; *Lily* and *Zoo* were each read in two schools. Both artists were interviewed at length and were supportive of the project. [1]

The schools

Seven primary schools participated in the research, ranging from multi-ethnic and economically deprived settings in north London to suburban schools in Essex. The schools were chosen to include those with differing intakes in terms of social class, though we did not systematically control for these variables, confining ourselves to collecting data on the proportion of pupils having free school meals.

All of the schools were to some extent multi-ethnic and multilingual, with the exception of School D in the south-east of England, where the pupils were predominantly white,

Table 1.1 Schools' socio-economic information

School	Population	Socio-economic information	Free school meals (%)
A	363	City council estate, mainly working class	22
B	466	Suburban, mixed housing, working/middle class	7
C	400	City, mixed housing, working/middle class	12
D	300	Suburban, middle class	9
E	518	Outer London borough, working class (32% ethnic minority pupils)	33
F	550	Outer London borough, working class (70% ethnic minority pupils)	30
G	898	Outer London borough, mixed housing (40% ethnic minority pupils)	52

monolingual speakers of English. This was in contrast to the London schools, where a whole spread of ethnic groups could be found, including a large percentage of refugees from the African and Asian subcontinents. Of the three schools in Cambridge, around 20 per cent of the pupils spoke more than one language.

The children

The interview sample was constructed in order to produce equal representation of boys and girls and to include children from diverse class and ethnic backgrounds. In addition, the class teacher's estimate of the reading ability of each child was obtained, providing a useful point of comparison when assessing children's ability to read pictures. Researchers had no knowledge of these reading abilities until *after* the interviews took place, though we had asked teachers to select two experienced and two relatively inexperienced readers. In the event, teachers took a fair bit of licence with our requests, including children who were fairly average readers and often selecting 'interesting' children whom they thought the experience would be good for. Overall, we had a sample of children from 4 to 11 years old with a wide range of abilities responding to the same questions based on the picturebook used in their school.

Approximately 35 per cent of the interviewed children were bilingual with varying linguistic backgrounds, from two pupils who had recently arrived in the UK with little knowledge of English to third-generation bilinguals.[2] Where necessary, interviews were conducted with a translator. A few children had slight learning difficulties associated with moderate dyslexia, autism and hyperactivity, but these were not found to interfere with their responses. Despite some shyness at the beginning of the interviews, and once they were assured this was not a test, most children were eager to participate, to answer the interviewer's questions and to draw, and by the time of the group discussion were almost always completely involved in the picturebook. When roughly one-third of the sample were re-interviewed a few months later, they remembered the initial interviews and could recall many details of the books even though most had not seen them for a few months. We have changed the names of all the children in the study, the pseudonyms taking account of ethnicity.

The questionnaire

In order to provide a context against which to set our results, we used a short questionnaire to find out about the reading habits of the pupils in the seven schools that participated in the study.[3] It invited information on their favourite picturebooks, television programmes, videos and computer games. A total of 486 children from Reception to Year 6 (ages 4 to 11) answered the questionnaire (see Appendix 1), which provided us with a glimpse of the reading backgrounds of pupils as well as of their interests by age and gender. We did not notice any significant difference in response by children who knew the authors' work we were using before the exercise began and those who didn't. What made a huge difference to the level of response was children's previous exposure to a wide range of texts. Having said that, it was also exciting to note the number of children without much apparent experience of books who showed great facility in reading pictorial texts.

The pupils' reading backgrounds

The data from the questionnaire revealed fewer differences between schools in terms of children's reading habits and preferences than we had expected to find. However, it was clear that the pupils in the three London schools (Schools E, F and G) had less exposure to books (at least in English) than pupils in the other schools. The economically disadvantaged catchment area of these schools was probably a reason for this, as well as the fact that English was not the first language in many of their homes. They also had less access to videos and computer games, but, like their counterparts in the other schools, their preference for these was far greater than for books.

The crucial role of the school in facilitating access to books at Key Stage 1 (ages 4–7) became evident through the questionnaires. Results revealed that approximately 60 per cent of pupils from schools F, G and A read mostly in school, while nearly 90 per cent of those in schools B and D (more 'middle-class' schools) read mostly at home. These figures changed at Key Stage 2 (ages 7–11), with students in all schools reading mainly at home. At this stage there was a slight increase in the preference for books, although videos and computer games were still more popular, and the reading of magazines and comics increased noticeably.

All told, the list of picturebooks mentioned by children was quite limited and 7 seems to be the peak age for reading them, with more girls than boys mentioning this genre. It was also when other reading, from non-fiction to magazines and comics, began to increase, presumably because children became more independent readers. The data from the questionnaire suggested that most of the children's contact with images had occurred through media texts rather than through books.

Overall, in 2003, the list for other types of texts far outweighed that for picturebooks. It would be interesting to see what differences would emerge if we applied a similar questionnaire in 2015.

The interviews

In-depth semi-structured interviews were conducted with 84 children, 21 of whom were followed up in a second interview several months later. An interview schedule was closely followed, normally 45 minutes long, with about ten questions common to all, and a further ten which were book specific (these questions can be found in the Appendices). We began by asking about the appeal of the cover and how it showed what the picturebook might be about (later in the interviews we asked if, in retrospect, the covers were right for the books). We asked children to tell us about each page or double spread that we had selected in turn, using both specific and open-ended questions. We invited them to show us their favourite pictures, to tell us how they read pictures and to talk about the relationship between words and pictures. We questioned them about the actions, expressions and feelings of the characters; the intratextual and intertextual elements; what the artist needed to know in order to draw, and the ways in which he/she used colour, body language and perspective, etc. In addition, we took research notes that included reference to children's body language (pointing, gazing, tone of voice, use of hand, facial expressions) while reading the books. All the sessions were taped and transcribed.

Group discussions

After the individual interviews, the children participated in a group discussion with other members of their class who had been interviewed, plus two extra children who had been identified by the teacher in case of the absence of the interviewees. In total, 126 pupils were involved in these discussions, which lasted up to an hour and which were normally conducted later in the same day. During these discussions, the researchers were free to review interesting issues that had come up in the interviews, open up new areas for debate, including those chosen by children, and give those who had not been interviewed a chance to grapple with the book.

Revisiting

Preliminary findings indicated that repeated readings of a picturebook could be an important element in pupils constructing meaning, so we were interested to find out whether significant changes in interpretation had occurred some time after the initial research. Accordingly, we decided to carry out follow-up interviews three to six months after initial interviews with roughly one fifth of our original sample, i.e. one child from each class. The children were chosen to represent a range of responses to the first interviews – from children who had been outstandingly articulate or passionate about the book the first time round, to those who had barely been willing to participate, from children with specific learning difficulties to those who were described by their teachers as more or less average readers. In the revisiting, the emphasis of the questions changed from detailed examination of individual pages to a consideration of the book as a whole.

Procedures

Five different researchers carried out the interviews in schools. Their role was to follow the interview schedules as closely as possible, while allowing for flexibility in following children's leads and pursuing further questioning when they thought it appropriate to do so. Analysis of the transcripts showed that each researcher had their own interviewing style, which influenced the results in intriguing ways. In some cases, particularly when working with young or bilingual children, the pupil's willingness and ability to talk determined the way in which the interview was conducted. Each of the researchers used their own criteria in deciding which questions or pictures seemed to elicit the most interesting responses from the interviewees and were free to choose when and where to probe further.

Children drawing in response to picturebooks

It was purely by chance that children drawing in response to picturebooks became such a major part of our study. We had noticed in our previous forays with children younger than 7 that their powerful physical, emotional and social responses to picturebooks, which we had closely observed over some years, were not always borne out in what the children had to say about the books when asked direct questions. In other words, and as plenty of research has shown, young children cannot always articulate their ideas and feelings – but they *can* often show their meaning-making through their artistic creations. We wanted to get as close as we could to understanding what the younger children in our study were thinking, so we decided to ask all the participants to draw in response to the book we had examined. The purpose of the drawing was to access some of the knowledge that may not have been verbally articulated during the interviews.[4] The researchers provided materials when necessary and the pupils were allowed time to draw, either while others were being interviewed, or later in the day. During the follow-up interviews, the children were asked to do a second drawing. The drawings are analysed by Kate Noble (previously Rabey) in Chapter 8.

Data analysis

The amount of data generated from the interviews and discussions was considerable and required many careful readings.[5] The transcripts from the initial and the follow-up interviews were analysed qualitatively, partially employing a grounded theory approach (Glaser and Strauss 1967; Strauss 1987), but also using codes derived from previous studies on response to text (for example Thomson 1987). We also took into account the data analysis carried out by two of the most systematic studies on response to picturebooks to date – Kiefer (1993) and Madura (1998). Kiefer developed categories and subcategories of response according to four of Halliday's functions of language: informative, heuristic, imaginative and personal. Madura took Kiefer's framework into account but grouped responses to the particular books she used into three main categories: descriptive, interpretive and the identification of thematic trends.[6]

Although we found these categories useful, both as analytical tools and as a means of corroborating our findings, *the most useful codes were developed from our own data which were successively modified through further analysis.* In order to facilitate this analysis, oral response was divided into two groups – although it was clear that these groups were closely linked. We identified one group as 'categories of perception' because the responses were based on codes derived from what the children took from the picturebook, such as, for example, the noticing of significant details, intra- and inter-textual references or the relationship between the text and the image. Responses in the second group, 'levels of interpretation', corresponded to the way in which the children made sense of these picturebook codes, for example, giving the interviewer literal, implausible or plausible explanations, interrogating or evaluating the text and/or images. This initial categorisation served as a framework for organising the data. Once this was achieved, researchers took the analysis in different directions, for example, looking more closely at response to visual features, ethical and moral issues, the interaction between written text and image (depending on the picturebook in question) or concentrating on the linguistic and cultural context of readers. The results of these diverse analytical approaches are discussed in Chapters 2–8. What follows are some of the theories and frameworks that guided us in our original study and still inform our work today.

Frameworks and theories guiding our original research

Lev Vygotsky introduced the seminal idea that language plays an indispensable role in mediating internal thought processes such as the ability to reason and to reflect and that social interaction through language is crucial for developing knowledge and thinking. Building on Vygotsky's insights, Jerome Bruner argued that the development of knowledge and the formation of concepts can be accelerated by 'scaffolding', particularly through the use of mediated language, as the more experienced inducts the less experienced learner into understanding. This is where Vygotsky's influential concept of the 'zone of proximal development' (1978: 86) comes into play. Both ZPD and scaffolding are important in confirming and expanding a child's understanding of a text, particularly a visual one, given that reading usually happens together with an adult, friend or sibling. Sipe (2008a) notes how 'child-centred' scaffolding in the classroom, in which the teacher guides the pupil towards multiple interpretation rather than comprehension, can enable literary understanding, especially when looking at picturebooks. It is not surprising that one of the most significant results from reader response studies from the last fifteen years is the influential role a mediator can have in encouraging deeper and, eventually, more critical meaning-making.

In our study, the results of co-operatively achieved learning were evident particularly in the semi-structured discussion of a group of children rather than through individual interviews. However, we also discovered that some of the most profound thinking about picturebooks occurred in follow-up interviews some months after the original interviews. Questions were not only working as tools for inquiry, but also as the 'planks' and 'poles' of scaffolding which allowed children to move further into their zones of proximal development. Researchers became facilitators, especially in terms of providing a language through which the children could talk about pictures, modelling concepts, using prompts and leading with questions. More experienced peers (those who had had greater access to the culture which produced the picturebook) unconsciously helped their schoolmates in their understanding as they talked about what they saw and how they made sense of it. This led us to concur with the idea that communal expertise played a more crucial role than individual logical mental operations in determining how far children could make sense of visual texts. We also noted the central role of language in developing thought and that when younger children could not communicate verbally their growing understanding could sometimes be shown in their drawings.

One schema which provided an illuminating framework for considering how the children in our study responded to picturebooks was Clark's description of four phases for appreciating visual works of art (1960: 69). First, he talks about a work of art having an *impact* on a viewer who gets a general impression of the picture as a whole, including subject matter, colour, shape, composition, etc. If there is no impact, nothing will happen, so an engagement between the see-er and the seen is an essential starting point. If understanding is to follow, the next stage is *scrutiny* – careful looking. Clark describes this as the purely aesthetic stage of response where the critical faculties come into operation and reminds us of the importance of patience and persistence: 'Looking at pictures requires active participation, and, in the early stages, a certain amount of discipline.' As viewers look at the image, the third stage of *recollection* may follow, where they make connections with their own experience and ask questions of the painting. Clearly, this stage of the process involves thinking and leads on to the final stage, which is *renewal*. The original image is re-examined more deeply, and features previously overlooked come into focus, perhaps fitting into pre-existing knowledge. This could be described as looking, developing into *seeing*, through memory, imagination and thought.

It was rare for the picturebooks to fail to make an impact on the children in our study, but in the odd individual (in one case a hyperactive child with a short attention span), little or no engagement occurred between viewer and text and so the activity was fairly worthless. (As teachers, of course, we would be concerned about those children and would want to develop strategies to aid concentration and help them find ways to take pleasure in books.) But for the vast majority of children in our sample, the impact of an appealing and challenging text encouraged them to move into the second phase of scrutiny.

Now scrutiny is obviously crucial: if real understanding is to follow, the child has to look carefully in a sustained way for some time. Looking is not easy. Yet that serious, sustained looking is what most of the children aged 4 to 11 willingly agreed to do with our chosen picturebooks. As you look, you have to think or, as Clark puts it, 'recollect'. This is also hard work, as the brain integrates the new knowledge with what we already know. But at the same time, other processes are likely to be going on which are more involuntary: memories of personal experience crowd in as the painting intersects with our lives in a text-to-life moment; ideas begin to bubble up and hints of deeper understandings begin to suggest themselves. This is the creative process at work which is a mixture of imagination, fantasy, recollection and wonder – the unconscious in collaboration with cognitive activity. This is the moment when a child says something insightful they didn't know they knew or had never thought about before. It's when, for example, Lara (10), suddenly realises the horror of captivity for animals after reading *Zoo*:

LARA: If you think about it, if you had to be put in a cage, that is where you would stay. You would stay there and I can't imagine living in that sort of conditions.
INTERVIEWER: Did you think of that before you read the book?
LARA: No, I just thought about it a moment ago.

Finally, renewal: over and over again we found the children going back to the books, looking at them almost with new eyes. In Clark's final phase of response, the viewer may be 'looking at his own everyday world in a way that was altered by looking at that picture' (Benson quoting Clark 1986: 138). And *over the course of several hours* the pupils in our sample made extraordinary progress in understanding. What couldn't they do if visual texts and art appreciation were given time and status and became a serious part of the curriculum?

Perkins, who was part of Gardner's Project Zero research team, provided us with illuminating observations about how looking at art engenders thinking and set us off on a fruitful line of inquiry. In *The Intelligent Eye: Learning to Think by Looking at Art*, Perkins shows how this works:

> looking at art has an instrumental value. It provides an excellent setting for the development of better thinking, for the cultivation of what might be called the art of intelligence . . . [and] a context especially well suited for cultivating thinking dispositions . . . as [works of art] demand thoughtful attention to discover what they have to show and say. Also, works of art connect to social, personal and other dimensions of life with strong affective overtures.

(1994: 3–4)

Perkins is interested in how exposure to works of art encourages children to think analytically. Rather than produce a model of aesthetic appreciation, he cites the characteristics offered to viewers by works of art and relates them to young learners. First, he talks about the *instant access* offered by a work of art which 'can be physically present as you think and talk, providing an anchor for attention over a prolonged period of exploration. . . . The image is here and now' (1994: 85). Instant access is followed by *personal engagement*: 'Works of art invite and welcome sustained involvement . . . by their very nature [they are] likely to stimulate one kind of spasm (sympathy, revulsion . . .) or another . . . thinking is a passionate enterprise [calling for] concern and commitment, spirit and persistence' (1994: 13). Many of the theorists in this chapter recognise the importance of personal engagement in looking at visual texts, but only Perkins alludes to the powerful reactions this can provoke, such as genuine passion in the eye of the beholder, something we observed in many of the children in our study.

Perkins goes on to talk about works of art addressing a range of symbol systems through *wide-spectrum cognition*, which generates the involvement of multiple sensory modalities (e.g. spatial, pictorial, verbal). Finally, Perkins argues that art is *multi-connected*, linking social issues, aesthetic concerns, trends of the times, personal convictions, different cultures, 'creating opportunities to bridge thinking dispositions across to diverse other contexts explored in tandem with the work of art' (1994: 85). He is particularly excited by 'the challenge of transfer' where learning in one context impacts on another. We noted this multiconnectedness in the responses of children from different cultural backgrounds and Coulthard's chapter (Chapter 6) highlights some of findings in relation to cultural transfer.

This 'model' is prefaced on Perkins' concept of *experiential intelligence*, 'the contribution of applied prior experience to intellectual functioning', and *reflective intelligence*, which refers to the knowledge, skills and attitudes that contribute to mental self-management.

> We can prompt our experiential intelligence, cajole it, aim it, redirect it, to arrive at more varied and deeper readings of the work before our eyes. . . . By cultivating awareness of our own thinking, asking ourselves good questions, guiding ourselves with strategies, we steer our experiential intelligence in fruitful directions.
>
> (1994: 82–85)

Perkins' two kinds of intelligence saw many echoes in our study, with the second, richer vein of thoughtful interpretation emerging after some time had elapsed from first looking at the visual text.

The most substantial developmental theory we found about the way people come to understand art is by Parsons (1987). He contends that children respond naturally from a young age to the aesthetic qualities of art. On the evidence of about ten years of somewhat eclectic research with a wide variety of adults and children, Parsons sets out stages of aesthetic response to art. The first stage he calls *favouritism* as 'an intuitive delight in most paintings, a strong attraction to colour, and a freewheeling associative response to subject matter. . . . Most young children understand paintings at this level' (1987: 22). This stage is characterised by simple responses such as liking the subject matter or the colour of the picture. The second stage is characterised by *beauty and realism*, where the viewer recognises other people's viewpoints as well as her own. At this stage, realism tends to be favoured above other styles of painting. The third stage Parsons describes as *expressive*, when the feelings provoked by the work of art begin to become more significant and the viewer becomes more interested in the artist's intentions. The fourth stage focuses on *medium, style and form*:

> The new insight here is that the significance of a painting is a social rather than an individual achievement. It exists within a tradition, which is composed by a number of people looking over time at a number of works and talking about them.
>
> (1987: 24)

In Parsons' final stage, *autonomy, judgement* and *dialogue* are the keystones: 'The result is an alert awareness of the character of one's own experience, a questioning of the influences upon it, a wondering whether one really sees what one thinks one sees' (1987: 25). This Parsons links with dialogue and reflection.

While we would agree with Parsons that most children's initial responses to art fall within categories 1 and 2, using his own criteria we can provide several examples of children fulfilling stages 3–5 in many regards. Accepting that all children reach level 1 as of right, let us take one of the key criteria in each stage and examine it in the light of our evidence.

Stage 2: realism

It is true that most children like realism in pictures. We had many examples of children making comments to that effect. One of the three picturebooks in our study was mainly realist in style (*The Tunnel*), while in *Zoo* Browne depicts the animals with almost photographic realism, contrasted with a mixture of realism and surrealism, as people turn into animals. However, the non-realistic aspects of *Zoo* were as appealing to the children as the realistic: while they loved the pictures of the animals, they were often as fascinated, by the strangely metamorphosing humans growing webbed feet, stripey bodies and tails. Kitamura's *Lily* does not use realism at all, drawing instead on a highly stylised method of painting, with many characteristics in common with the cartoon world into which most children have been saturated by exposure to television. None of the children seemed to find *Lily* less interesting or enjoyable because it deviated from realism. Our findings suggested that, although children do favour realism as a style of painting, they can find other styles of art equally absorbing and understandable. Many other best-selling picturebook authors, like John Burningham, David McKee, Eric Carle and Maurice Sendak, do not use realism in their work. It seems more likely that children favour styles of art that amuse, delight and challenge them and that the range of styles which they take pleasure in and understand is much wider than Parsons suggests. Of course, the fact that his study only included paintings by famous artists, rather than narrative texts geared to children, may make a significant difference.

Stage 3: expressiveness

Children from 4 to 11 showed strong emotional reactions to the picturebooks. *The Tunnel*, a tale of conflict and reconciliation between siblings in a part modern/part fairy tale setting, provoked fear, sympathy and joy in equal measure; empathy and revulsion were the strongest feelings expressed about *Zoo*, which unleashed a debate about captivity and freedom; whereas the children who read *Lily* were aware of the menace in the text, but could distance themselves from it through the humour and the contrasting viewpoints of the two central characters. In response to all three books, the children not only talked about their feelings or related the subject matter intelligently to their own experience, but often considered the artist's intentions most thoughtfully when invited to do so by the interviewer (see Chapters 2–8). Our evidence suggests, therefore, that many of the children in our study reached level 3 of Parsons' hierarchy in the interview and discussion situation. How much this was brought about because of the nature of our questions and how much the children would have spontaneously achieved this by themselves remains a question.

Stage 4: medium, style and form

In this category, Parsons is concerned with understanding the social and artistic context of a work of art and the sense of the artist working within a tradition. This is a sophisticated position which Parsons assumes only a minority of viewers will achieve. However, we should like to emphasise the number of times pupils made references to other books by the same artist, comparing and contrasting what they were doing in the book in question with his other work. For example, 4-year-old Amy is devoted to examining *Zoo* for the 'changes' she knows Browne makes in other books, including *Changes*. Before she was 3 years old, Evelyn's daughter, Isabel, on entering an exhibition of picturebook artists, shouted 'Lily' on seeing examples of Kitamura's work on the walls. These particular pictures were not taken from *Lily*, which she was familiar with: Isabel had simply recognised Kitamura's style of painting. Many of the children in our study were very interested in how the artists had painted the pictures, what medium they were working in and why they used a particular style, voicing their opinions with confidence ('He's a good artist because . . . '). We would suggest that many of the children in our study fulfilled significant elements of stage 4.

Stage 5: autonomy, judgement and dialogue

We want to emphasise the serious, careful way most children examined the texts in our study. The interviews gave children the opportunity to take their time to think about the books in the supportive context of a one-to-one conversation with an interviewer. The discussions gave them the chance to listen to what others had to say, to exchange views with their peers and generally to collaborate in their learning. In so doing, their judgement was being extended by the research situation.

Revisiting picturebooks

Several months after the initial interviews, we decided to revisit one-third of our original sample to see if there were any significant changes in the responses made by the children. Having selected a mixture of children, from those already making sophisticated analyses of image to those just beginning that journey, we set about asking questions which were more demanding than the first time round and which focused on the book as a whole and the artist's likely intentions. For example:

- What goes on in your head as you look at pictures?
- How do you think the artist decides what to write as words and what to draw as pictures?
- Tell me about the way Satoshi Kitamura draws lines.
- How do the endpapers of *The Tunnel* take you into the story?
- What is Anthony Browne trying to tell us about the differences between humans and animals in *Zoo*?

We also repeated a few of the original questions which the children had found challenging initially and asked for new drawings in response to the text.

Our first impression was that although the children returned to the books eagerly enough and remembered a great deal about their earlier encounters with them, there was little evidence of any major new thinking. However, after we scrutinised the transcripts we became aware of small, subtle developments. Amy (now 5), for example, pounced on *Zoo*, declaring: 'I just noticed a funny difference I never noticed before . . . the colour helps you to find the differences between the animals and the humans' (Amy had meticulously searched for what she called 'changes' in Browne's work the first time round). Her statement about the mother was more clear cut than before: 'Mum is sad and she thinks the animals should be going free.' She also told us that, 'I imagine the pictures. I see them with my brain', while Yu (4) concluded that, 'I think of pictures when I go somewhere else.'

Erin's (7) thoughtful interpretation on the first visit was again evident on re-interview. Her summing-up of *Zoo* as a whole showed her usual insight: 'Humans change into animals to learn how it feels; animals look a bit like humans so they know what it's like to be free.' She liked Browne's work because 'it makes you keep thinking about things'. Perhaps most noteworthy was Erin's different style of drawing. Her first picture is spontaneous, attractive and expressive, full of the experimentation she enjoyed in Browne's work; five months later she seems to have entered the phase which Davis (1993) calls 'literal translation' and she is now more concerned with naturalism and a sense of morality, so evident in the drawings of the older pupils. In all cases, the children went a little further in their understanding of the picturebooks.

The evidence for all the points we have been making in this chapter about the often remarkable ability of children to interpret challenging picturebooks with great insight can be found in Chapters 2–8 to follow.

Notes

1 The interviews can be consulted in 2003 edition of this book.
2 Nationalities included Greek, Italian, Turkish Cypriot, Turkish mainland, Kurdish, Tanzanian, Nigerian, Afghan, Chinese, Colombian, Kosovo-Albanian and Sri Lankan among others.
3 Because this was mainly a qualitative study, the questionnaires were meant to provide descriptive examples, comparisons and contrasts rather than results of statistical value. The questionnaire format was adapted from Davies and Brember (1993).
4 Because of the difficulties involved in articulating verbal response to a work of art, Gardner suggests that 'nonverbal means, preferably involving the medium itself, would seem preferable for determining the full range of the child's competence' (1973: 180).

5 All the interviews were transcribed. In the examples used throughout this book, the use of (. . .) indicates a gap in the transcription.
6 As far as we are aware, no previous study has analysed children drawing in response to picturebooks. The data analysis in this instance (Chapter 8) was based mainly on aesthetic interpretations of children's drawings.

Chapter 2

On a walk with Lily and Kitamura

How children link words and pictures along the way

I think you need the words really, to take the story along.

(Lauren 11)

Lily is a cheery little girl who likes going for walks with her dog, Nicky. She watches the sunset, buys groceries and flowers, looks at the stars, says goodnight to the ducks, arrives back in time for supper and finally goes happily to bed. This is Lily's story and it is the story told by the words. But to understand why the smiling Lily is accompanied by her anxious-looking dog, Nicky, we need to 'read' the story told by the pictures. As Lily and Nicky take a walk, the pictures show us that the dog encounters (or he imagines), among other things, a snake, a tree with a wicked grin, a fierce-looking post-box, lampposts with eyes, a vampire-like man emerging from a poster on the wall and various monsters. When they get home, Nicky seems to be trying to tell Lily and her parents what he saw, but they are not paying attention. Exhausted, he finally lies down, only to be plagued by a group of mice trying to get into his basket with a ladder!

Seeing things from a different perspective

Like the hen in *Rosie's Walk* (Hutchins 1970) who apparently never notices the fox that is following her, Lily goes out and returns home seemingly unaware of the creatures that frighten her dog. The text tells us that 'even if it is dark, Lily is not afraid because Nicky is with her'. Is she so confident with Nicky that she is oblivious to danger? Or is Nicky so neurotic that he will see monsters wherever he looks? Is it irony? Or perhaps, as one of the young readers we spoke to speculated (and not without reason), Lily is not afraid because she and her family are also ghostly monsters, a point which we will take up later.

Lily is a postmodern picturebook in the sense that it leaves the reader to deal with the questions mentioned above, fill in the gaps and resolve the ambiguities of the pictorial text (Styles 1996). These aspects belie the apparently simple narrative and lead the reader into a world of alternative meanings where fears can be dealt with through humour and irony. This picturebook is also illustrating one of the defining aspects of its genre: the relationship between image and written text. Lewis writes that, the picture book always has a double aspect, an ability to look in two directions at once and to play off the two perspectives against each other . . . the picture book is thus not just a form of text, it is also a *process*, a way of making things happen to words and to pictures.

(Lewis 1996: 109–110)

In *Lily* we have two characters, each literally looking in a different direction, and as their perspectives play off against each other, readers find themselves participating in the process of making a story happen. They perceive at least two contrasting versions of the same events at the same time and perhaps understand that reality is never quite simple. If this seems too complicated a concept for young readers, it is worth quoting Kathy (7) even if she is struggling to express her reply to why Lily and Nicky might always be looking in different directions: 'Because they might have different like . . . say if Lily heard a joke and Lily laughed but Nicky couldn't laugh because he didn't get it . . . so they might have different possibilities.'

Nikolajeva and Scott (2000) call this particular dynamic 'perspectival counter-point'; it stimulates the reader's imagination because of the different possibilities of interpretation.[1] In the case of *Lily*, Nikolajeva and Scott argue that this dynamic is 'highly developed' and that '[t]he counterpoint between the two perspectives and the ambiguity of the actual events shape the book's impact and the reader's involvement in decoding it' (2000: 234–235). Certainly we found that, when the readers became aware of the counterpoint pattern, they began to anticipate it and to show they appreciated the humour of 'the jokes in-between the pages' (Lauren 11).

As in many of his other books, Kitamura's 'jokes' are part of a serious game he plays with the relationship between the illustrations and the written texts. In this particular picturebook he invites his audience to join Lily and Nicky as they walk along, encouraging readers to become aware of the complexities in postmodern narrative. As Meek (1988) tells us, it is the text that teaches what readers need to learn. It may be that some inexperienced readers will require more help in this understanding, and this is where the teacher should come in as the more experienced reader who listens to the children's responses and asks the questions that will lead them to develop critical awareness of the text and of their role as readers.

But how do young readers learn how picturebooks work? How do they join the artist's game, if in fact they do? How do they make sense of the discourse of the pictures? How do they relate it to the words? And how do they deal with the incoherent and the incomplete? We now explore some of these queries as interviewers as the children we worked with followed Lily and Nicky's footsteps through the picturebook.

Walking with Lily and Nicky

At all ages, the children became interested the moment they saw the cover and became keener as they turned the pages. The cover sets the tone for the rest of the book: the seemingly innocuous title which is Lily's story, together with the threatening background of blank, dark windows, empty streets and frightening monsters. It shows a smiling Lily carrying her groceries towards the left side of the page while Nicky stands facing the opposite way with a frightened look on his face, his eyes are wide open, his nose, ears and tail are pointing upwards and his mouth crumpled into a worried grimace. From Nicky's expression, the children – from the youngest to the oldest – gathered that there would be something menacing to come. This lured them to find out what he was scared of and to read the rest of the book. As Keith (10) said, '[You think] what's the dog scared of? So you like turn the page and then look and then just carry on reading and there's some more monsters and you just want to see the rest of it.'[2]

Despite the sinister atmosphere, the children expected a 'scary' but, at the same time, 'funny' book, because they were reassured by the cartoonish style of the drawing. Colin (8), for example, predicted it might be 'a bit like a comedy'. Readers become involved when they can form analogies between the text and their own experience. For example, Judy (6) was immediately interested because of a building which looks like a church she goes to; others spoke of their own or other people's dogs. Interestingly, for many readers (myself included), it was not until the first reading was over and the cover was scrutinised again, that they discovered what it was that Nicky was looking at: a frightening face made by trees with fierce-looking nostrils, bent lampposts as eyes, and a mouth full of tree trunks with iron railings for teeth. At this point there was unanimous agreement that the cover was a good one for the book because, as Janet (4) put it: 'it looked like what was going to happen in the story.'

The title page belies the cover in that the dog is actually looking quite happy to be going for a walk. Perhaps this is because they are just starting out or because Lily is actually looking at him for once. Several children noticed the house in the background and wondered whether it was Lily's home. On the next page, back on the pavement, both characters are looking at the reader: Lily is smiling but Nicky is already looking anxious and seems to be inviting us to share in his apprehension.

Empathy also encourages involvement, and it was not surprising that most readers were more concerned about the feelings of the over-imaginative dog than with the child, while at the same time laughing – not unkindly – at him. This also allows quite young readers to enjoy the experience of feeling a little more mature than the characters in the book. Some of the children reasoned that the dog was worried because he was hungry or tired, but most of them realised it was because of what he might see on the walk. Several children commented on this direct gaze. Flavia (10) said it was as if someone was taking a picture of him from outside the book, while Selma (11) noted that they were looking at 'us, the reader'. Nikolajeva and Scott (2000) equate Lily's lack of observation or imagination to that of an insensitive parent (although they also question the dog's reliability), though this does not correspond to the representation of Lily as a child who enjoys the sunset and the stars and who likes animals (even bats!).

Next we have a double-page spread (like all the remaining pictures in the book), which shows them once again in the country or a park. Lily has her back to us as she admires the sunset, but Nicky is startled to see a snake as he lifts his leg against a bush. Several children said this was their favourite spread because of the rich colours, especially the blues and greens, and they also commented on the way the grass and the trees were drawn. Carol (10) liked the 'texture' and the way the trees looked 'scribbled' but were actually 'very carefully done'. As Lily walks along towards the right-hand corner of the page, Nicky's imagination really starts working. He looks behind him to see a tree giving him a wicked grin. Then, when Lily stops at the grocer's stall, his eyes widen in terror when he sees a post-box leaning over, with its open top full of pointed teeth and letters dropping from its 'mouth'. Some of the children mentioned the empty can and other litter in these two spreads, and, as we will see, they followed this trail and later reached the conclusion that Kitamura was saying something about pollution.[3]

As it gets darker, we find ourselves in one of the more frightening places on the walk: while Lily looks up at the stars, Nicky sees a face in the tunnel, a wide gaping mouth with lampposts for eyes and traffic cones for teeth (see Figure 2.1). The alley is dark and deserted like the rest of the streets, except for a skip full of rubbish. Most of the readers commented on the menacing atmosphere, the older ones being more specific about which details made it frightening:

> It's kind of scary, but it's funny because . . . street lights with just a tunnel wouldn't scare you at all, but it's just because it's together it makes it look real, like it's actually alive. . . . All the detail, like even the skip with the rubbish falling out, and another reason why it's frightening is because not only that the dog's not looking at her, but because the dog's on the other side of the wall looking at something and she's just kind of talking to herself.
>
> (Keith 10)

A younger child, Judy (6), was probably making an association with her own fears: 'Scary, there might be baddies' houses and as it is dark I thought there might be a baddie in [the skip].'

The evening has become purple and, on the right side of the page, the moon appears and becomes one of the eyes, together with the clock on the tower, of an owlish-looking face with tree trunks for teeth and a lamppost nose. Nicky stares at it in horror while, on the other side of the page, Lily seems to be looking directly at us, although the written text says that she is waving to a Mrs Hall. Mrs Hall is not depicted: she would have to be facing Lily where we, the readers, are. This gap, the 'missing' Mrs Hall, was only a problem for the younger readers, some of whom said that she must be in one of the windows *behind* Lily. The older ones said rightly that she must be off the page: 'It's like you're Mrs Hall because she's looking at you, because you can't actually see the window . . . so she's waving to you' (Keith 10).

As she continues her walk, now almost in the dark, Lily points out to Nicky how clever the bats are, but he is shaking at the sight of a strange-looking man who is tipping his top hat with one hand and holding a glass of blood-coloured juice in the other. He seems to be coming out of a poster advertising tomato juice, bending a lamppost in the process and spilling tomatoes on to the pavement. Keith observed that the dog was not 'round' but 'fuzzy', which meant he's 'even more scared'. When asked what sort of man he was, the children used the picture's clues to define him as a witch, 'because it's got a witchy hat and coat' (Janet 4) or a vampire, 'because it's got very pale white skin and it's got a blood stain there [on the cuff]' (Hugh 9). Anne (9) even gave him a part in the narrative: 'He has that sort of spiky collar and maybe he's pretending that's blood, blood juice and also there is a bat swooping around and going "Oh do not get near this poster or the evil bloodsucking vampire will have you for dinner!"' (see Figure 2.2).

she stops for a moment
to look at the evening star.
'Look, Nicky', she says.
'That's called the Dog Star.'

Figure 2.1 From *Lily Takes a Walk* by Satoshi Kitamura

Source: Illustration reprinted by permission of Catnip Publishing

Bats flitter and swoop in the evening sky.
'Aren't they clever, Nicky?' says Lily. 'Not far, now.'

Figure 2.2 From *Lily Takes a Walk* by Satoshi Kitamura

Source: Illustration reprinted by permission of Catnip Publishing

The next spread shows Lily saying goodnight to the ducks and gulls on one side of the bridge, while on the other a dinosaur or Loch Ness monster-like creature stares down at Nicky, who is rooted to the spot despite his fast-moving legs. All the children were able to explain why Nicky seems to have eight legs in this picture and some exemplified it by moving their own legs very quickly. In this spread, it is Janet (4) who gives a voice to the monster: '"Aaaggg!" He's getting burnt [as he leans over the lamppost].' There are still a few more monsters to terrify Nicky, popping out at him from rubbish bins before he and Lily get home. According to Keith (10) they looked '3D' and Carol (10) described how Kitamura's lines make them look scary: 'He's made them all like all different angles and all different triangle shapes and all sticking out and stuff and this one's just all straight, then zig-zagged.'

Once at home, over dinner, Lily tells her parents about her walk. We can see the father smiling but we can't see the mother's face. On the opposite page, Nicky has his mouth open, surrounded by little bubbles with the pictures of the monsters he has seen. Many of the children again showed their familiarity with the cartoonish style by saying these were the dog's 'speech' bubbles (one compared them to those in the Asterix and Tintin books): 'Well you can see the mother asking Lily and she's just like saying some nice things and he's just thinking of the things he's seen' (Martin 7) (see Figure 2.3).

As the text says, it's time for bed and Lily sleeps happily underneath the duvet with her name written all over it (only the older pupils noticed this). Nicky has also settled into his basket and is just about to relax when, as the flap over the last page opens, a group of mice give him a final shock by trying to climb into his basket with a ladder. When asked how they felt about this picture before and after opening the flap, some of the readers remarked on the cosiness and messiness of her bedroom (and immediately compared it with their own) and at the same time remarked upon details which reminded them of the uncanny atmosphere, such as the fact that three of the stuffed animals look rather worried and sad, that the tiger in what is presumably Lily's drawing looks scared and that dark, blank windows are looking into her room. As Anne (9) rightly pointed out, it doesn't seem that Nicky will be happy anywhere because he will always find something to be frightened of: 'It's a place that Lily can be really comfy in and very happy, but Nicky can be like "Ooh this room!"' There's just something about everything that he can get very scared about.'

Doonan notes that 'The omnipresence of musical and artistic instruments reveals Kitamura's focus upon the inner life, as well as providing intertexual reference to the artist's own creativity, and indicates a source for the self-reliance and independence of his characters' (1991: 108). Although there are no musical instruments to be seen in this picturebook, Lily's room is decorated not only by a Kandinsky-like poster, a calendar and a seagull mobile, but also by her own drawings (or maybe original Kitamuras?), and her table is covered in art materials and a sketch of Nicky. Perhaps Lily, unlike Nicky, channels her imagination into her drawing, making her unafraid of encountering monsters on her walks.

Reading further into the picture

As readers and researchers walked along with Lily and Nicky, the responses gave us an insight into the more complex discursive aspects of this book in particular and of

Lily's mother and father always like to hear what she has seen on her walk.

Figure 2.3 From *Lily Takes a Walk* by Satoshi Kitamura

Source: Illustration reprinted by permission of Catnip Publishing

picturebooks in general. As we have noted, the most distinctive feature of *Lily* is the counterpoint between perspectives and it was this aspect we were keen to explore with the readers. In other words, we wanted to find out how they made sense of the interaction between words and pictures. Other responses that provided insights in relation to this main aspect were the following: readers' appreciation and awareness of visual features of text and artistic intentions; the implied reader and the children's own reading/viewing process and appreciation of the significance of the book as a whole.

Interaction between words and pictures

Almost without exception, the children thought the pictures were more interesting than the words. They felt that the book would still be good if you only had the pictures, but if there were only words it would be boring, especially, they added, for 'children'. There was definitely a belief that books with pictures (lots of them) were for younger children and the amount of pictures in books decreased in inverse ratio to the words as books were intended for older readers. However, some children did realise that only having the words would change the meaning of this particular book. Hugh's (9) comment about having only words was typical: 'You wouldn't be able to see what was happening.'

About the relationship between words and pictures in *Rosie's Walk*, Nodelman says, 'In showing more than the words tell us, the pictures not only tell their own story; they also imply an ironic comment on the words. They make the words comic by making them outrageously incomplete' (1988: 224). A similar interaction is taking place in *Lily* and it means that the reader must link not only the two different narratives – that of the printed text and that of the pictures – but also what the pictures are telling us about the printed text. As Nodelman says, they are showing them to be incomplete and therefore enhance the comedy of the narrative. It is not surprising that most of the younger readers struggled to express their understanding of this interaction; what is surprising is that some of the older ones managed to explain it quite clearly.

INTERVIEWER: Do you think the pictures are telling the same story as the words?
SELMA (11): Yes plus a bit more . . . [the pictures] seem to bring out the story.

When asked if the words and pictures told the same story, most readers found it hard to separate them and answered yes, but some of the more engaged ones recognised they were different:

INTERVIEWER: Do the words and the pictures tell the same story?
KATHY (7): A bit of a yes and a bit of a no because it doesn't say that like Lily is pointing to the leeks or something, but it does say 'today she . . . '
INTERVIEWER: So if the words are telling that story, who's telling the rest of the story?
KATHY: The dog.

The older pupils were more able to articulate the difference between the meanings derived from the written text and the pictures. For example, Flavia (10) pointed out that 'the pictures tell you about the monsters and the words just tell you what Lily thought'. Keith (10) described this in more detail, weighing up the contribution of both words and pictures:

> [If it were only the words] it wouldn't be good because it would just be a happy book because it doesn't say anything about anything being scary. It's just saying she's not scared and she'll do her shopping, she looks at the stars, she walks past someone's house and waves. You wouldn't see the bats or any of those things that make it scary. . . . Some books are better without the pictures because then you can make up your own thing, but I think this is better with the pictures . . . the words need the pictures more than the pictures need the words.

Invoking his previous experience as a reader, Keith recognises the difference between the two signifying systems and how they work upon the reader (the pictures make it scary). His statement also shows us the analytical process by means of which he arrives at a conclusion and makes a judgement on the value of these systems. It is an indication of the processes that are going on in the reader/ viewer's head as they attempt to construct a story structure using different kinds of 'building blocks'.

Appreciation of visual features and artistic intentions

Questions about visual features were asked throughout the interviews with prompts about colour, pattern, perspective and body language. We also asked if they had found similarities with other Kitamura picturebooks. Most of the children mentioned colour and referred especially to the different shades of sky (later, many of them made an attempt to portray these skies in their drawings). They also noticed the cartoon-like patterns of the 'wobbly' lines, the uneven bricks, the flat wheels and the crooked windows. One 10-year-old boy described this style as 'realistic but not realistic'. This 'cartoon-like' style helps widen the distance between the straightforward textual narrative and the fantastic images. Other visual features that were mentioned included perspective (how the trees became smaller in the distance); where the characters were placed (for example, that Lily is always on the side furthest from the monsters and Nicky is nearest); and intertextual references (to other Kitamura picturebooks, such as *A Boy Wants a Dinosaur*).

The less experienced readers tended to provide less plausible explanations (with no basis in the text) for the way in which Kitamura draws lines. For example, they said the steps were wobbly because: 'they belong to a witch', 'they've been there for thousands of years' or 'a heavy man stepped on them'. The more experienced readers tended to give reasons that had more to do with logic (rightly or wrongly) than with the author's intention. Kathy (7), for example, said: 'It is hard to draw steps so he might wiggle a little bit 'cause he is worried about it, that he's going to do it wrong, so he's a bit shaky.' And Martin (7) considered how they added to the atmosphere: 'It's to make it scarier and to stand out more.'

Other children commented on the atmosphere created by the continual appearance of dark colours, the blank windows and empty cars. They described it as 'spooky' and 'upsetting'. Carol (10) spoke of the difference between these dark backgrounds and the way in which Lily and Nicky 'brightened it all up'. Martin (7) also remarked on this contrasting effect:

> It's very good, his use of colour, because he's like used all bright colours on her. . . . I reckon he could have picked different [flowers] like roses or daffodils . . . but he probably just chose a really bright colour: yellow. And he's chosen a really dark colour for the houses.

Both Kitamura's characteristic colour and line were reflected in most of the children's drawings as they attempted to recreate the atmosphere in his pictures. Further examples can be seen in Chapter 8.

The implied reader and children's own reading/viewing processes

Perhaps because the 10- and 11-year-olds had little opportunity to look at picture-books both at home and at school, *Lily* was initially considered a book for younger children. This was also true of some of the 8- and 9-year-olds, because, they argued, if it were for older children it would have more writing and 'a bit more detail'. However, by the end of the interview, this opinion was revised by many of the older readers, such as Peter (9):

> I think this book's interesting because . . . children enjoy picturebooks but I think it's also better for older people because if they read it carefully they can like spot things, like what we're doing now, they can sort of have fun with it and spot things.

This and other answers show how their previous experience of books and their knowledge of the type of fiction we were reading comes to bear on their responses. Kitamura's cartoon-like style was an indication that it would be both a fictional and humorous book. Anne (9), for example, when asked if the monsters were real or imaginary, said: 'Well in books really anything can actually happen, it's just your own imaginary world so that could actually be happening.'

Asking a reader to describe what happens when he or she reads is always fascinating, especially when they are young children who are searching for a way to describe it (these processes are described further in Chapter 7). Many answers revealed the importance that detail has for them. The older children described how they spot 'the problem' or the unexpected and then return to the 'normal' and put the two together:

PETER (9): I look carefully and I see what may be the problem because you see the dog notices things that the girl isn't noticing so then I split the book into half and I see what Lily's seeing and really what she's saying . . . seeing and doing, and I will look at the dog and see what he's doing.
INTERVIEWER: So you get sort of one side and then the other side?
PETER: And try and put them together.

Peter's description of what is going on in his head as he reads give us an indication of what children are noticing as they look at pictures. As they read, they are looking at the whole picture and connecting it to the words, as well as seeing through the characters' eyes and trying to pull all this information together. Their processes of deduction involved both imagination and common sense. Judy (6), for example, spoke of looking for clues to 'get things right'.

Readers were aware that they were joining in a kind of game which allowed them to go back and forth through the book to look for details they had missed in order to solve the puzzles. In this case, they had to work with two different characters, comparing and contrasting their actions and words (at least Lily's words) with the written and pictorial narratives (which also meant imagining what Nicky would say if he could). They were willing to work hard at making connections and coming up with explanations; evidently they were deriving great satisfaction from participating in the meaning-making process by piecing the picture together.

Significance of the book as a whole

One of the most difficult tasks for any reader is to be able to stand back from a text and view it as a whole; it is perhaps even more difficult when we are dealing with a book where two different discourses must be dealt with at the same time. Yet the children in the study showed that they were beginning to consider overall meaning at various levels. To begin with, we asked children whether they would describe *Lily* as 'funny' or 'serious'. Many of the younger readers said it was simply 'funny', while some of the older readers said it was both. They pointed out the humorous elements of the picturebook and the way in which Kitamura 'makes you laugh'. Hugh (9) summed it up by saying, 'It's funny because the dog keeps getting scared and the little girl smiles'. In the children's drawings, Nicky is depicted as worried and Lily always smiles.

As the interviews and discussions progressed, the children raised moral and ethical issues which demonstrated that they were able to perceive more profound implications of this deceptively simple story. This occurred mainly in the group discussions. Often the researcher led up to some of these issues, but in other cases the readers arrived at some surprising conclusions as they discussed possible and alternative meanings. For example, in the following extract from a group discussion, 6- and 7-year-olds are debating whether the 'monsters' were really there or if they were a product of Nicky's imagination:

KATHY: I think he's just looking at it and then he thinks 'Oh no!'
JUDY: No, because it is in the dark, because he's staring in the dark and it makes them look different to what they really are.
JOHN: No, I think he's been watching TV about all this stuff. . . . He's thinking of all this stuff and when he looks he sees them there, when they are not really there.
MARTIN: (Maybe it's a) person holding things up . . .
SEAMUS: I think that it's that he looks at them and then he imagines that they're scary.

The children put forth their hypotheses, trying to explain it to themselves and the others, based on their own experience of dealing with imaginary terrors. Together they are struggling to reach beyond the literal to a level of understanding that shows psychological insight into the dog's behaviour.

The environmental issue was raised by some children who noted that litter appears in many of the pictures. Carl (8) read this as a message Kitamura was trying to put across through his book: 'He might be trying to tell people in just a picture in a little way to clear up your rubbish . . . he might be saying to people who read the book to clear up your rubbish.' This idea was also brought up in the group discussion between 7- and 8-year-olds, and for one girl it involved an important consideration about viewpoint and perspective:

INTERVIEWER: So the dog does notice all the rubbish doesn't he?
LAUREN: Because he's so small he might see it more, because it's a bit bigger than him.

By means of the two stories running alongside, Kitamura leads us to understand that the world can be seen from different perspectives. Selma (11) applied this idea to the fact that the 'vampire' and Lily's dad look quite similar. It is interesting to note that she also speaks of the importance of looking carefully at the text in order to notice this sort of detail and understand what she called 'the moral': 'People may look different in a different suit but they could be the same person. Some people may not realise that, they just look through it and they don't actually see the dad.'

The interviewer picked up on the idea of 'the moral' and as the children worked collaboratively, they reached a more satisfying explanation of what is going on in the book:

INTERVIEWER: Would you say that there were any other morals in this book?
LAUREN (11): People believe in things but not everybody.
ANGUS (9): From the dog's point of view when you are little things scare you more than when you are bigger . . . when you are little sometimes your imagination just wanders and then when you are older you can tell things look like that or not.

The last statement shows a grasp of how characters' perceptions can be different and how these differences may be responsible for their emotions and actions. It also shows an analogical understanding of how the ability to discern between reality and fantasy develops with age. Like Angus, by the end of the group discussions, many other children were showing signs of a much broader comprehension of the picturebook.

Looking and walking with Kitamura

In English schools, picturebooks are not often re-read and re-discussed because of the constraints of the curriculum. This means that many children remain at a more literal level of comprehension, in which they understand the plot sequence, facts and details, but find it difficult to construct meaning at a more critical level. We found that at first the children were trying to make literal sense of the gaps and incoherences, instead of being able to take a step back and comprehend how they worked within the whole of the story structure. The reading of books like *Lily* confounds the reader's expectations in a playful and at the same time thought-provoking manner. It forces even older readers such as Keith to look more carefully, resulting in a greater understanding of how the visual and verbal narrative can work together as well providing a greater enjoyment of the text.

We also found that some of the children who were considered by the teachers to be 'struggling readers' turned out to be some of the more experienced and articulate interpreters of the visual; even those students who had particular learning disabilities were able to make meaning and in some cases actually expanded the possibilities of Kitamura's pictorial text. Such was the case of Charlie, whose slight autism made him speak slowly and not very distinctly (his extraordinary drawings are analysed in the vignette). It was Charlie who reasoned that Lily's white face, the fact that the family were drinking the same tomato juice as the vampire and the father's resemblance to this vampire, meant that Nicky was, ironically, living with a family of ghostly monsters. No wonder Lily wasn't afraid of the dark!

An earlier version of this chapter appeared in M. Anstey and G. Bull (eds) (2002) *Crossing the Boundaries*, Sydney: Pearson.

Vignette – 'getting the pictures in my head' (Charlie 9)

Charlie was not one of the four children interviewed individually about Kitamura's *Lily*. I first met him for the group discussion, where his extremely slow and hardly intelligible manner of speaking, as well as his reluctance to meet my eye, made him stand out from the rest of the children. He spoke so slowly that he was constantly interrupted (something he seemed to be used to) and it was a struggle to make the others let him finish. I was intrigued, however, by his interventions – short as they were – and particularly impressed when I saw his drawing. So much so, that I decided to re-interview him five months later after a brief talk with his teacher. She described him as 'slightly autistic' and said that he was registered as having special needs. However, she added, 'although he's slow, it's all up there'.

Charlie's first drawing is based on the 'tunnel monster' picture, where Lily is looking up at the stars (see Figure 2.4). All of it is drawn with thick, determined lines. The left half of the picture is dominated by a brick-lined arch filled with vivid turquoise blue pencil crayon. On either side of the arch stand two lampposts bent inwards underneath the top of the arch giving the impression of two staring eyes. Inside stand two nearly identical houses with a perfectly balanced window and door in the centre of each. Nicky's state of mind is revealed by the squiggly, uncertain line that is his mouth. As with the rest of the drawing, Charlie has paid great attention to detail and the dog is carefully patterned with spots and black paws. Both Lily and Nicky are drawn in profile and this is particularly interesting because only a few of the other children attempted to draw the characters from this perspective. In his attempts to get it 'right', Charlie has rubbed out Lily's face once before carefully redrawing her hair and the shape of the side of her nose.

At the beginning of the re-interview, I asked Charlie why he had chosen to draw this particular picture. He said it was because that page 'looked really spooky, because it looks like a horrible monster, like the mouth'. It was also his favourite picture in the book because

(continued)

(continued)

Figure 2.4 By Charlie (age 9)

of 'the way the path goes like into the mouth' and the way Kitamura had drawn the lines. As these comments reveal, Charlie was very perceptive about Kitamura's actual drawing style. He mentions the 'lines' twice and also that 'the colours are good and like that's quite scary . . . because her [Lily's] skin is very white'.

The other aspect of Charlie's reaction to the pictures revealed by these comments was his sensitivity to the atmosphere in the book. He explained that the lines made things look scary, 'and the black walls too, the rubbish on the ground is also scary, and kind of crooked tyres and crooked sticks'. He mentioned that he often had trouble going to sleep after watching a scary video. Kitamura's images also haunted him: 'When I read this book it made me think of bats when I was in bed.'

During the group discussion he scrutinised a copy of the book, pointing out the monsters to the others. After several interrupted and unintelligible remarks, he pointed out that the father in the penultimate picture looks 'just like' the man in the poster and that Nicky was feeling 'a bit sick and thinking, "No, go away!"' to those horrible things in his mind'. When at the end of the discussion I asked the children what they would like to ask the artist, Charlie said, 'Well I'd like to ask him if that was Lily's Dad and were these things actually really happening or Nicky was just thinking he'd seen them'. It seemed to worry him whether the monsters were 'real' or just a product of Nicky's imagination. When I spoke to him five months later I asked him what he remembered most about the book. He said: 'The looks of things . . . they look like spooky things.' I asked him what Kitamura wanted to make the readers think. He replied: 'That the town is haunted . . . he's trying to say that there are monsters and horrible scary things, or maybe he's [Nicky] just imagining them.' Charlie thought he could make out more monsters in Lily's room (made of windows) and claimed: 'If [Nicky] looked out the window he would see more scary things.'

During the re-interview, I read the book to him slowly, letting him comment during the reading if he wished. Then I asked him the same questions I was asking the other re-interviewed children but tried to give him as much time as possible to answer. Even so, he did not say very much because of the effort it took him to speak, and much of what he said was refining the ideas he had tried to put across during the group discussion. He had no problem understanding what the story was about: 'Lily is having a good time but Nicky is not having a very nice time on the walk . . . the pictures tell his story and if he tells it the people wouldn't believe him.' So he had noticed that the words and the pictures were telling different stories.

The picture he chose to represent in his second drawing was the one with the 'vampire' man and the bats, which had evidently made a strong impression on him and, like the first one, it shows an outstanding ability to draw as well as an understanding of Kitamura's style. In this drawing there is also an example of his handwriting, which reveals his meticulous interest in shape. The letters have been laboriously delineated as if he had been thinking carefully about each of them. The drawing bears many of the characteristics of Kitamura's original drawings such as the accurately hatched blue sky which dominates the composition. Apart from the predominant blue colour, the picture is drawn almost entirely in black felt tip, with a red sea of tomatoes on the poster spilling down onto the pavement.

In this drawing Lily has become more 'ghost-like' because only her yellow hair and red shoes are coloured. The man coming from the poster is very similar to that of the original, with his round cartoon eyes, U-shaped nose and arching semi-circle smile – again, carefully thought-out shapes. Lily and Nicky are drawn in a similar position and profile to the first picture but here is a more accurate depiction of the side on view with only one arm showing. Charlie's drawing also shows development in terms of movement (another aspect which few pupils tried to depict) with Lily's back leg bending at the knee as she walks forward.

Of all the drawings we showed him, it was Charlie's that most caught Kitamura's eye when he saw them; he even said he wished he had thought of the composition himself! Kate Noble, who analysed the other 'Lily' drawings in the study (see Chapter 8), also found that Charlie's art work stood out, particularly in its attention to detail (e.g. the lamp on the post is shaped exactly with pointed pattern on the top, split into two panes and anchored on three triangular-shaped supporting struts). She was also surprised by the boldness of his line and use of colour, suggesting it reveals a confident, definite use of drawing materials. She surmised this must be a child who draws a great deal (noticing, for example, the repeated schema of the house and the figures, almost identical but subtly improved in between the two sessions). It also seemed to me that he was carefully trying to reproduce the menacing atmosphere which so impressed him.

Not surprisingly, Charlie told me that he prefers pictures over words 'because they help you with the story; only words would be boring'. When faced with books without pictures, his approach is to 'get the pictures in my head, imagine them'. He certainly did not lack imagination, especially when he reasoned that Nicky was so afraid because he

(continued)

(continued)

realised the whole family were ghosts! He came up with this idea after pointing out Lily's face is 'white' (colourless), that the father is like the 'vampire' and that the family were drinking tomato juice.

Fortunately, Charlie's teacher was aware 'it was all up there' and the fact that she selected him for the interviews meant she was confident that he would have something to say about pictures. The obstacles in verbally expressing himself completely disappeared when he communicated through the visual. His engagement with the picturebook was intense and it is this intensity he manages to express to us only through his drawings.

Notes

1 Nikolajeva and Scott (2000 and 2001) include a section on *Lily* both in their book and in an earlier article.
  Their insights on the word/image dynamic is useful for understanding *Lily*, however, we differ in the interpretation of some of the images, as they see the 'monsters' as more menacing than humorous and seem to have misinterpreted some of them, such as the 'giant', which is not emerging from a shop window but from an advertising poster (and playing with advertising billboards is a common feature in Kitamura's work).
2 Keith was described by his teacher as of 'middle ability'. He was a bright, articulate boy who spoke of *Lily* as a book for younger children, yet he became more and more involved in it and particularly in the relationship between words and images. He is therefore frequently quoted throughout this chapter as an example of the way in which picturebooks can stimulate older children's understanding of visual literacy.
3 When asked about this particular point, Kitamura admitted that he might have made the reference unconsciously.

Chapter 3

A gorilla with 'grandpa's eyes'

How children interpret ironic visual texts – a case study of *Zoo*

I always remember pictures. I sometimes forget words.

(Amy 5)

He doesn't just want to say the animals want to be free – blah, blah, blah. He leaves you to find it out a bit better . . . makes you keep thinking about things.

(Erin 7)

A visual analysis of *Zoo*

The story is an account of a family visit to a zoo, which interrogates the ideological concept of zoos, and of man's relationship with animals, delivered in a multi-stranded narrative. . . . The family and its backgrounds are depicted in comic book style, with clean outlines, minimal modeling and (with the exception of Mum) in plenty of bright, saturated hues, in lightly framed pictures generally, which occupy about a third of the page area. The animals and their enclosures are portrayed in black framed full plates, painted in Browne's meticulous non-photographic realist style, with intense care to selected details and textures. Each animal has a grave and beleaguered natural beauty set in contrast with unsympathetic materials – concrete, brick, cement shuttering – from which their environments have been structured. . . . The composite text both questions the value of caging wild animals for the casual pleasure of the majority of visitors, and at the same time communicates the sad truth that humans also construct metaphorical cages through the ways in which they construct the world.

(Doonan 1999: 36–37)

With her usual flair, Doonan gives a telling description of Browne's prize-winning book. The dramatic cover features black and white, vertical, wavy lines which most children interpret as reference to a zebra which is, in fact, missing from the list of animals encountered in the book. 'Well, it's just like a zebra, the stripes of a zebra I think and . . . that's kind of symbolising a zoo really' (Joe 10). It is also suggestive of the sort of puzzling optical illusions so favoured by artists like Escher. It could be a postmodernist joke, as *Zoo* is an unstable text with surrealistic fantasies side by side with hyper-real illustrations. Instead of zebra stripes, those lines could represent the bars of cages dissolving before our eyes. Nothing is what it seems. From the cover in, it is clear this is not going to be a conventional family outing (although that is more or less what it is in the written text) and the reader will be taken on a confusing but rewarding journey.

There is also a book-shaped insert of the central family on the cover with an over-sized father, a small, young-looking mother, plus two boys. The male family members are in the foreground looking happy and confident, wearing bright, colourful jerseys, whereas Mum (reminiscent of the mother living in a sexist household in Browne's *Piggybook*) almost disappears into the background, looking straight at the reader with a serious face. Unusually, the only lettering on the front or back cover is the title and the name of the author which are in large, white, bold print. The typography hints at eyes (gazing on the reader?) in the two 'O's of ZOO. In contrast, the word 'Zoo' is picked out in black lettering on the title page, which also depicts a hamster in a cage full of accoutrements, the same colours as the clothes of Dad and the boys.

The dominance of black and white is further emphasised in both endpapers, one side white, the other black, an unusual choice and clearly there for a purpose. It suggests there is going to be a debate going on in this book; or perhaps it is raising the issue of right and wrong, good and bad, two sides of the same coin? It is for readers to decide by analysing the pictures; Browne raises questions rather than providing answers and the story told in words is often at odds with what is revealed in the pictures. Young readers soon learn (if they haven't already discovered from earlier encounters with Browne's books) that everything in the visual text is significant and they are going to have to work hard to carve out the meaning for themselves. Fortunately, this is an enjoyable process, as Browne is extremely funny and children laugh a lot as they read the book.

Ironic picturebooks

Most children read *Zoo* as a book which is severely critical about animals being held in captivity, but there is no reference to this in the written text except for Mum's final comment: 'I don't think the zoo really is for animals. I think it's for people.' Otherwise, all the evidence for an authorial stance critical of zoos comes from the pictures. For children to judge that this is a book about how humans treat animals and about captivity and freedom, they have to be able to interpret irony and read moral ideas into pictures.

Zoo could be described as a prime example of an ironic picturebook as Kümmerling-Meibauer explains: 'Ironic meaning comes into being as the consequence of a relationship, a dynamic, performative bringing together of the said and the unsaid, each of which takes on meaning only in relation to the other' (1999: 168). This irony makes demands on the reader to use inference to detect contradictions between what is said in the written text and illustrated in the picture. She goes on to underline the difficulties irony poses for younger readers, suggesting that:

> children do not acquire a full understanding of this concept in comparison to other linguistic phenomena until relatively late. . . . The groundwork for understanding irony is often laid first not in verbal but in graphic images that act as visual equivalents to tone in oral storytelling and that can serve to play with or cast doubt on a straight-faced text.
>
> (1999: 167)

Nodelman (1988: 222) devotes a whole chapter of *Words about Pictures* to consider irony in multi-modal texts: 'They come together best . . . when writers and illustrators use the different qualities of their different arts to communicate different information. When they do that, the texts and illustrations of a book have an ironic relationship to each other.' While Nodelman argues that picturebooks are 'inherently ironic', Kümmerling-Meibauer prefers to emphasise the reader's role in recognising irony through paratextual clues and other visual hints which often contradict or subvert the written texts. These operate as triggers to suggest that the viewer should be open to other possible meanings, thus encouraging the development of metalinguistic skills. She also emphasises the hard intellectual work involved in interpretation of such indeterminacy which forces the reader 'to prise open the gap between the text and the pictures, working on the relationship between them' (1999: 167–176).

Nikolajeva and Scott (2001) also talk about the tension between the two different sign systems creating 'unlimited possibilities for interaction between word and image in a picturebook', also using the term 'counterpoint' to describe the dynamic between them. They go on to outline different kinds of 'counterpoint', many of which apply to *Zoo*, that is counterpoint by genre (e.g. realism and fantasy side by side), style (e.g. use of different artistic styles), in perspective (e.g. contradiction between ideologies), and of paratexts (e.g. titles and covers). It was evident in our study that most of the children, even the very young, were aware of, and responded to, tensions within *Zoo* and that this was one of the features of the book they found so challenging and absorbing.

Seeing and thinking

Browne uses surrealist techniques to make connections between human beings and animals; people begin to metamorphose as the visit progresses. At first there is just the hint of a tail, a banana, or a fur coat, but soon we have people growing webbed feet, hooked noses and monkey faces. On most double spreads animals, sometimes alone, are presented within their cages with the colours, light, caging and body language emphasising their isolation. On the left-hand pages, in contrast, Dad, the boys and other visitors to the zoo appear in bold colours, often in bright sunlight under a blue sky with billowing Magritte-type clouds, something the children always notice. The visitors often behave thoughtlessly, intent on their fun and dismissive of the animals. Throughout the book the animals are portrayed sympathetically in contrast to the bizarre-looking humans, displaying (often most amusingly) shallow and boorish behaviour. Although the zoo is newish, architect-designed and relatively clean, the emphasis is on harsh, synthetic materials; the reader is positioned outside the cages until half-way through the book when the standpoint moves just inside for an even closer experience of the misery of captivity.

What came over most forcefully in the interviews and group discussions based round Browne's *Zoo* was the children's engagement with the text and their willingness to spend time analysing its meaning. What we saw, even with the young children, was what can only be described as intellectual excitement with the ideas raised by the book and aesthetic pleasure in the images. It was as if *Zoo* offered an invitation that children felt compelled to take up. Here are Lara (10), Joe (10), and 5-year-old twins (part of the pilot study) explaining why the pictures were a priority for them.

LARA: The writing doesn't explain everything what you think about . . . the writing only explains what the book is about and what is happening, but it doesn't explain what you feel and what they feel. *So I like the pictures better because then you can think more stuff* [our emphasis].

JOE: I think I found the pictures more interesting really because the text does help me to know what is going on in the family, *but the pictures show what it's really like* and what's going on with the animals [our emphasis].

R AND F: Pictures are better.

F: Cause we can understand it more. We can't read very well, but *we can understand it by the pictures* [our emphasis].

Motivation was high from the moment children started looking at the front cover of *Zoo* and, almost without exception, they were eager to engage with the book after it had been read to them by their class teachers. Although this enthusiasm was evident in all the children (whether they had seen the book before or not did not seem to make a difference), those below the age of 7, unsurprisingly, found it much harder to answer the questions in interviews than those of 7 and above. Furthermore, children below the age of 7 were usually satisfied with seeing things in the text; older pupils wanted to pursue the how and why of Browne's artwork.

By the group discussions at the end of each interview day, it was always evident that the children's thinking had moved on. Aspects of the book that individuals had failed to comprehend in interviews were often sorted out when they began talking together. Group dynamics were interesting. For example, Joe was regarded by his teacher as a very good reader and was the most academic of the 10- and 11-year-old children. He made thoughtful responses in interview, but held back during the discussion. This could be for reasons of personality; perhaps he was confident enough to form his own opinions without voicing them aloud, or perhaps the more forceful members of the group held him back? However, if there was any doubt about his emotional investment in *Zoo*, a glance at his powerful drawing of an elephant would cast it aside.

The children were assiduous at noticing details in *Zoo* and were keen to interpret every last image. They all enjoyed the humour, but thought the book more serious than funny. This is probably one of the reasons for Browne's popularity with young readers: the combination of intellectual challenge, aesthetic pleasure, amusement and intriguing 'puzzles' to unravel.

Perplexing features of visual texts

There were some instances of imagery which adults tend to find straightforward, once they have been pointed out, but which proved perplexing to most children. For example, on the first page a snail is poking out of the top right-hand section of the picture, ahead of the traffic jam leading to the zoo, while cars and people acquire animal characteristics. This is presumably an ironic joke by Browne, saying that the traffic is moving so slowly that even a snail could go faster. We should not have been surprised that children found this difficult since Kümmerling-Meibauer reminds us that such irony requires sophisticated metacognitive awareness and, perhaps, familiarity with metaphorical linguistic terms and their application, such as 'going at a snail's pace' or 'the traffic was crawling along'. Children came up with every conceivable suggestion for the snail's role on the opening page. Here are some examples by groups of 5-, 8- and 10-year-olds:

YU (4): To make it beautiful.

ASHOK (5): Because *Bear Hunt* had lots of different things and perhaps he thought he could put lots of different things into this book as well [a nice example of inter-textual awareness].

PAUL (5): I think he's jumping off the roof.

ASHOK: Because he wanted to get to the lions first.

SOFIA (8): Well, the man in the van must have like pushed him off.

EYLEM (8): It shows you to like . . . change the page.

INTERVIEWER: It tells you to . . . go to the next page. Is that what you mean?

EYLEM: Yeah [a good try, but incorrect].

MIKE (10): Well he might like snails.

GIOVANNI (10): 'Cause he can see the traffic jam, people shouting and arguing and it gives you an idea of the snail is fed up and he's trying to get away from it.

In the final discussion, most children of 7 and above solved the snail conundrum together with some guided questioning by the interviewer. The children's problems with interpreting the snail serve to highlight the extraordinary analytical ability shown elsewhere by so many children about other pictures in the book.

Affective and moral dimensions of Zoo

One of the reasons the children were encouraged to work at an analytical level in examining *Zoo* is that they were emotionally involved with the book. Vygotsky taught us about the interrelationship between the intellect and emotion, arguing for 'a dynamic system of meaning in which the affective and the intellectual unite . . . every idea contains a transmuted affective attitude towards the bit of reality to which it refers'. Vygotsky believed that thought processes were inevitably linked to 'the fullness of life, from personal needs and interests, the inclinations and impulses of the thinker'. And he goes further: 'Imagination and thought appear in their development as the two sides of opposition . . . this zigzag character of the development of fantasy and thought . . . reveals itself in the "flight" of imagination on the one hand, and its deeper reflection upon real life on the other' (Vygotsky 1986: 10).

There were some features of the book that most children, regardless of age, were able to comprehend and articulate. Perhaps most noticeable was an empathy with the suffering of the animals, often linked to statements of personal analogy. This was generally accompanied by criticism of the way humans behaved towards animals. Joe (10) summed up the book's message neatly: 'I think he's trying to get across that we are more like animals than animals really . . . like it says on the last page . . . the zoo is more for humans than animals.' Most of the children interviewed were critical of the poor conditions in which the animals were held and very concerned about their apparent unhappiness. (Again, this is never mentioned in the written text and has to be inferred from the pictures.) The older the children, the more concerned they were with the ethics of keeping animals in captivity. This strong moral viewpoint was also evident in the drawings of this age group, which either showed humans and animals in role-reversal situations or pictures which contrasted the misery of the animals in captivity with the joyousness of freedom, expressed in the use of bright and dull colours. Sue (10) joined the discussion, but was not an interviewee. She had only had one quick reading of *Zoo*, but she quickly gets straight to the heart of it:

> Well, it was about how lonely [the animals] were in the zoo . . . and the people were being nasty and just wanted to look at the animals. . . . They didn't seem to realise how miserable the animals were . . . it is not just a trip to the zoo. It is thinking about how the animals feel and how the people. . . . They should be given more freedom. . . . The animals are acting better than the people. The people are acting like animals or what we think animals act like.

The children read emotion in Browne's pictures with great subtlety and their empathy was often extended towards the mother who shows concern for the animals' plight and appears ashamed of the bad behaviour exhibited by her husband and children. Here is Sue again, observant of Mum, and understanding what it means to show rather than tell: 'Perhaps she felt sorry for the animals, because all the way through it suggests it.' Les (10) also noticed that Mum might be disapproving as 'she's just standing there and everyone else is smiling'. Even 5-year-old Amy was able to articulate in her second interview that 'Mum is sad – she thinks the animals should be going free.'

AIDAN (10): She doesn't like the animals being in the cage 'cos when they was looking . . .
I think it was at the gorilla or something like that . . . she said 'poor thing'.
I: Right. So she doesn't . . . like the animals being caged in the zoo?
MIKE (10): Because she's a very serious-looking lady that she er thinks the animals should be free, so she probably ain't in that picture because she's like wandering off all upset that the animals are trapped.

Many children found the image of the orang-utan very moving. Browne emphasises a sense of desolation as the animal crouches dejectedly in a corner of a domestic-looking cage with his back to the jeering visitors. The only objects in its space are bits of faeces and empty shells. In contrast, the increasingly animal-like visitors (who include Magritte, Catwoman and D. H. Lawrence!) bang on the glass in derision. Here is an extract from the discussion of 10-year-olds who humanise the orang-utan, perhaps for greater identification with him:

SUE: Because he is sort of similar to a human, he should be treated like a human.
LARA: Because he looks like he's got hair coming down . . . it has got really long hair.
SUE: And it has got hairy ears.
TONY: And it has got grey hairs like an old person.
SUE: He looks like he's got his hair in a bun at the top and like . . .
INTERVIEWER: How do you know he's sad?
JOE: Because you don't just crawl up into a corner, just turn away, for no reason. You can't be happy when you're like that, you can tell that he is not happy.

A 7-year-old in interview showed how she could read the environment:

INTERVIEWER: How do you think the orang-utan is feeling?
ERIN: Very sad.
INTERVIEWER: What makes you say that?
ERIN: Well if he's not showing his face then it might be because he's sad and he just doesn't feel like it.
INTERVIEWER: Is there anything else that suggests he might be sad?
ERIN: Well if you look really, he hasn't got anything around him. Like the elephant, no natural habitat.

The 4- and 5-year-olds in interview also realised the orang-utan was unhappy:

INTERVIEWER: How do you think the orang-utan is feeling?
AMY: Sad.
INTERVIEWER: You think he's feeling sad? And what makes you think he's feeling sad?
AMY: Because he's sitting in the corner.

Analysing visual imagery

Kümmerling-Meibauer discusses the textual markers and paratextual clues that encourage readers to recognise irony in picturebooks operating 'as triggers to suggest that the viewer should be open to other possible meanings, thus encouraging the development of metalinguistic skills' (1999: 168–176). What follows in the next few sections are some examples of children recognising textual markers, noticing switches in artistic styles, analysing colour imagery, noting changes in points of view and filling in semantic gaps.

Younger children were fascinated by the changes that kept appearing in Browne's humorous, comic-style art work. They also kept commenting that reading this text was like solving a puzzle.

ARJANIT (10): You know where the 'em the gorilla is . . . that looks like a puzzle and it's like . . . he's puzzled they're looking at him like that.
INTERVIEWER: Why do you like his pictures?
AMY (4): Because he hides things.

There were many examples in the transcripts of the children's understanding of how Browne used frames to emphasise the captivity theme. Doonan (1999: 39) notes:

> There are hand-drawn frames thin as threads (depicting humans), their outlines wavering and bulging at times almost like breathing. . . . There are rigid frames (for the animals), black save for one yellow, and one grey. The apparently small detail like type of frame becomes a vital sign in the discourse.

INTERVIEWER: Why do you think he puts that big black line round the animals?
AMY (4): Because the edge of the cage is black.
ERIN (7): They're all barred up like they can't get out, and it's not very nice.

TINA (10): Yes, on the little picture there is hardly any, but then on the big pictures (of the animals) there is a big, black outline round the pictures . . . on this page it hasn't got a border at all, so it is like he's an animal and he is also free.

The children were also able to talk about how the viewer was positioned, confirming their hunches about the text with reference to Browne's use of colour imagery, perspective and body language.

TINA (10): I've got two things to say. That the big animals have got little bits of wood and the things like the gorillas and the monkeys and the lions have all got bars, so really they haven't got much freedom. And it doesn't look very healthy around there, because it is all really grey on the page.

SUE (10): He's chosen quite pale colours and nothing too bright . . .

TINA: It is like the giraffe; it's got all dull skies around it, so it seems like there's a factory somewhere near the zoo and letting lots of fumes just near it.

They were also quick to notice Dad's behaviour linked to body posture.

SUE: Because he's a more dominant person and he's shouting and bossing people about all the time.

TINA: He's always big in pictures and there's one picture where he is standing up and he's got two clouds like that and he looks like the devil.

The children had no difficulty in analysing most of the visual metaphors. For example, Browne is clearly making a pointed analogy when he paints a butterfly, perching freely on fresh green grass in identical colours to the tiger who paces across the parched grass of his high metal cage (Figure 3.1). This was not lost on some 10-year-olds.

LARA: He is kind of like saying the butterfly is free but the tiger isn't.

TINA: It makes you think the tiger has been walking around that bit for ages and made a shape of himself.

The 7-year-olds:

ERIN: Well outside they're free and happy, but inside he's really sad.

And the 4- and 5-year-olds:

AMY: The butterfly's the same colour as the tiger.

INTERVIEWER: Why do you think he put a butterfly out there on the grass?

AMY: Because butterflies live outside.

INTERVIEWER: And do you see the colour of the grass there [lush green outside]? But what about the colour of the grass in his cage [dull green inside]?

PAUL: Because it's like a desert inside his cage.

This example shows development of visual understanding linked quite clearly with age. The youngest children have noticed connections between the butterfly and the

Figure 3.1 From *Zoo* by Anthony Browne

Source: Illustration from *Zoo* by Anthony Browne, published by Jonathan Cape (Artwork © Anthony Browne), reproduced by permission of The Random House Group Ltd.

tiger and the first glimmerings of understanding that they represent the concepts of captivity and freedom. Although this is a sophisticated idea for 4- and 5-year-olds to grasp, we believe their responses show that they do. This is backed up in the children's drawings. Five-year-old Amy observes the size differentials between the family members looking at the tiger with fierce claws dwarfed by his large cage. She also notices the grass outside the cage. Ten-year-old Bella is trying something quite sophisticated and 'Brownesque' as the tiger's stripes appear to be melting into the background. Both depict the butterfly outside the cage (the children's drawings appear in Chapter 8).

Paul's analogy, likening the grass to a desert, shows his imaginative interpretation of the picture. By the age of 7, children were able to provide a simple explanation, linking freedom with happiness and captivity with sadness. (The word 'sad' was probably the adjective used most frequently in relation to *Zoo* by children from every age group.) By the time they reach 10 years old, children are capable of articulating the visual dichotomy. 'He is kind of like saying the butterfly is free but the tiger isn't.'

A gorilla with 'grandpa's eyes'

The image of the gorilla is one of the most powerful in *Zoo* (Figure 3.2). This digni-fied, thoughtful, wise-looking gorilla seems young at the top of the picture and older at the bottom, depicted against a structure which could be a cage or a window, but also forms the shape of a cross. (Browne himself once described this picture as 'my first crucifixion'.) Adults may be familiar with such symbolism from religious paint-ings and visits to churches, though most do not see the connection until it is pointed out to them. None of the children were aware of the religious iconography suggested by the gorilla framed within a cross during individual interviews. Joe (10) came clos-est and did notice it in his interview, but he wasn't quite ready to go one step further to make the connection with the crucifixion.

JOE: I think it's interesting the way they've made a white cross right through the mid-dle of the picture and I think it's to show that he's trapped inside this cage. That he drew this thick line to show the cage lines . . . and he can't get out and he looks . . . he's got a really sad expression on his face.

INTERVIEWER: What might the cross symbolise?

JOE: I think it symbolises that he's just . . . he can't get out because there's all these wires stopping him . . . and he just doesn't have the freedom and he can't run around in the wild. He can just sit there while there's all these people staring at him.

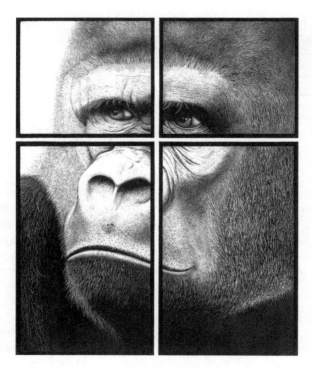

Figure 3.2 From *Zoo* by Anthony Browne

Source: Illustration from *Zoo* by Anthony Browne, published by Jonathan Cape (Artwork © Anthony Browne), reproduced by permission of The Random House Group Ltd.

One researcher did not pursue this line of questioning in the group discussion since none of the children had made reference to it. The other researcher, however, was very interested in the symbolisation of the gorilla as a Christ figure. Consequently, she was tenacious in her questioning on this issue, not least because she believed the children themselves were aware of some symbolic meaning, judging by their voices and their body language.[1] After discussing Browne's use of frames, cages and bars in the group discussion with the 10-year-olds, she draws their attention back to the cross:[2]

INTERVIEWER: Look at this shape. Does it remind you of anything else? We've said windows; we've said bars of cages. Is there anything else this shape reminds you of?

TINA: It reminds me of a sad thing that happened, when Jesus got crucified on the cross and like the monkey is thinking that he might . . . [voice tails off]

Children as young as 7 eventually noticed the connection in the group discussion.

INTERVIEWER: Yes, but there's something else. There's something else. Look at that cage. There's something else in that cage.

ERIN: There's been no white bits in between . . . because like it looks sad and kind of like he don't want to see in his . . .

CHLOE: It's like Jesus's cross.

Finally, here's Amy (now 5) and Yu on a second interview, answering the question, 'Why do you think Browne makes us look at things this way in the gorilla picture?'

AMY: It's like a cross . . . makes me feel sad . . .

YU: He's got like . . . a grandpa's eyes.

Empathy and personal analogy

On the final spread, the boy who is the narrator of *Zoo* sits with head in hands while the bars of a cage are shadowed against his body (Figure 3.3). All the mischief seems to have ebbed out of him and we are left with a small boy in a subdued and reflective body posture. On the opposite page, we see the zoo buildings in silhouette, dwarfed against a beautiful moonlit sky with two wild geese flying off into the distance. The buildings are angular with straight lines; there are, perhaps, echoes of concentration camps – even a tree appears to be imprisoned – which contrast with the soft roundness of the moon and the curved lines of the geese in flight. The images made a big impact on young readers. Here is Chloe (7), an inexperienced reader who is struggling to articulate her thoughts.

INTERVIEWER: What do you think the last two pictures are about?

CHLOE: Like he's a little bit sad because we're leaving the zoo now . . .

INTERVIEWER: How do you know he's sad?

CHLOE: Yeah, because you know he's going like that (points to his crouched position and bent head) he don't feel very well.

INTERVIEWER: So you're reading his body posture, aren't you?

CHLOE: Yeah . . . and he feels like sad because he's like left the zoo and he's like thinking like a dream. He's thinking like a dream. He's like thinking about the gorilla and he's dreaming about it at the same time.

Similarly, Dan (7), also an inexperienced reader, felt a sense of moral injustice on reading *Zoo*, again linking it sensitively with his own experience.

DAN: He's in a cage and been all sad and all that lot.

INTERVIEWER: Do you think the boy was feeling bad about the visit to the zoo?

DAN: Yeah, and sometimes when your worst dreams, you like cry in the middle of the night and all that lot. . . . I like this page because it's all black, dark and all that lot. And then birds come along and fly away. And it's nice and peaceful in the dark, I find it is, and I just like these mountains and all that . . .

INTERVIEWER: What do you think Anthony Browne wants us as readers of the book to feel about it?

DAN: Well I think they should read it . . .

By the age of 10 some children, like Joe, were able to express their ideas more forcefully.

INTERVIEWER: What do you think Anthony Browne wants us as readers of the book to feel about it?

JOE: He wants us to stop and think about that zoos may be fun to go to and look at all the animals but it's really horrible for the actual animals . . . they need to be happy. But they're just stuck in cages for our own entertainment.

INTERVIEWER: Do you agree with him ?

JOE: In the end I agree with him and when I go to zoos I just don't stop and think about how they might feel.

Figure 3.3 From *Zoo* by Anthony Browne

Source: Illustration from *Zoo* by Anthony Browne, published by Jonathan Cape (Artwork © Anthony Browne), reproduced by permission of The Random House Group Ltd.

As we have tried to demonstrate, a significant finding from the research was that, while some children who were fluent readers of print were also good at reading image (such as Joe), it was also noticeable that many children in this study labelled as below average readers (such as Lara) were capable of subtle and engaged analysis of visual texts within an enabling environment: with an interested, experienced reader who listens carefully to their responses and gives them time to think; in a situation where the emphasis is on talk and image rather than written text and writing; where carefully constructed questions supportively challenge their thinking; through the facilitating process of talking in a focused yet open-ended way with peers and a teacher/researcher with high expectations of what the children could achieve; using a text that is intellectually, affectively and visually interesting and that motivates engagement and scaffolds learning – in other words, a text that teaches (Meek 1988). Indeed, as we read the transcripts, it is almost possible to watch the children working through their particular zone of proximal development into deeper understanding.

LARA: It's a good book because it gives you the feel of what it's like, because I never thought what it would be like in a cage.
INTERVIEWER: You've never thought of that before.
LARA: No, but then when I read this book it made me feel different. *It's a serious book* [our emphasis].

An earlier version of this chapter appeared in *Children's Literature in Education*, 32 (4) 2001, 261–281.

Vignette – 'I think she feels the pain of the animals' (Lara 10)

Lara was impressive from the outset. She listened and watched eagerly as her teacher read *Zoo* to the class and clearly couldn't wait to contribute to the discussion. Her answers showed her to be alert, sensitive and fairly articulate. As I knew that one of the two girls I was interviewing must be an experienced reader, I assumed (wrongly as it turned out) it was Lara, and was very surprised to discover later that she had literacy problems. Lara was eager to be interviewed and took an active part in the group discussion later in the day. Her drawing in response to *Zoo* was ironic, featuring a defiant, fashionably dressed woman with a bare midriff behind bars, shouting 'What's everyone looking at?' as families of pigs, foxes and bears jeer at her with cheeky, speech bubble remarks – 'Look at that thing!' 'Hey kids, look at that.'

The most noticeable aspect of Lara's response to *Zoo* was her empathy for the animals' plight which she often highlighted through powerful personal analogy. Looking at the picture of the penguins, she remarked, 'If I had to live in a cage, I would live in the penguins' cage because it has got nice turquoisy colour water and it looks like it's been looked after.' Speaking about the elephant which she has described as 'lonely . . . because it is in the dark in the corner doing nothing', Lara goes on to say: 'I think he [Browne] is trying to make us feel what you would feel if it was you being trapped in a cage.' She imagines the orang-utan 'is missing his family and wants to be at home where he used to

(continued)

(continued)

live instead of being trapped in the zoo, because most probably he doesn't want everyone looking at him all the time . . . and staring and shouting and waving and looking at him all the time. He just wants to be left alone.' Unsurprisingly, Lara was sensitive to Mum's feelings: 'I think she feels the pain of the animals. They want to be left alone and not pushed about and shouted at.' And later: 'The Mum is looking very miserable still because she has got dark patches around her eyes.'

This attention to pictorial detail also helped Lara analyse visual metaphors. She realised that Browne created a dramatic cover for visual impact: 'it makes it different from other books.' She correctly identified the imagery of wild geese on the final page: 'making it look like they're free, but the animals in the cages aren't.' She was also able to read the silhouette of bars against one of the boys: 'they've swopped around, so the boys are in the cage instead of the animals.' Lara was strongly aware of colour symbolism and the emotional intentions of the artist.

INTERVIEWER: How do you think Browne shows us the elephant's loneliness?
LARA: Because it is in the dark, in the corner doing nothing. It is all bright then they just go to into this other page and it's all dark . . .
INTERVIEWER: And do you think Browne did that deliberately?
LARA: Yeah, to make you feel what it is like to have everyone looking at you . . . it doesn't look a very nice place to be in, so that makes you think what would you feel if you were trapped up all the time in a horrible little cage.

Lara's teacher was surprised that she had made such a positive impact on our research, yet the extracts above show that she was deeply involved by the ideas in the book and articulate in exploring them. Did this largely pictorial text enable Lara to show what she was capable of when not held back by problems with decoding print? Did the images provide an enabling structure in which she could develop her ideas? By analysing a sophisticated picturebook (unlike the relatively simple fiction she could manage on her own), was it the case that, for once, the complex ideas, images and issues thrown up by this text matched Lara's need for challenging literature? She was so absorbed by this book that it led us to question the diet of texts struggling older readers like Lara exist on, how many chances they normally get to engage with satisfying texts, and whether visual texts should not have a greater part to play in reading development? It also raised questions about whether the short, highly focused approaches to extracts from books in literacy lessons had replaced more ruminative exposure to literature, where there was more time for young readers to explore texts in their own ways.

We had intended to re-interview Lara, but on the day in question she had the chance of taking part in a special maths game and chose that activity above ours. (Another child was re-interviewed in her place.) It was a useful corrective for a researcher all too ready to make assumptions about Lara's passionate commitment to picturebooks!

LARA: How would you feel . . . trapped up in a cage and everyone looking at you, staring at you, shouting at you. Treating you really bad. . . . If you think about it, if you had to be put in a cage, that is where you would stay. You would stay there and I can't imagine living in that sort of conditions.

INTERVIEWER: Did you think of that before you read the book?

LARA: No, I just thought about it a moment ago.

Notes

1 This shows the difference the knowledge and preferences of teachers can have on learning outcomes even in a situation where teachers were trying to follow a common script.
2 This was certainly a leading question, but one that the interviewer had used regularly with adults on other occasions, many of whom had failed to see the connection.

Chapter 4

'Letting the story out'
Visual encounters with *The Tunnel*

INTERVIEWER: Why do you think the ball and the book are together on the final page?
SENTHURAN (5): Because now the ball and the book can cuddle.

Sinatra defines visual literacy as 'the active reconstruction of past visual experience with incoming visual messages to obtain meaning' (1986: 5). This simple definition emphasises that visual skills are essential for encouraging an active and even critical interpretation of textual and visual information. In proposing to investigate how visual texts are read by children, we attempted to find out what skills children already possess, how they think about image and participate in the meaning-making process, and how this participation can be extended. *The Tunnel* provided an ideal means of exploring these areas, given that the printed text and the richly detailed illustrations only release their story when they are linked to other narratives and pictures. Yet because of Browne's careful use of symbols, even children as young as 4 are able to make these links and find meaning in *The Tunnel*, perhaps even better than many adult readers who have lost touch with the fairy-tale world in which Browne immerses his reader.

We found that even in their earliest impressions of *The Tunnel* it was evident that the children were drawing on their previous experience of books and their knowledge of the world. For example, one of the youngest children, Luke (5), spoke of things that couldn't happen in real life, 'but in books they can'. More importantly, from their reading experience – especially of the picturebook genre – they brought the expectation that what they saw carried meaning and that they would have to look for and construct it from the illustrations. Thus Simone (10), speaking of the first set of endpapers, said rightly: 'I think it might mean something that might be there later on in the story . . . it might mean the meaning of the story.' Even those children who were not familiar with Browne's work realised that they would have to look carefully in order to make sense of the story.

Gemma (9), however, was familiar with Browne's picturebooks and spoke of him as one of her favourite authors. She provided an example of how an experienced reader approaches a picturebook. She had read *The Tunnel* at home and also done some work on it at school 'for our literacy'. From her interview, we can gather that she lives in a house where reading and talking about books is commonplace. She writes stories, and visits the library every weekend to 'do some research on my favourite children's books'. When asked what was special about the illustrations for *The Tunnel*, she summed up the three most outstanding characteristics of this book:

'detail', 'characters' and 'colour'. In what follows, these characteristics and the way in which they were linked by the children to the characters and overall meaning of the story will be discussed at length.

Entering the tunnel

All the children regardless of age were enthusiastic about reading the book, and those who had not read it before were intrigued by it from the beginning. On the front cover a young girl can be seen, halfway into a dark tunnel; next to the entrance is an open book with drawings suggesting fairy tales. The children described the cover as 'interesting', but also as 'exciting', and arousing 'suspense'. It suggested something strange or wonderful would be found inside or at the other end of the tunnel and this made them want to read on:

> It makes me feel like there's going to be a fantasy story. . . . Like there's going to be like lots of stuff happening in there. And it's got really good titles [so you] know it's going to be a really good story.
>
> (Matt 8)

The narrative tells us about the resolution of the conflict between siblings. As the protagonists – Rose and Jack – are introduced, a visually alert reader will have begun to make connections between the girl and the boy and the book's endpapers, which are striking because of their contrasting patterns: leaves and flowers on one side and a brick wall on the other (upon closer inspection both of them turn out to be wallpapers). These images enhance the textual description of a sister and brother constantly at odds with each other because of their different temperaments: she likes to read and dream indoors on her own; he likes active games outside with his friends. We learn more about the children in the next spread where Jack is playing on Rose's fear of the dark by coming into her room with a mask. The wolf shadow cast by the boy, a red cloak, a picture inset of Little Red Riding Hood by Walter Crane and a lamp in the shape of a fairy-tale cottage are the first of many intertextual references to fairy tales the reader encounters in this book. As Doonan points out, all of Browne's picture-books require 'knowledge of other texts and discourses – folk and fairy tales, classics, and his own works, fine art, cinema, comics, advertisements; the intertextual process is his whole business' (1998: 1).

When they are sent outside by their mother, Jack finds a tunnel in a bit of waste ground and decides to explore. Rose becomes so worried when he does not return that she puts aside her fears and follows him through the dark and damp tunnel. On the other side is a wood that soon becomes a terrifying forest, with strange shapes on the trees and other objects reminiscent of fairy tales. After running through the forest, Rose arrives at a bleak clearing to discover a stone statue of her brother. Tenaciously she hugs him and smiles in triumph as he recovers his human form and hugs her back. The dark woods have become lighter and less dense, the sky is blue and the ring of small stones around Jack has become a ring of daisies. In the last picture, a happy, knowing Rose smiles at her brother. We read (because Browne does not show us Jack's face) that he smiles back. Their hair mingles and the warmth of the light from the window is reflected in her face.

Rose has confronted her fears and conquered them through love. The ball and the book, pictured together on the endpapers underneath the brick pattern, confirm the siblings' new-found closeness.

As we read and talked together, most of the children recognised the motifs that keep appearing throughout the book, such as the ball and book, the leaf and brick patterns and those related to the story of *Red Riding Hood*. In some cases, listing these and other objects sidetracked them from discussing the significance of the particular images, but more often it led them to speculate why the artist had put them there. Some children, for example Mark (8), proposed that Browne was playing a game to involve the reader: 'It makes you look at the picture [and] you use your imagination.' Other children suggested that he was creating a certain atmosphere: 'making it scary', said Simone (10) who thought that Browne 'included bits of stories into his book to make it have more feeling [. . .] that scary feeling and all sorts of feeling.'

During the interviews the children were fascinated by the many 'details', as they called them, and kept pointing them out – especially in the woods and the waste ground. As Dave (8) said, 'the more you look at it the more you find'. The significance of these details and their connection to the narrative usually began to emerge as the interviews and group discussions progressed, sometimes aided by the interviewer's questions. The following excerpt from the group discussion with 9–10-year-olds shows how the pupils build upon their peer observations to make meaning and also relate this meaning to their own life experiences. It is also an example of the way in which they analysed visual imagery and linked it to the characters' different temperaments:

SEAN: Look, salt and pepper!
INTERVIEWER: What about the salt and pepper?
SEAN: The pepper's black and [is interrupted]
CORINNA: And the salt's white! It's kind of like they're having an argument therefore they see things in a different way.
TAMSIN: Like me and my sister when we argue about something [see Figure 4.1].

As well as intertextual references, there are intratextual ones. The text and illustrations keep referring back to themselves and this leads to re-readings and moving back and forth between the pages and between the words and the pictures in order to make yet more connections between the incoming visual messages. Browne skilfully uses his craft to make these intratextual references, using colour, pattern and symbols. All these references are there for a purpose, as Browne himself says, 'whenever I put anything in like that [an image or reference within a picture] nearly every time, it's there for a purpose, it's there to help to take the story somewhere else, to tell something about the story'.[1] In *The Tunnel* these 'puzzles' (as Browne calls them) must be taken seriously and put together like a jigsaw in order to make the story meaningful. In order to arrive at a deeper understanding of this story, the bits and pieces of fairy tales which appear throughout the illustrations must be 'puzzled over' and sorted out. The next section reveals something of the children's reconstruction processes and how they contributed to the meaning of the story as a whole.

Whenever they were together they fought and argued noisily. All the time.

Figure 4.1 From *The Tunnel* by Anthony Browne

Source: Illustration from *The Tunnel* by Anthony Browne, copyright © 1989 Anthony Browne, reproduced by permission of Walker Books Ltd.

Fairy-tale land

The children's responses revealed their familiarity with the fairy-tale genre in their recognition of the intertextual references (especially to *Little Red Riding Hood*, but also to *Hansel and Gretel* and *Jack and the Beanstalk*). They used their knowledge of the genre in constructing explanatory narratives: for example, Gemma (9) pointed out that Rose's fears come from reading a lot of 'bad fairy tales'. Another example was when they gave explanations for Jack's statue-like form, such as that a witch or 'mythical character' (like 'the Medusa') had put some kind of magic spell or curse on the boy and 'marked their territory' with the stones. Another explanation was that Jack and the flowers had been 'frozen', probably an unconscious reference to the boy's 'cold' attitude to his sister. Several children contrasted his coldness to her warmth, and although they seemed to mean it literally, it is not difficult to see that they have a sense of the children's personalities: 'Because her body's warm-blooded she hugs him and then because she's warm all of her sweat and body makes the stone go away' (Shanaz 8).

Maria (8) literally linked his freezing to not having a coat (unlike his more sensible sister) and the dampness of the tunnel. This girl's imagination also led her to create a whole additional storyline where the witch's hat and black cat outside Rose's window were 'warnings' about what might happen to her brother, and the animals in the wood were 'giving her a message' that her brother was hurt. This imaginative but implausible deduction can be contrasted with the metaphor Gemma (9), the experienced reader we mentioned above, struggles to use in order to explain her more subtle grasp of the sibling relationship. Although at first glance her comments seem confusing, closer scrutiny shows Gemma has caught the tension in the relationship quite well:

> Maybe two things that didn't agree with each other bumped in and then like water doesn't agree with a computer because if you knock it down then . . . the computer'll go funny so if two things aren't happy with each other then something bad will happen.

Some explanations for the stones turning into flowers were integrated into the fantasy narrative although a few were also quite literal. Stewart (11) thought the stones or rocks were preventing the plants from growing, so when Jack moved they were able to shoot up again. Simone (10), like several others, thought the sun melted the stones. Gokhan (8) was the only child who mentioned God: 'Maybe God done it 'cos God was happy what she'd done. She saved her brother.' And Tamsin (9) was the only one who interpreted them as symbols:

> Because the [flowers] are beautiful. Or because maybe the artist thinks that rocks are not that peaceful because people throw them at things and they get breaked and flowers are peaceful because kids make chains as presents.

This kind of imaginative deduction, trying to thread together the events and objects in the pictures was an ongoing process. The readers were determined to make sense of the story, to try and explain why things appeared in the illustrations, to fit it into a coherent whole (within or without the folk/fairy-tale genre). This coincides with Gardner's description of the child's early development with respect to art: 'As the child gains facility in using language and reading pictures, he [sic] manifests a very strong tendency with respect to these symbols. Put directly, the child searches for meaning or reference in every perceived symbol or object' (1973: 156). This was especially apparent in the interview with a recent immigrant from Africa, Sam (11). He had no knowledge of European fairy tales, yet because of the strong visual images, he recognised the genre and worked hard to assemble the pieces of the story, grafting these to traditional tales from his own culture that deal with magic and witches (a more detailed analysis of his interview can be found in Chapter 6).

When the children got hold of an idea that began to make sense of all the 'details' and the general story, they became very excited, as in the group discussion below (with 8- and 9-year-olds). They all began speaking at once, racing ahead of each other with their ideas:

BOBBY: In that picture . . . that could be the Candy Cottage or something, it could be like a fairy-tale picture like, and they could have crawled into the picture.
MARIA: That's what I said, I said that!
RUTH: Well as they went into the tunnel, it might be like they're going into the fairy tale as well . . .
BOBBY: Yeah, oh no, maybe everything's the other way round in here.
DAVE: Yeah, it's a different world, everything's got the other way round. It's a fairy tale. He [Jack] must have gone into the pictures!

This group developed the fairy-tale motif more than other discussion groups did and, in the example above, it is clear how they encouraged each other towards an understanding of the story. They are also using previous readings to imagine that Rose and Jack 'entered' another world, one where 'everything is the other way round' (a reference to *Through the Looking-Glass*?). Although only a few children like those in this group actually described the other side of the tunnel as 'fairy-tale land' or described Rose's adventure as a fairy tale in itself, it is evident from all the responses that there was a continual exploration of the possibilities which would help construct a schema for interpretation. As the children saw more intertextual references, they refined this mental schema, actively extending their own and, in some cases, others' understanding of the story.

Brothers and sisters

The character of the siblings and their relationship is the other focal point of the book. In some cases the children reduced the plot to a simple 'they didn't like each other and now they are friends', but in others there was a more complex understanding of their relationship. Many children made immediate analogies between the relationship in the book and their own experiences of these relationships (fighting, making up with their siblings):

> Like me and my sister. We don't actually get along very much, because we fight a lot, well when she's upset, I really, well I don't feel good.
>
> (Ruth 8)

Here we have the bridging of life experience with the visual experience, a text-to-life link that also allows the reader/viewer to create meaning from art. It is also life experiences that the artist builds on and in this case we have Browne's recollections from his childhood, not only of a dangerous game he used to play with his brother, swinging their legs over an abandoned tunnel, but also of being left alone in the woods.[2]

Although at the beginning not everyone was able to say what the wallpapers represented, by the end of the book most linked the patterns that appear throughout the illustrations to the differences in the children's characters. Even Polly, who had just turned 5, was able to see this: 'I've noticed that the boy always has bricks there and the girl always has patterns.' From the picture of the waste ground, readers were also able to infer something about the sibling relationship and their insights went well beyond the obvious ones based on body language (not facing each other) and symbolic objects (the pipeline or pole that physically separates their spaces). For example:

> Well [the picture] tells you that the brother don't like the sister because the sister's sitting like far away from the brother. The brother's standing quite far away. You can see the brother don't want her near, because you can see the pole and he don't want his sister to cross it.
>
> (Matt 8)

Because of the contrast between the siblings, the story lends itself to gender analysis.[3] In one school, during the reading of the story, a few boys snorted when the teacher read that Rose was scared to go into *The Tunnel*. Like Jack, *they* would have gone inside with no hesitation! Some of the older boys also seemed impatient with her fears about witches and goblins and, like her brother, probably thought she was being a 'baby'. The wallpaper patterns were considered to represent the children because 'girls like flowers' and boys play football on the 'grass' (the green bit of carpet). Reading was definitely felt to be a 'girl thing' and playing football a 'boy thing'. Cliff (10) said that looking around in waste ground was also a 'boy's thing': 'I think he's more at home there because I know that boys like exploring in a junk yard.'

The most profound insight into the general question of gender and the fairy-tale genre was made by Dave (now 9) during the follow-up interview. When asked to talk about the last picture (when Rose is smiling at Jack), he seems suddenly struck by an idea:

> She thinks she's been to a fairy-tale land and she's like [long pause] instead it's the other way around! It's usually the lady who gets stuck and the boy who rescues, usually, and here the girl rescues the boy. Like in nearly every fairy tale when the lady is stuck in the tower, a man comes along and rescues her or she gets chased by the fox and the woodcutter chops his head off another man. And this time it's a girl. [Browne's] changed it [Interviewer: Why?] To make it feel, don't know, like if this little girl . . . she might feel she couldn't do anything so now she can do something the boy can't.

Revealed in Dave's response is one of the achievements of Browne's artistry which can be described in Grumet's words, 'the work of art simultaneously draws the viewer to it; engaging expectations, memories, recognition, and then interrupts the viewer's customary response, contradicting expectations with new possibilities, violating memories, displacing recognition with estrangement' (quoted in Sinatra 1986: 31). Dave's expectations of gender roles were contradicted and hopefully these 'new possibilities' will lead him to 'see' further or keep an open mind before applying the usual gender stereotypes. Although the other pupils did not seem to be aware of this change of roles, with further guidance from a teacher, most of them would probably be able to achieve similar insight into this and other gender issues in *The Tunnel*.

Another aspect that strengthens the bond between the siblings is that at the end of the story they share a secret, a secret that is kept from their mother. They are smiling in the final page, not only because they like each other now but also because no-one else knows what happened and it will be their special secret. This was also a matter for empathy and analogy:

> She's smiling because their mum don't know what happened, and they do. That's the kind of look I have when I steal some ice cream from the kitchen.
>
> (Tamsin 9)

For most of the readers, it was the sibling relationship which was seen as conveying the main message of the book. One child who came from a family of Jehovah's Witnesses managed to find 'a lesson' in the book: 'So it must have been like a lesson, maybe. [Interviewer: What sort of a lesson?] Maybe you should always like your family and enemies, your friends.'[4] Dave (8) did not say it was a 'lesson', he just boiled the thought down even further: 'Don't be angry with people, be friends.' In general, when the children were asked if the book could be described as 'funny' or 'serious', although some parts were found to be 'funny' (such as where the brother scares his sister with the mask), because of this message or 'lesson' the book was mainly considered 'serious'.

In the initial endpapers only the book appears, but both ball and book sit side by side in the final endpapers. Their explanations for the change of focus in the endpapers were sometimes quite literal, such as that he was outside playing with it or 'maybe the brother didn't like football then' (Shanaz 8). Although some of the younger children still missed the point about the ball and the book on the final end-papers, most realised they stood for a closer relationship between the siblings, as Natasha (10) said: 'Because they're together, that means they're getting along.'

Watson, reading *The Tunnel* with 4½-year-old Ann, also tells us that she recognised the symbolism of the ball and the book: 'Ann knew at once that the illustration was a metaphorical representation of reconciliation, or friendship, or what she thought of as *kindness*.' Watson points out that this interpretation involved 'more than an instant revelation about an image; it involved a kind of "backward reading" and the ability to hold in her mind a full and holistic sense of the story and the way the narrative web is strung together' (1996: 148). This stringing or piecing of the narrative was being done all along the way, gathering force as the readers had more time to think about it and make more connections. The way in which certain visual features, such as the use of pattern and colour, helped strengthen these connections (book/flowers and ball/bricks) will be discussed in the next section.

Drawing 'the real' and other visual features

The visual features mentioned most often by the children were colour (particularly the use of dark and light) and the hyper-realist style of the illustrations. They make Browne's work easily recognisable and memorable. Matt (8) immediately compared the two picturebooks he was familiar with: 'In *Zoo* he uses colours quite light, and in *The Tunnel* he uses them quite dark.' According to the children, it is these two features that make a 'good' artist: the colours make the pictures 'stand out' (e.g. Rose's red cloak and the wolf's red eyes) and his detailed and what they saw as realistic style make them 'lifelike'. The use of shadows – another of Browne's trademarks – also provoked positive comments. Some children (probably echoing adults) praised him for 'staying in the lines', colouring them in 'nicely' and 'not smudging'!

Several respondents revealed a keen interest in the technical aspects of his drawing, such as his use of different kinds of paints and brushes. Although they may have been incorrect in supposing what kind of brush Browne actually used, it perhaps made them think of their own artistic experiences and it is clear how much they would have benefited by discussing the pictures with an art teacher. One of the children who spoke most about Browne's techniques was Maria (8). Her comments show how carefully she had examined each picture. Asked to talk about the first set of four pictures (where the characters are introduced), she referred to colour and tone:

[On the girl in the room and the boy outside] I like how he's mixed them colours up. Like there's light green, then a little darker then really dark and then lighter again. He's mixed all the colours up together to make them look like they're from the sunlight [as] it's shining onto the curtains and you can see the shadows as well, from the boys [outside].

She also spoke of the transformation caused by the use of light and dark in the sequence when Jack turns from stone back into a boy, regaining his own colours while the sky goes from grey to blue. Like many of her peers, Maria easily linked this change to the mood of the narrative: 'Then instead of being dark, it comes to . . . light and then more light, and then light. That's why I like that, because they probably done that because of the happy ending.'

Tamsin (9) was another discerning viewer and both she and Maria tried to explain how the perspective in several pictures worked. Although precise technical terms are not used, we have a detailed appreciation of Browne's artistic techniques as well as value judgements based on his ability to capture reality through body language, colour and detail as well as perspective:

MARIA: I like (Browne's) bird's eye view from up above.
TAMSIN: It looks like it's a really long way, the picture [of Rose entering the tunnel]. But it's just one piece of paper and you're looking down.

In developmental models of aesthetic experience, the middle childhood years are usually considered to be a time when children express a preference for realism. This could be one reason for children's attraction to Browne's style, as things are drawn as they supposedly really look. Benson questions this theory by citing Goodman's distinction between 'pictorial fidelity' and 'pictorial realism', fidelity being the representation of the object corresponding to the properties which are ascribed to it and realism depending on 'how easily this information (in a picture) is yielded to the viewer by the picture' (1986: 125). Benson argues that middle childhood is characterised by both pictorial realism and pictorial fidelity and this is related to their first experiences with literacy in school where they are encouraged to understand the word–thing relationship as denotative, thus reducing the ability of pictures to render meaning if they do not clearly denote objects or actions with which they are already familiar.

It is interesting that Browne's hyper-realist drawings were frequently compared to other types of visual media with which the children were familiar, for example: videos, 3-D ('not just a flat picture'), film and a 'play'. Simone talked about the way Browne 'set out' the picture of Rose going into *The Tunnel* as if it were 'in slow motion'. Dave liked the way the graffiti on the walls looked like 'proper spray'. References to the way movement looks in real life were made about Rose running in the forest. Children talked about 'smudging', 'all the bits going off' and how colour contributed to this effect: 'Because when you run . . . you can see the colours, they kind of run away' (Tamsin 9).

This raises questions about the value children accord to what they see as 'realistic' and what many of them also enjoy but is definitely 'unrealistic', such as cartoons. Could it be that in the case of *The Tunnel* a more 'realistic' style of drawing allows them to relate to the characters in more depth? Further research is clearly needed in this area to understand how children read and value different styles, not only in the technical sense but also in terms of their emotional and intellectual response.

Following Benson's line of thought, although Browne's picturebook apparently 'yields information' quite easily to the viewer, it then causes a disruption in their expectancies of narrative because readers are forced to consider objects that, although 'realistic' in style, denote something beyond themselves – such as the ball and the book. The objects in the waste-ground picture are a good example too, because of the eagerness with which the children identified them, and also because they had to consider why they were there not just as 'junk' but as symbols of the siblings' relationship (like the pipe or pole that divides them) as well as intriguing intratextual references (the shoes, the cat face). With the interviewer's prompting, many of the pupils in this study did consider the links between these references (and many of them appeared in their drawings; see Chapter 8).

'Describing' words and 'helping' pictures

In *The Tunnel*, the relationship between the words and the pictures is more straightforward than in some of Browne's other books (such as *Zoo* or *Voices in the Park*). The written and pictorial texts reinforce one another, with the pictures adding symbolic and intertextual dimensions to the story. The children, especially the younger ones, found it hard to differentiate the stories told by the words and the pictures. Most of them thought the pictures were more interesting than the words; they felt that the words without the pictures would be 'boring', whereas the book could still be good without the words. However, some of the older children considered the words equally important. Stewart (11), for example, said Browne was a good illustrator but he also 'throws these little words in very well'. The pictures were considered aids to understanding and a better way of showing details which would take too long to describe in words, as Kemal (8) explained: "cos if it doesn't say she's running, on the pictures you look, you can see her running.'

Jason (9) had an interesting theory about the different narratives (textual and visual): that the forest picture was 'from the girl's point of view . . . because she's scared and if you're scared, you imagine stuff like that.' Simone (10) also attempted to explain the difference:

> They tell different stories because there it says they went to a piece of waste ground and here you can see it but you could actually tell it in a different way to the writing (because) he can get more descriptive words and you can see the pipes and all sorts of stuff.

Gemma (9) was one of the few who talked in more detail about the written text and found it hard to choose between one or the other:

> He's very good at illustrations and the words he used to describe things and the nouns he puts in makes it look . . . makes you want to read more [Interviewer: What kinds of nouns make you want to read the book?] He doesn't just sleep softly, he sleeps soundly. He doesn't just sleep normal. So the words he used are very effective. Well I couldn't really choose between them [words or pictures]

because the illustrations are excellent and the words he uses just capture your imagination and then if it didn't have any pictures you would still understand because the words he uses describes it very well.

Even though Gemma seems to actually be referring to adjectives rather than nouns, she reveals an understanding of the interaction of words and pictures and how both of them move the story along.

According to the children, having pictures make it easier for the book to appeal to younger audiences. They seemed to agree that *The Tunnel* would be 'good' for all ages ('from age 1 to about 13', according to Dave) because both younger and older children would enjoy looking at the pictures. Jason (9) recommended the picturebook 'for parents to read to their children when they're quite young, about 5 or 6', because if the children were 'beginners' the pictures would help them understand the book better. Natasha (10) added: 'They will be able to read the pictures because children have a good imagination.'

Conclusion: rites of passage

Browne has commented that, among the many letters he receives from his readers, the ones about *The Tunnel* are the most interesting and that children seem to be 'really thinking' about this story. Our study confirmed that children 'really think' as they read and look, so much so that, as Watson writes of 4-year-old Ann also apropos *The Tunnel*: 'Reading illustrations was not a mere list-making activity or an inventorying of her observations; it was a complex and dynamic process, mediated through conversation' (1996: 151). Throughout the interview day (and in some cases in the follow-up interviews) it was possible to observe how their thinking processes developed and their mental schema changed as they became more familiar with the story. Many of the children, for example, tended to get 'stuck' in their 'inventories' of the objects in the pictures. Once they had taken their time to look and had been gently prodded by the researcher's questions, they were able to consider how these objects contributed to understanding the 'bigger picture'.

Doonan uses the words 'psychological journey' in a possible interpretation of *The Tunnel*,[5] and Browne speaks of the story being about the boy and the girl 'coming together in some sort of balance'.[6] Although the children obviously did not have the knowledge and experience to articulate these interpretations of the story, their responses showed that, through the dialogue with the interviewers, they were widening their Vygotskian 'zone of proximal development' and beginning to appropriate more mature structures of meaning.

Gardner grants the status of 'audience member' to children when they reach the age of 7 because they are capable of 'experiencing pleasurable sensations and changes of affect in the presence of symbolic objects, by appreciating the difference between artistic illusions and real experiences, and by achieving some understanding of the symbol system' (1973: 234). However, he stops short of according 'critic' status to children because, although 'the genuine antecedents of the critical faculty seem dependent upon some degree of competence with symbols', they cannot articulate their reactions and evaluations in a systematic manner (1973: 118). Our study indicated that all of the children we worked with could be considered 'audience members', including those under the age of 7, and that some of the more experienced 'viewers' required only a little help in order to become 'critics'. These are precisely the abilities and skills that need to be taken into account in a curriculum which claims to emphasise 'literacy'.

As Sinatra says: 'The visually literate are those who have acquired the ability to make viable judgements about the image they perceive' (1986: 56). Just consider the following comment by Tamsin (9), which reveals acute observation of artistic features, emotional involvement and critical appraisal:

[About the siblings at the table:] 'Cause the way the shade's done on that, it's lighter then it gets darker, cause the sun is on the part of the roof, it makes this part dark and this part light and how it's just chosen like, the arm is going around and it's not just like flat. I think it's really wonderful the way they've done the shadow, it's good.

The children were definitely learning to be 'visually literate' and only lacked the words to express their aesthetic experiences. In fact, in some ways their choice of words – notwithstanding grammatical structure – went further in describing aspects of the work than many adults would probably do. Gemma (9) best summed up Browne's accomplishment in *The Tunnel* as: 'the way he does the illustrations, it just lets the story out.'

An earlier version of this chapter appeared in *Reading* 35 (3), pp. 115–119.

Vignette – 'If you can read the pictures you can tell another story' (Dave 8/9)

As I was writing this vignette, I glanced at the answers Dave gave to our questionnaire on reading habits and preferences. They were no different to those of most of the 8- or 9-year-old boys in the study (in brief, he liked reading picturebooks, comics and stories but preferred computer games to books), except that his handwriting was more illegible than most and, where I could read it, his spelling seemed based on his own particular phonetic rendition of a word: 'Bloow peter' (*Blue Peter*), 'Benow' (*Beano*), 'Supooer Mareeyow' (*Super Mario*), 'Dinsi pichus' (Disney pictures). I had not seen this questionnaire at the time of the interview, nor did I know that he was a pupil who 'struggled with reading and writing' as his teacher later told me.

As we went through the interview questions and looked at Browne's *The Tunnel*, I was struck by Dave's engagement with the narrative, his capacity for noticing pictorial details and his frequent references to visual techniques (including terms from other visual media such as comics, photography, film and computer games). It was obvious that he found the images compelling from the very beginning:

The pictures just look so good. You just want to read it . . . you think, 'Oh, what's going to happen to her, is she going to die, is she going to live, what's going to happen?' It just makes you read it.

(continued)

(continued)

Dave grasped not only the basic plot but also some of the finer details of the narrative after just a couple of readings, an achievement many of his fellow pupils did not manage immediately. He realised the differences between the siblings, he recognised the allusions to fairy tales and summed up Browne's message: 'Don't be angry with people, be friends.' During the group interview he went a step further in his interpretation:

> 'It's a different world. It's a fairy tale. [Jack] must have gone into the pictures.' Five months later during the re-interview he came up with the most insightful interpretation of the book of all his contemporaries, in terms of Browne's subversion of typical gender roles: 'It's usually the lady who gets stuck and the boy who rescues, usually, and here the girl rescues the boy. He's [Browne] changed it . . . like if this little girl she might feel she couldn't do anything so now she can do something the boy can't.'

Dave's interpretation of the story was based on his attention to detail and his ability to make sense of it within the narrative. During the group interview he said he liked the details because they 'make you look at the picture [and] you use your imagination'. He noticed the flowers on Rose's mat and the explosion on Jack's as they sit at the table, as well as the line between them created by the shadow on the wall. He linked it to the different wallpapers which show 'they don't have nothing in common' so 'they hate each other'. Then, speaking of the coming together of the siblings at the end of the book, he says 'the stones mean hate and the flowers mean love'. But he's also noticed other significant details:

> The pictures have got detail in them because if you look in this picture there's no trees, but when the sister comes to get him there's like some trees, like they just re-grow . . . when she touches him. [It's] gloomy, then lighter and lighter. Look here, she's nearly avoided it, like her brother, going into the ring.

The last sentence refers to a 'detail' I had not noticed and which I presume few readers of *The Tunnel* ever notice: there is a shadow which one can assume is of Rose's head, just at the edge of the circle of stones where her brother has been 'frozen'.

On several occasions Dave described Browne's style as 'realistic' and this realism extended to other aspects such as 'the way they [the characters] stand'. When asked how Browne made things look 'real', he showed me the entrance to the tunnel as an example and explained that it was of 'all the creases . . . and all the shading, it looks like 3-D not just a flat picture, it goes darker'. These details were painstakingly reproduced in his own drawing of Rose going into the tunnel, where he attempted to show these creases as well as the shading. He was particularly sensitive to different textures, the graffiti on the waste-ground wall, for example, looked 'like proper spray, it's smudged'.

He also noticed the tiny blue dots covering the image of the boy lying on his bed and speculated that Browne had used a blow pen for spraying it.

Because Browne is such a 'good artist', according to Dave, he could make a picture-book without words and 'you'd still know what's going on'. The problem was when you had a book with just words, because 'it would be a lot fatter book because there'd have to be more writing, describing and everything'. Dave said that before he could read, he'd 'make up the words in my head', but he also said that he'd recently had trouble 'making up the pictures' for a book for 'older children' which he had found difficult to understand.

It seems Dave's extraordinary capacity for making sense of visuals was not helping him face the printed word. However, during the interviews he mentioned another of Browne's picturebooks, *Voices in the Park,* and it was evident he had been struck by the different print fonts which distinguish each character's version of the story. In this case, the letters themselves had become visual objects:

[*Voices*] is good because one person has different writing and speech, like one has slanty writing . . . some is printed like on computer, some big bubble letters, some was writ [sic] quite small.

Would it be possible to use these sorts of observations to make print more accessible to Dave? Could this be a way forward for helping Dave in his reading and writing? But would his teacher notice and, even if she did, would she have the time and knowledge to build upon these visual skills? Finally, I ask myself, during his schooling, will anyone realise there is 'another story' to be told about Dave's literacy skills?

Notes

1 All quotes from Browne are from an interview we conducted in January 2000 which can be read in full in the 2003 edition.
2 The first incident is mentioned in Doonan (1998: 2); the second was mentioned in Chapter 10 of our original volume.
3 In discussing *The Tunnel's* setting as support for characterisation, Nikolajeva and Scott comment that: 'we must accept that there is considerable gender stereotyping in this book' (2001: 105). It seems to us that Browne is actually using these stereotypes in order to make a point about how they can be subverted.
4 A reminder of the children in Roadville who were expected to find the 'moral' in stories, in Heath's 1983 study, *Ways with Words.*
5 Doonan (1998: 2–3): 'The story may be interpreted as a psychological journey of male and female principles moving towards integration, or the unity of ego and id, or as contrast between conscious and unconscious worlds, or simply as being about two children of different temperaments of either sex.'
6 Browne (interview 2000, quoted Chapter 10 in 2003 edition): 'I think it's also a book about coming to terms with different aspects of your own character. In a way it's about a brother and sister, but it's also in a way the two aspects of oneself. I mean I think, I identify with both the boy and the girl in that. And in the end you have them coming together in some sort of balance.'

Chapter 5

Putting yourself in the picture

A question of talk

Helen Bromley

'What is the use of a book,' thought Alice, 'without pictures or conversations?'
(*Alice in Wonderland*, Lewis Carroll, 1865)

Introduction

A good story's got to have a problem and the problem's in the pictures.
(Kathy 6)

Picture, if you will, the following scenes. Running her fingers over Kitamura's evocative blue sky in *Lily Takes a Walk*, Kathy says softly, 'Back in Majorca we had some colours with that all across the sky . . . and also in the sand, blending.' Judy ponders the reasons why Kitamura has drawn steps with wobbly lines and says, 'They are very old. My church is very old and it has steps like that.'

These snatches of conversation illustrate the power of the picturebook to stimulate children to reflect on their past through the window of the present. Invited into the miniature world of the illustration, children and indeed the adults who are prepared to take time to look, contemplate and talk with them, have access to both individual and shared histories. The illustrations in the book encompass the individual's past within the present time and everyone's experiences are authenticated. In this chapter I shall look at how this shared context created by the pictures provided a foundation for some fertile and reflective conversations.

Tell me . . .

In discussing *Lily* with the children, both as individuals and as small groups, I became increasingly conscious of the role that the pictures played in creating a shared world. Although the memories which the pictures triggered in me could not be identical to those of the children, it became clear that through the pictures it was possible to find 'common ground' – areas of experience which, despite the differences in our ages and personal histories, overlapped and formed a shared foundation for conversation – a site for genuine collaboration. The creation of this shared context was supported by the pace at which the interviews were conducted. It was as if the pictures were being shared, savoured and relished in the manner of friends looking at photographs, rather than as a lesson in looking.

How might all this appear in practice? Here is Kathy (6) discussing with the interviewer a double-page spread which shows Lily and Nicky standing on a bridge. Lily looks at the ducks on one side of the bridge, while on the other Nicky is aware of an enormous dinosaur. His legs are moving frantically; we know this through Kitamura's use of the conventions of animation – numerous legs on the dog, and movement indicated by small lines around his paws. The text on the page reads simply 'She stops by the bridge to say good night to the gulls and the ducks on the canal' (Figure 5.1).

The discussion went as follows:

INTERVIEWER: Tell me about this picture.

KATHY: She might have found some things in the bag that the ducks might like to eat. And she is throwing them out and Nicky is looking at them and I think it might be a dinosaur, it might be a big duck!

INTERVIEWER: You see that as a big duck?

KATHY: But it hasn't got any wings.

INTERVIEWER: No it hasn't got any wings, yes it is the funniest-looking duck I have ever seen, I have to say!

KATHY: It hasn't got any beak.

INTERVIEWER: No. No beak. I think we can safely assume it's not a duck.

KATHY: It might be a dinosaur.

INTERVIEWER: It might be a dinosaur.

KATHY: But how could there be a dinosaur in the water and also, there wasn't people when dinosaurs were alive. But there was a couple but I suppose they killed 'em to eat the meat.

INTERVIEWER: Oh, well the dog's got problems in that case. How do we know then that he is moving, this little dog, how do we know he is moving?

KATHY: Because he is going like that [waving arms in the background]. He might be doing the can-can . . .

Chambers says that the words, *Tell me*, 'suggest a desire for collaboration, indicating that the teacher really does want to know what the reader thinks, and that it anticipates conversational dialogue rather than an interrogation' (1993: 49). This certainly seems to be true in the example above. By this point in the interview Kathy has been asked to tell the interviewer about other pictures in the book and so realises that her views are valued, and that there are no right or wrong answers. In fact she feels so secure that she is able to make jokes and enter into a playful relationship with the interviewer. What is not apparent from the transcript is the mischievous grin and the tongue-in-cheek tone as she says, 'It might be a big duck.'

In the conversational exchange that follows (where both participants use irony), the joke is played around with, and indeed various possibilities explored, until Kathy herself suggests that it might be a dinosaur. The adult's responses are also important here. To have closed the exchange at this point, and decreed that the creature was indeed a dinosaur and that Kathy was 'correct' might well have closed the conversation down. What came next might not have been heard at all and yet is one of the most interesting parts of the conversation. She knows that the likelihood of there

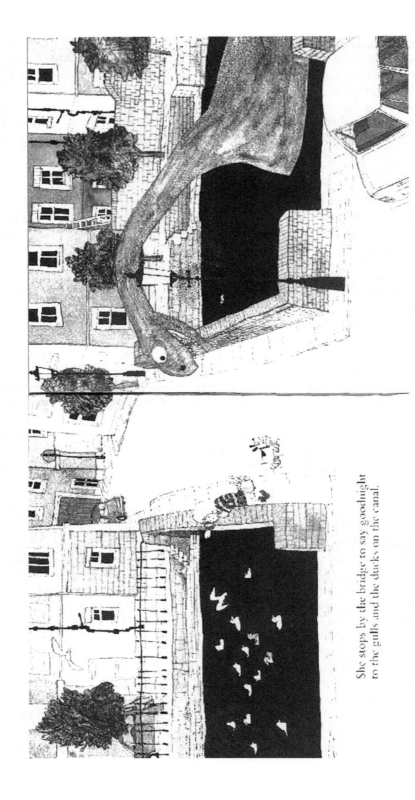

She stops by the bridge to say goodnight to the gulls and the ducks on the canal.

Figure 5.1 From *Lily Takes a Walk* by Satoshi Kitamura

Source: Illustration from *Lily Takes a Walk* by Satoshi Kitamura reprinted by permission of Catnip Publishing

being a dinosaur in the water is slim for a number of reasons: there aren't dinosaurs now (implied, but not stated) and they did not roam the earth at the same time as people. However, what she can see in front of her is indisputable: dinosaurs and humans in the same picture. This juxtaposition of remembered facts prompts the sanctioning of the widest range of possibilities. What is apparent here is a child 'turning around' her own schema. Her memories of what she knows about dinosaurs have to be reconstructed in order to fit the context in which she is working. Kathy has what Bartlett (1932: 206) would describe as 'the capacity to turn around (her) own schemata and construct them afresh'. In the conversation in which she is participating no single type of knowledge is privileged over another – thus creating an atmosphere where Kathy feels that she is able to reflect on and manipulate her memories to solve the problem that the picture poses.

Kathy's humorous approach continues when the adult returns to the interview schedule to ask about the dog's legs. The sort of complex concepts that Kathy is dealing with and the way that she deals with them are made manifest through her conversation. In order to subvert facts, you need to feel secure in your knowledge of them, and she does this remarkably well. What we have here is visible thinking. Kathy's ability to use her remembered knowledge and make connections between it and the context in which she is currently working are as worthy of note as her interpretations of the picture. The *Tell me* focus has effectively given Kathy permission to ask and answer her own questions.

It is important, too, to note how identities and roles are created through the discussion around a picture. In this small piece of transcript Kathy positions herself in several ways: a dinosaur/prehistory expert; an animation expert; a user of irony; a thinker; a conversationalist. She does not position herself in the traditional role of 'pupil' – a receiver of knowledge. The identity that she creates for herself (through talk) is of someone who is on equal terms with the adult in the conversation, who is confident to take turns with the adult, and who can manipulate the pictorial symbol system assuredly. There is a genuine non-competitiveness about this exchange which makes it all the more worthwhile. Both participants co-operate in the negotiation of meanings, which no doubt encourages Kathy to talk about her ideas. As Wells points out, 'It is the collaborative approach . . . that encourages children to explore their understanding of a topic and gives them the confidence to try out their ideas without the fear of being wrong' (1986: 115).

Judy (6), another child from Kathy's class, also used her prior knowledge to make meaning of this particular double spread. Asked to tell the interviewer about the picture she begins:

JUDY: He is in the water, he must be swimming but he can't put his neck in there because he is too big he might knock all the houses down. He [the dog] is scared because there is one of them [referring to the dinosaur].

INTERVIEWER: How do you know he is scared?

JUDY: Because he is big and she is looking at the ducks. They're looking different ways again because he probably doesn't like duckies and they're probably scared of the dog. She has put the flowers down.

INTERVIEWER: She has put the flowers down. I suppose it is difficult to feed the ducks if you are holding the flowers. Why is he drawn like that though?

JUDY: He's gonna run away from that probably.

INTERVIEWER: So what does it mean then?

JUDY: He is shouting.

INTERVIEWER: Mmm. Dogs don't have eight legs do they, so why has he got lots of legs in that then?

JUDY: Is it because his legs are shaking?

INTERVIEWER: Yes, I think you are right.

JUDY: That's what happens, because I had this thing and she only had two wings and arms and when they ha! turned around and then she had lots [Judy is referring to a toy].

As with Kathy, Judy clearly demonstrates how problems can be solved through conversation. Importantly, she was asked to explain how she knew something. This supplementary question led ultimately to Judy being able to explain a complex visual phenomenon (persistence of vision) and how it can be represented in two dimensions and not three. Judy continues to speculate about the picture for some considerable time, discussing such wide-ranging topics as the possibility that all the houses are empty (because their occupants are at the pub), and what would happen if the dog was to be eaten by the dinosaur. Throughout her interview Judy was able to use her experiences of life to interpret the miniature world encapsulated in the pictures of Kitamura. Her answers and interpretations are even more remarkable when one considers that she was positioned in the 'lowest ability' group in that classroom.

It is fascinating to look at the different types of experiences which the girls draw upon in interpreting the pictures. In both cases they use their own first-hand experiences – feeding the ducks in the park, for example, or playing with a moving toy. There are also those experiences whose reality is of a different nature. Kathy's knowledge of life in prehistoric times comes from books read, films or TV programmes seen or museums visited. Looking at Judy, one can see the same types of knowledge being used: the reality that was her spinning toy, the reality that is feeding the ducks, and the knowledge about dinosaurs – their size and strength. This thoughtful and reflective dialogue with their past provides the children with a powerful means of moving forward in their thinking.

It is talk which empowers this. Asked to *Tell me* about the picture through writing, it is certain that for Judy at least, such complex understandings would never have been revealed. The task of writing would have masked her considerable ability to reflect on the pictures in front of her. Dialogue is also important – while a writing journal, or a 'thinking book' would have gone some way towards supporting and enhancing these behaviours, the teacher would also have needed to be an equal partner in the written dialogue.

The pictures are undoubtedly the key to the children's success. Both participants in the dialogue have equal access to the ideas represented by the illustrator. This would not have been the case had we been discussing written text. Trying to hold the ideas presented by the written word and reflect upon them would have been too demanding for both Judy and Kathy. More importantly, dealing with the written word, the adult would have undoubtedly been the expert. Pictures provide a landscape in which minds can meet for contemplation rather than competition.

Griffin and Cole, quoted in Edwards and Mercer, say that 'a zone of proximal development is a dialogue between a child and his future; it is not a dialogue between the child and an adult's past' (1987: 164). It is interesting to consider this quote in the light of the children's discussions. It is obvious that the children's past histories are of considerable importance to them as ways of constructing meaning. It is as if the pictures act as a trigger for a host of memories – each one personal to that child. The adult's past is also important in these discussions. It is the over-lapping pieces of these autobiographies that help child and adult understand each other, finding commonalities of experience as well as being able to explore differences. The possible worlds created by Kitamura, child and adult, overlap. Each participant in the discussion has their experiences widened through incursion, not only into the worlds of the picturebook, but also into the remembered vistas that are the landscapes of memory.

Reading together

Kathy, interviewed for a second time, is prompted to draw upon a whole new refer-ential framework to discuss the pictures in *Lily*.

> Bats flitter and swoop in the evening sky. 'Aren't they clever, Nicky?' says Lily. 'Not far now.'

KATHY: I don't really like bats.
INTERVIEWER: Don't you?
KATHY: NO.
INTERVIEWER: We get some in our garden sometimes. I think they're quite curious. They move very funnily.
KATHY: My nan gets foxes, well she used to.
INTERVIEWER: Does she? Did she used to feed them, Kathy?
KATHY: No.
INTERVIEWER: No. Do they come for her dustbins?
KATHY: Well, once actually, my Dad was sleeping over my Nan's for some reason I don't know, and he left his trainers outside and the foxes came and sort of bited the laces and stuff and it was all horrible. And there was all holes in his trainers and everything.

This vignette of family life so powerfully provided by Kathy may at first glance seem to consist mostly of 'off task' talk; however, this is not the case. The comment prompted by the picture of the bat is picked up on and the discussion enlarged, and culminates in the sharing of an amusing anecdote and, less importantly, an insight into the habits of urban foxes. It is as significant as the contemplation of the meaning behind the picturebook or Kathy's comprehension of the story. This type of talk builds relationships and creates shared contexts which may act as reference points for future learning.

Knowledge about the children as individuals can only be gained through conver-sations such as these. Through these spoken stories Kathy's ideas and interpretation of events are available with an intimacy, immediacy and authenticity that would be difficult to match in a conventional activity. Yet it is too frequently the case that, in the classroom situation, the adult needs to drive on with the 'educational' agenda of the day, hiding wisdom and understandings such as those displayed above. Conversations like these also build the relationships needed for children to feel emotionally secure and predisposed to learn. How good to know that the grown-up with whom you are working is interested in you as a person, and not just as a recipient of an adult-designed and -delivered curriculum. Wells (1986) speaks of how 'the content of the curriculum becomes increasingly to be presented symbolically through uses of language that are more characteristic of writing than of conversation'. He goes on to argue that children for whom it is difficult to cope 'with the linguistic representation of ideas that are disembedded from a context of specific personal experiences' become less able to meet the demands of the school system, and become judged as academically limited. The use of pictures overcomes these difficulties.

The older children in the study tended to be less conversational in their responses. While studying the picture of the dinosaur that gave the younger children such food for thought, the older children's comments included: 'Lily's looking at something nice . . . all the swans and ducks swimming around, but all Nicky sees is a big dinosaur' (Tina 8). Unlike Kathy, Tina returns directly to the book in her description of the picture, but on this occasion chooses not to expand on the theme of the dinosaur. Seamus (7) pursues a line of thought prompted by the drawing of Nicky: 'I like the way where they've put the dog. You've got like four legs at the front and four legs at the back and he's trying to get away. The water's kind of really dark. . . . A little bit of black, not exactly blue.'

To Seamus and Tina, the juxtaposition of the dinosaur with a human being does not pose the problem that it does for Kathy. For Seamus, the picture simply amuses him; and we could argue that Tina also 'got the joke'. Their reflections, however, did not seem to take on the dialogic nature of either Kathy or Judy's comments. This may be, of course, because some of the dialogue has become internalised. Transcripts alone cannot show the way that the children examined the picture, their heads to one side in contemplation.

Looking at the same picture, Lauren (10) comments:

> There's a bridge in the middle page with houses in the background and then Lily is looking at the ducks and she might have been feeding them or something like that. I mean on the other side where Nicky is looking it seems like there is a dinosaur, a Loch Ness Monster.

Lauren makes reference to her knowledge of mythical monsters, but does not feel it necessary to pursue that line of thought. However, as with the younger children, she is interpreting the picture through the use of remembered experiences – in her case knowledge of the Loch Ness Monster. In common with the other interviewees, she recognises that the large number of legs on the dog signifies movement and can attribute her knowledge to media texts. In response to the question 'What is Nicky doing?' she replies 'Getting really scared. Like in cartoons, and they run with their legs.'

It is in comparing this response with that of Judy, who used the flying toy to interpret the picture, that the different learning styles of the children become apparent and how important it is for all experiences to be brought to bear on a problem-solving task. Judy has undoubtedly watched cartoons, but it is clear that playing with the toy has been the most powerful tool for her interpretation of the picture. Neither child is more 'right' than another. Knowing their different ways of thinking would undoubtedly help teach them more effectively.

Making pictures

Throughout the conversations with the children it became apparent that they were as interested in how the pictures had been constructed as they were in their content. The children's appreciation of colour, depth and tone and of the way in which Kitamura had constructed the pictures suggests that this is an area which should be developed further in schools. Discussion about how illustrations are made have parallels with deconstructing written text – in both cases children are contemplating the use of tools and of symbol systems, as well as thinking about the efficacy of the whole and its relevance to them as people.

Here is Kathy (6) in discussion about the colours in the book:

INTERVIEWER: What do you think about the colours in this picture, how do you think he has used the colours?
KATHY: Maybe the sky might be sort of like he might have got some dark colours and then made it lighter and then lighter, and maybe he didn't put no water on it for a long while.
INTERVIEWER: Yes. I think that you could be right there. How do you think the colours make you feel?
KATHY: Like back in Majorca, because back in Majorca we had some colours with that all across the sky . . . and also in the sand, blending.

Kathy is not only able to speculate on the possible construction of the picture, but also to link the colours in it to her prior experience – in this case a happy family holiday. The wistfulness in her voice suggests a longing to relive that experience, something that many of us could identify with. There is no doubt that the colours in the book are evocative – the use of blue was mentioned by most of the children and there was a determination to replicate this colour in their own drawings. Their comments included the following:

I like the way the sky . . . like it's gone quite dark and into the light.

(Lauren 10)

They are well done because they are like . . . the sky has been done very well. Like dark and erm light blue, and I like how it has been done.

(Judy 6)

I like the way he's done the colours, and made them really blue and swirly colours and it's a bit like black.

(Seamus 7)

Seamus in particular made comments which showed how he understood the role that the pictures played in helping to tell the story, rather than merely showing us what is happening. His comments arose through being asked why he felt that Lily and the dog were constantly looking in different directions.

> Erm, I think Nicky, it's getting dark, so I think he's a bit worried so he's going to look around and make sure nothing tries to snatch him or anything. See, because at the beginning it's broad daylight and she's out for the whole day. If you turn the pages, it gets darker and darker and darker.

Seamus was also asked about the lines in the illustrations. Reflectivity on the part of the children was supported by the conversational nature of the interviews and the time given to them to formulate their answers. His reply is a good example of the way in which all the children pondered their initial responses and built on them, offering supplementary answers:

INTERVIEWER: How do you think he [Kitamura] used lines?
SEAMUS: It doesn't look like he used a ruler or anything.
INTERVIEWER: No, that's true, it doesn't look like he used a ruler, no.
SEAMUS: I don't think he knows about rulers, it's a Japan thing.
INTERVIEWER: I wonder why there are so many lines. Because there certainly are, aren't there, on each of the pages?
SEAMUS: He's put a lot of them in. I don't think he knows of a word called blank!

It is interesting to note that the children related their own ability to discuss the construction of the pictures (materials, perspective, etc.) to the knowledge of art that they had gained from watching children's television. Programmes such as *Smart*, *Art Attack* and *Blue Peter* were mentioned by the children, and creating their own works of art at home was obviously an important pastime for many of them.

The pictures and the type of questions asked about them clearly supported the children in formulating personal responses to *Lily*. Martin and Leather (1994: 48) comment that 'Perhaps we need, as teachers, to indicate much more clearly the kinds of response that are possible, so pupils see that it is a natural part of reading to make links between the book and the 'real' world. Drawing significant moments from a book offers children one such alternative response.

The 'pleasure principle'

It was apparent throughout the interviews that the children took great pleasure in the pictures in *Lily*. Interestingly, what was initially rejected by the older children as an 'easy book' had its hidden depths revealed by closer inspection:

> When [the class teacher] read it out loud to us I thought, 'Oh, no, why is he reading us this baby book? But then the jokes got more and more and I realised it wasn't a baby book.
>
> (Selma 11)

With this realisation, Selma allowed herself to take delight in the book, particularly the pictures, which are where the jokes are told, and then was able to respond to them through speculation and reflection. In these discussions pleasure was not denied; indeed, it was validated and encouraged. The enjoyment of the text was linked to the pleasures that existed for these children outside school – family holidays, trips to the market, watching television, reading the *Beano*, to name but a few.

These pleasures formed part of the unique experience that was each child's response to the text. As Evans, quoted in Martin and Leather (1994: 117), writes, 'It is no part of the teacher's business to reduce that uniqueness to uniformity.' Fortunately, neither art nor language provides the security of a single interpretation. However, as adults working with children, we need to provide the security for multiple interpretations to be shared and made explicit. As soon as children think that there is a 'correct' or true answer to be had, then diversity vanishes and along with it children's willingness to take risks and to develop their use of spoken language as a tool for thought. The conversations with the children around the pictures in this book were some of the most enjoyable that I have ever had in twenty years in schools.

For all the children in the study the pictures provided a means by which they could move from using talk for appreciation, to using talk for critical understanding, particularly through the group discussions. This is a very important development for them to make. As Bruner (1986: 129) tells us:

> The language of education, if it is to be an invitation to reflection and culture creating, cannot be the so-called uncontaminated language of fact and 'objectivity'. It must express stance and counter stance and in the process leave place for reflection, for metacognition. It is this that permits one to reach higher ground, this process of objectifying in language or image what one has thought and then turning around on it and reconsidering it.

For the children who participated in these discussions, invitation was key. They were quite literally, invited to take part, invited to share their views and invited to participate in group discussions. The language of the conversations was never going to be that of fact and objectivity – the nature of the questions prevented this. Children expressed stance and counter-stance in many ways: these included debating issues with themselves (for example, Kathy and the dinosaurs), debating issues with the interviewer (Seamus and Kitamura's use of rulers) and, of course, with each other during small-group discussions.

Many children came to the group discussions full of enthusiasm for the renewed opportunity to reflect on the text and to create new understandings. In returning in this way they had been given space to reflect on their initial comments and to sound out their ideas in the company of their peers. Many of them quoted their earlier interviews: 'Do you remember when I said . . . '; 'I said about the sky didn't I . . . '; 'You liked it when I said about the lamp posts. . . . ' These comments indicate how important the discussions had been to the children.

The shared memories of some 10-year-olds led to profound interpretations of the book which no child on their own had managed to make. This is just a small extract from one discussion.

INTERVIEWER: A lot of you noticed the rubbish in the book. What do you think the significance of the rubbish is?

SELMA: I think all the bits and everything makes it a bit more amusing.

ANGUS: I think it is just because the monsters are around that all the rubbish is in the book. I think it just adds things to the picture.

INTERVIEWER: If we think about what Angus said, there might be a relationship, there might be something to do with the monsters and the rubbish. How do you think they might be related?

SELMA: I think it is like all the monsters making the rubbish, so like they are knocking everything over.

ANGUS: I don't think Lily has seen any of the rubbish.

INTERVIEWER: Do you think it says anything about the way people treat the planet?

SELMA: Yes, they are a bit careless, not minding what they are doing and just not bothering about anything, just making all that rubbish and not bothering.

ANGUS: It is teenagers. They think they are big stuff and just throw their rubbish where they want.

INTERVIEWER: So the dog though, he does notice all the rubbish doesn't he?

LAUREN: Because he is so small he might see it more, because it's bigger than him.

Supported by the interviewer and working within each other's 'zone of proximal development', the children elaborate their interpretation of the text. Although the adult provides the focus for discussion, it has come directly from observations that the children have made on their initial readings of the book. Their responses support and enhance each other, moving thought processes forward to 'the higher ground'. Look at how Lauren, through a series of statements, builds on her first thoughts and encourages Angus to offer personal opinion and develop his own earlier ideas. It also becomes clear in this discussion that Lauren, who does not contribute as frequently as the other children, nevertheless makes a pertinent point which contributes significantly to the way that this discussion continues: that animals are more at risk from a polluted earth than humankind.

Seven-year-olds worked in a similar way to allow Seamus to reach this conclusion: 'It might be because erm . . . because they might be quite erm. . . . As well as showing this they might, he might be trying to tell people in just a picture in a little way to clear up your rubbish.' The tentativeness of the way Seamus offers his opinion powerfully demonstrates the crucial significance of involvement in such a discussion. He is developing and redrafting his thoughts as he speaks. For children like him, the group discussion provides an opportunity to listen to the ideas of his peers, and to feel safe to offer his own thoughts. Children were also able to pool their individual expertise. Each child was differently aware of the dramatic potential of each picture. As each of these double-page spreads was a fragment of narrative that formed part of the wider story, bringing the children together in discussion was rather like completing a jigsaw puzzle of meaning. They could support each other in putting missing pieces into place, literally putting the whole picture together.

Implications for teachers

The significance of carefully planning questions to use with the children was key to the success of the project. Asking questions which tantalise children and which provoke thought is not a new or revolutionary idea, yet in practice very little planning for questioning takes place. In his book *Teaching Thinking* (1998), Fisher discusses at length how to use stories for philosophical enquiry, and how cognitively demanding it is for children not only to answer questions of a philosophical nature, but to think of such questions for themselves. He also proposes creating a 'community of enquiry' in the classroom. This research project provided the opportunity for the children involved to be part of a modest community of inquiry. The interviewers gathered valuable insights into children's motivations, ways of thinking and learning styles, as well as sharing personal anecdotes which cast valuable light on the children and their lives.

Quality conversations such as those described by Wells (1986) were evident throughout our research, only a few extracts of which are shared here. It is apparent that the children were committed to these conversations and answered at length, in stark contrast to recent findings about the discourse of the Literacy Hour (Mroz et al. 2000). (Children involved in conversations about the number of phonemes in 'pig', for example, have a limited option of possible answers and little likelihood of showing the thinking skills so clearly demonstrated by the children here!) Teachers need time to hold such discussions with children, either individually or in a group. They also need time to contemplate the questions they might ask, getting to know books well before using them with the children.

Our discussions were clearly held in high regard by the children; most of those who were involved in the re-interviewing process quoted themselves, or opened statements with 'When you came before I said . . . '. And they were generally right. How often do we allow children to return to a topic of discussion months, or even weeks later? After participating in this research, I have no doubt of the value of revisitation, particularly for the purpose of developing metacognitive skills. In his re-interview Seamus looked at the final page of *Lily* where a lift-the-flap device is used and exclaimed 'Oh, now I get it', and leant back in his chair with great satisfaction. We need to build in more opportunities for children to savour their learning in this way. As Bruner says: 'Much of the process of education consists of being able to distance oneself in some way from what one knows by being able to reflect on one's own knowledge' (1986: 129). The discussions about the picturebook provided the children with a meaningful context to reflect not only on what they knew, but most significantly on how they knew it. The research project allowed for such reflectiveness to be made possible over a period of time. Children were able to distance themselves from their initial readings of the text and, through interacting and talking with others, were able to reflect on their own learning.

The significance of being able to discuss the pictures was neatly summarised by the oldest children. I asked them to try and remember how they felt when the class teacher first held up the book.

INTERVIEWER: What exactly was in your head at that moment, have you changed your thoughts from this morning?

ANGUS: I don't think I really saw the *Spooky Surprise Book*, and I thought it was a book for Year 2.

SAUL: Now I have read it I thought it was quite good, but at the start when Mr Smith held it up, I thought 'Oh no, another boring story.'

ANGUS: From where I was sitting, I couldn't see any of the pictures, so I didn't know what it was about, apart from what the words said.

INTERVIEWER: Now you have had a chance to see the pictures your opinion's changed . . . ?

SAUL: Yes – they seem to bring out the story.

Putting yourself in the picture

When asked if she placed herself in the book as one of the characters when she read, 10-year-old Lauren came up with a very powerful description of the reading process. 'No, I'm not one of the characters. I am in there though, but I'm watching them.' Kathy (6) was asked not only about how she read, but also 'What happens in your head when you read?' Her responses were very illuminating. '[When I read] I'm always thinking, "I wonder what's going to happen next", "I wonder what's going to happen next", even though I know it's already been decided.' Asked if it was the same when she watched television or played computer games, she was able to shed further light on how she copes with the complexities of being a literate child in the twenty-first century:

> When I play solitaire [on the computer] I'm thinking, 'Come on, come on', especially when I need something I'm wishing would come. When I watch TV it's usually with a friend and I would say, 'What do you think's going to happen?', something like that.

Thus Lauren deals with such intricate thought processes as prediction, problem-solving, the joint construction of knowledge and, of course, the toleration of uncertainty that all readers face, whatever the text.

As well as showing how they could read images, during the research I was also aware of children's facility to paint pictures with words, regardless of age or academic ability. Each time the curtain rose on Kitamura's pictures, the scene was set for new characters to populate the narrative. The props in the pictures, from shopping bags to ducks and dinosaurs, required concentration and experience. Readers used these props to put themselves and those around them 'in the picture'. To do so, they drew on the frozen fictions of their minds – re-creating moments of the past to interpret the present. I hope that the pictures painted in words throughout this book by the children in our study will empower educators to give image the same status as words in their discussions with pupils. To return to *Alice in Wonderland*, I would add, 'How much *more* use is a book with conversations about the pictures'.

An earlier version of this chapter appeared in *Reading* 35 (2), pp. 62–67.

Chapter 6

'The words to say it'

Young bilingual learners responding to visual texts

Kathy Coulthard

The transformative power of visual narrative

The teacher was nearing the end of the story. As she revealed the final page of *The Tunnel*, Sam's (10) face was transformed by a smile so immediate and engaging that I neglected to observe the reactions of other pupils. What was it that Sam had seen? What had spoken to him so directly to cause this involuntary expression of empathy and understanding? Tantalising questions, as Sam had arrived in this English classroom from Tanzania only three months ago. It was easy to assume an incongruity between Sam's experience of growing up in a different tradition and the Englishness of Browne's book, but something had transcended language, place and culture to enable Sam to find himself within and be touched at the deepest level.

The Tunnel tells the story of Rose and Jack, a seemingly ordinary sister and brother who are 'not at all alike'; and it is Browne's representation of this difference in the endpapers that gives us the first clue about Sam's engagement with the book. These endpapers portray two patterns which, on closer inspection, reveal contrasting wallpapers, one with brick and one with leaves and flowers. A closed book lies in front of the latter. Pointing to the brick and then the flowery wallpaper, Sam expresses his understanding of the endpapers as a way into the book and goes straight to the symbolic meaning: 'this means the place where the boy is playing. And here means the girl where she likes sitting and reading the books because she likes flowers.'

Sam's response to the night-time scenario suggested that he was looking at this text in the light of his own experience. We see Jack creeping into his sister's bedroom wearing a wolf mask with the deliberate intention of scaring her. As in all Browne's books, this picture reveals so much more than the written text. Sam notices the red coat hanging on the side of the wardrobe, the shoes arranged in a sinister way, the tail under the bed and the 'scary' picture of a 'wolf talking with a lady'. The story of Red Riding Hood is not part of his oral or literate tradition but other folk and fairy tales are and it is this genre experience that enables him to clue into the menacing intertextual messages:

> This picture means the brother is . . . at night. Because the brother knows her [his] sister. She's afraiding of dark. Now she [he] always comes down. Sometimes night she [he] comes and make her to afraid and cry. That's why. And then she [he] goes away.

Sam's response, however, demonstrates an understanding that goes beyond the immediate situation. He knows exactly how to scare someone like Rose:

> Because you know how she's afraid of him because she [he] just come and stop here in the shadow and makes her afraid. Because she doesn't see a person. She just see a shadow and the shadow doesn't show this.

Both the written and visual text deal with the here and now and neither hints at a possible outcome but Sam can predict how this drama will end: 'When they [he] goes she starts crying. The boy goes away and says I'm not the one, I'm just sleeping.'

To arrive at this state of 'innerstanding' (Heathcote 1983), Sam had to mediate the cultural differences between himself and Jack and Rose. The obvious differences are in appearance and the context and landscape in which they live, of which he has no intimate knowledge. There must be numerous cultural motifs beyond his experience and textual features to be reconciled but, despite these differences, he understands why the characters act as they do and the consequences of their actions. Although he stops short of analogy, there is a powerful resonance of personal experience in his interaction with this particular visual text.

And now we arrive at the final page of the book and the resonance is even more powerful in Sam's involuntary reaction when presented with a smiling Rose facing both her brother and the reader. They have been through a transformative experience. Rose has conquered her fear; the sibling bond has been tried and held fast. Sam chooses this as his favourite picture because 'they look happy and are happy to each other' and explains their mutual smile in this way (see Figure 6.1): 'Because they love each other now . . . You see now that's why they were smiling and they will be together everywhere.'

Following our session together, I learn from his teacher that Sam's sister had died in a tragic accident in Tanzania only weeks before. Sam did not talk about this but his involuntary smile during the class reading and his struggle to unlock and communicate the symbolic meaning of Browne's secret images attest to a profound critical engagement with this story of sibling relationship. In discussing the complex nature of narrative, Rosen (1989: 159) writes: 'Even so stark an ending as death is only an ending when we have made a story out of life.'

Is Sam engaged in making a story out of their life together and has Browne's text helped him to revisit, remember and reassess? He is so eloquent in articulating the symbolism of the story.

> I think this football and book means when they like each other now the sister and the brother she made a friend the book and the football like each other . . . Or maybe the brother will tell the sister play football after half time maybe they start to read a book telling each other about their book.

Cummins (1996: 91) stresses the absolute importance of texts that second-language learners can relate to their own personal histories or their understanding of the world, but equally important is the opportunity to have one's voice heard. Sam's first language is Kiswahili, which he also reads and writes, yet so engaged is he with *The Tunnel* that he struggles for an hour to make himself understood in a language

Figure 6.1 From *The Tunnel* by Anthony Browne

Source: Illustration from *The Tunnel* by Anthony Browne, copyright © 1989 Anthony Browne, reproduced by permission of Walker Books Ltd.

that is not his own. He uses every resource available: gesture, mime and facial expression are as valuable as words and intonation. He takes enormous risks as the drive to communicate meaning takes precedence over correct use of language. Sam has something to say and finds the words to say it.

Why did he bother to make the effort? The choice of text must go some way towards answering this question. For Sam, *The Tunnel* is an emotionally powerful text to which he can respond from inside his own life experience and, significantly, the focus on making meaning from the visual image enables him to do this. Another possible reason is that the interview context is authentic. I genuinely want to know what Sam is thinking and he enters into a dialogue about his understanding in the certain knowledge that he is not being assessed on his ability to decode unfamiliar words or the extent of his developing sight vocabulary in English. The interview questions exemplify reading as a quest for meaning and it is in this quest that we observe him working at a higher conceptual level than his current literacy in English would suggest. To demonstrate this, he has needed a book worth reading, the opportunity to explore and time to think and reflect. Under these conditions, the effort seems to be worth it.

From 'intimate' to 'extra personal' responses

Unlike Sam, Mehmet finds the interview situation overwhelming and takes refuge in silence despite the presence of a Turkish-speaking interpreter whom he knows. He is just 6 years old and has only been in British mainstream schooling for two terms, so clearly does not feel comfortable to be away from the support of his teacher and friends. The interview is abandoned. I am surprised but delighted when he chooses to join the group discussion at the end of the day although there is no interpreter available. At the time of the discussion Mehmet is a beginning reader and learning to read in a language that is not spoken in his home or community. He is unable to read the words of *The Tunnel* but has listened attentively and been engaged in looking at the pictures during the class reading. The focus on reading pictures is significant as it removes a barrier in terms of the written text and puts him on a more equal footing with the rest of the group. Visual literacy, however, is no easy option when the text being read is as complex, multi-layered and fragmented as *The Tunnel*.

At one point in the discussion I focus the group on the bedtime scene as their individual responses had been predominantly descriptive. They had noticed details such as Jack wearing a wolf mask, a wakeful Rose, Crane's picture of Little Red Riding Hood and the open book lying on the bed, but had not perceived or attached significance to these and other deliberate hints of menace. In discussing how readers bring meaning to text, Smith (2000) suggests a primary stage in which the responses are 'intimate' based on 'who I am' and 'what I know'. This is especially true of young, inexperienced readers. The children's initial response to this visual text came from inside their own experience of bedtime.

The questions are now framed to support the group in discovering another layer of meaning, by helping them to reflect on images that had been previously unnoticed or which had been treated as benign. I draw their attention to the shoes under the bed. The explanations are still pragmatic: 'Because she's gone to bed. If she put them in her wardrobe she would maybe forget where she put them' (Alison 6); 'You should put your shoes together in a dresser then you wouldn't get mixed up' (Tosin 6).

It is only when the children's attention is drawn to the position of the shoes that the schema about this night-time scene flips from one of domestic familiarity to one of menace. Mehmet notices that they are lying at an awkward angle and remarks: 'I think someone's under the bed.' It is his response to this pivotal question that leads the group into greater awareness and insight: 'There's a man under the bed' (Manisha 6). The floodgates open and they begin to notice a wider visual vocabulary. Luke's (5) eyes travel to the other side of the bed and see 'a sort of rope hanging out' which Mehmet elaborates on: 'Somebody can be under it [the bed], it's supposed to be a monster.' Tosin clarifies that it is a tail and this prompts Michael (5) to suggest that what is also lurking under the bed is more likely to be an animal such as a lion or tiger. With the growing realisation that these images are extremely significant, the cosy bedtime scene ceases to exist. The group has moved from the 'intimate' to the 'extra personal', Smith's second layer of response, in which we observe them reading the images and constructing meaning beyond their personal experience but within their knowledge of how the world can work.

There is now the distinct possibility that another story is unfolding and this leads the group to a further layer of response, the 'intertextual'. Mehmet makes an observation that shapes the group's expectation about the nature and narrative possibilities of this story. He spots the picture above the bed and recognises it as Red

Riding Hood, a folk tale found within his own cultural tradition and which he has obviously experienced in Turkish. He demonstrates his familiarity with the story:

INTERVIEWER: What's scary about the picture?
MEHMET: A wolf and Red Riding Hood.
INTERVIEWER: What happened in Red Riding Hood that was a bit scary?
MEHMET: The wolf was trying to eat Red Riding Hood.

The realisation that Red Riding Hood is haunting the scene influences subsequent readings as the children bring their narrative experience to Browne's carefully planted motifs. Attention now turns to the red coat hanging on the side of the wardrobe. It looks particularly menacing with the pointed hood shaped like the head of a fox or some surreal creature. Mehmet makes the intertextual association: 'I think it's Red Riding Hood's and it might come in real life.' His syntactic error is powerful in fuelling Tosin's imagination. *Coming in real life* rather than *coming to life* suddenly moves this scenario from the world of books to the world of the mind. So completely has she entered into this pictorial text that the line between fact and fantasy becomes blurred and she is filled with foreboding. The hints of menace are potent. She wants to stop: 'I don't want to do this. It's scaring me.' Tosin's fears are reflected in her simple but striking drawing of the open cupboard, a strange creature lurking by the door and the girl in bed (see Figure 6.2).

Figure 6.2 By Tosin (age 6)

Seeing, talking and thinking

This small section of the transcript opens a window on a group of 5- and 6-year-olds developing their individual and collective responses to this visual text. We witness their initial observations of the images and their movement through a zone of proximal development, from 'seeing' to 'thinking', led by a guide who points out significant landmarks along the way and allows those on the quest, time and space to explore. With limited experience of English and schooled literacy, it would be easy to assume that Mehmet would take a more passive role but the transcript tells a different story. Out of a possible one hundred speaker turns, he takes twenty-four and, far from being passive, he is pivotal at certain points in leading the group to greater insight and deeper layers of meaning. He clearly did not feel confident in the one-to-one interview but, surrounded by his classmates and with the emphasis on enquiry, he feels safe enough to speak out. At times this requires him to use some quite sophisticated aspects of English, most noticeably when he is engaged in expressing insights or feelings. Responding to questions about the waste-ground picture, Mehmet communicates his thoughts about Jack's character and intentions, drawing on intratextual references to Rose's fearfulness and her brother's obsession with football:

> I know why the brother brings the girl here. Because the brother wants to scare the girl. . . . The brother, yeah, cares about the sister not coming with him so that he can play football if he wants or so that he can go down the tunnel.

These are complex issues. He is having to piece together the jigsaw of images and hypothesise their significance in relation to this page specifically and the story in general. He then has to articulate his thoughts in English, a language he has been learning for only six months. Since the questions are open-ended and invite discussion, he is involved in producing more extended explanations than single-word answers. The task is cognitively demanding but the contextual support in this pictorial text and in the collaborative group ensures that Mehmet is positioned to succeed. We are reminded that this is exactly the context in which cognitive and linguistic growth is stimulated and second-language learners (indeed all learners) flourish:

> At a cognitive level, writing about or discussion of complex issues with the teacher and peers encourages students to reflect critically and refine their ideas. As learners connect new information with what they already know, their cognitive power increases. They are enabled to understand more of the content and language that they hear or read.
>
> (Cummins 1996: 81)

Constructing virtual texts

In discussing the kinds of literature that influence children's writing, Barrs and Cork (2001: 36) suggest that those with most potential require readers to become active and involved in the world of the text. Their references to 'performance of meaning' (Iser 1978) and the construction of 'virtual text' (Bruner 1986), as part of the process that readers go through to make the text their own, helped me understand that there is something more going on here than miscue. Both the words and insistence suggest that Mehmet and Sam are engaged in constructing a virtual text which is being acted upon and shaped by the actual text, their own experience and imagination. Mehmet feels confident that he knows what Jack is up to and this leads Manisha to predict what will happen:

MEHMET: I know why the brother brings the girl here. The brother wants to scare the girl.
INTERVIEWER: And if she's scared what will happen do you think?
MANISHA: She's all scared, she'll scream.

Manisha is so clearly involved in the world of the text and so comfortable in this collaborative exploration that it is easy to forget she is right at the beginning of learning a new language. What is it that has enabled her to see herself as an active meaning-maker, to have a voice and to feel confident to use that voice at a time when she might be most sensitive to making mistakes? My expectation that she will behave like a reader is a crucial factor. Implicit in this is a belief in her as a learner and an acknowledgement that she already has a first language, French, and a history of home literacy experience to bring to the task. Since she is not new to the world (only new to English), she also brings a rich array of personal experience which she will need to make sense of the text. The fact that this experience has been shaped by another place and culture can only be a bonus in a group that is engaged in negotiating meaning.

This brings me to another important factor. If Manisha is to use all her resources, she must have a text that allows her to do so. Meek (1988) describes such texts as 'texts that teach' and recognises the skill of the illustrators who produce them as being able to 'link what children know, partly know, and are learning about the world, to ways of presenting the world in books'. *The Tunnel* is just such a text and for an inexperienced reader, like Manisha, its rich visual imagery is more accessible (and more inviting) than the written word. There is no doubt that she has been able to decode the images and engage with Rose's loneliness and fear. After all, these emotions are experienced so profoundly by children like herself who arrive in school not knowing anyone, not speaking English and not understanding how school works. What she has to say is important and must be heard but how does she find the words and the confidence to say it?

In my experience this happens naturally when the text and context are right and by 'right' I mean challenging but supportive. These features of the learning environment have already been discussed but one other is essential to Manisha's engagement. Both learning a language and learning to read involve taking risks and making mistakes, a daunting prospect when language and culture are unfamiliar. We have all been in coercive situations and know how paralysing they can be, as well as counterproductive, for all they usually achieve is a further retreat into silence. There is no pressure on Manisha to speak, but, importantly, there is time for her to listen and tune in until she feels comfortable to speak. This happens more quickly if the emphasis is on making and communicating meaning rather than correctness. After a reticent start, she becomes engaged and language arises naturally from the interactions within the group. Her syntax and pronunciation may not always be correct but the meaning is absolutely explicit. Not only is she learning valuable lessons about reading through language, but she is also learning how language works and how to manipulate it. Since language is at the core of reading, what better way to learn about both?

Exploring visual detail

Before we leave this group of 5- and 6-year-olds, I want to turn my attention to Tosin. She was born in this country to Nigerian parents and is growing up in a home and community where she hears English and Yoruba spoken. She was interviewed for the study as well as taking part in the group discussion and it is the expression and development of her ideas in both contexts that I want to explore. Within minutes of meeting Tosin and the interview starting, I was alerted to her sensitivity to visual detail as she noticed a host of images on the front cover of *The Tunnel*. Some carry meaning in relation to the story while others encode different kinds of meaning (for example, the Walker Books logo and the strip pattern marking the edge of the picture). The open book at the entrance to the tunnel is the first image she notices and is attracted to because she likes reading. She does not develop this response further but goes on to demonstrate a more insightful reading in the group discussion by linking the characters in the abandoned book with Rose's personality and the unfolding story. These links are not explicit but her words suggest an implicit perception about Browne's intentions: 'I like the cover because the girl's in the tunnel, yeah, and I think, and because she's saying that there's witches and stuff like that and then because there's witches in the book.'

There are other instances when there is an obvious progression in her thinking during the course of the day. Her first response to the endpapers inside the front cover, for example, go straight to the symbolic representation of difference suggested by the two walls covered in contrasting wallpaper:

TOSIN: I think this one [brick] was in the book because the brother went out with his friends and played football.
INTERVIEWER: And what does this one [flowers] make you think of?
TOSIN: The girl sitting down because of the book.

In the group discussion she reiterates this interpretation with greater confidence but develops it by drawing on intratextual links to justify her reading of the images. In the interview Tosin's keen eye for visual detail had noticed the flowery wallpaper recurring in the hall outside Rose's bedroom. Her recognition of the wallpaper's significance is particularly insightful as Browne has talked of his obsession with wallpapers remembered from his own childhood and their inclusion in the book as a personal expression of early memories. Tosin made an intuitive connection between the pattern and the focal character, a connection which she affirms and consciously recognises through words in the discussion:

It's meant to be the sister for two reasons. One is that because we're going to see it in the middle of the book and two is that we know it's for the sister because there's a book there.

I am reminded of Watson's (1996) observations on the changing understanding of 4-year-old Ann during re-readings of *The Tunnel* and how, as time passes, she is able to 'make explicit' what has previously been implicit but 'remained unsaid'. In Tosin's case, time is not days or weeks but a few hours between sessions, long enough it seems for some reflection (conscious or otherwise) to have taken place and for understandings to shift. These understandings are not fully formed, however, but continue to be acted upon by the pushes and pulls of other children's thinking as they look and talk about the images together.

The representational wallpapers at the beginning of the book are repeated on the final endpapers but with significant differences. Jack's football has appeared in front of the brick wall, lying beside and slightly overlapping Rose's storybook. Tosin is immediately alert to these changes and can tell me the exact position of the book on the opening endpapers but offers no thoughts about meaning. This is explored further in the discussion; and the images are recognised by other members of the group as a pictorial metaphor for reconciliation, but another puzzle opens up. Why has Browne put the ball and book on the brother's page? Mehmet makes a pragmatic suggestion and one which probably reflects the perceived pecking order in the world of the 6-year-old: 'Because the boy is bigger than the girl.' It is the light and shade in the backgrounds, however, that suggest an alternative explanation to Tosin: 'I think it's because that one [brick wallpaper] has got no hard colours on it and . . . it's been painted soft.'

I have to confess to being perplexed at the time, as I associated the hardness and coldness of brick with those traits in the brother's character, but Tosin taught me to look in a different way. As I pored over the endpapers, trying to make sense of her interpretation, I saw that Browne has indeed used predominantly soft, warm, muted colours for the bricks and that they are cemented in place by rather malleable-looking mortar. Although the brick wall is a recurring image in his work, he has described this as his 'first significant brick wall' (Arizpe and Styles 2003: 208), drawing attention to the suggestion of wallpaper and the diverse shades and patternings of his handmade bricks. Just as she had perceived the importance of the wallpapers, she now seemed to sense that the execution of such minute detail was for a purpose and demanded attention (far more than I had given it). My eye then travelled to the contrasting wallpaper. The fluid leaf and flower shapes are painted in a spectrum of greens from light to dark and stand out boldly against a cream background. I began to see how hard-edged they could look.

My understanding deepened when I revisited the transcript of Tosin's interview and detected an intratextual connection behind the reading. In the story, Rose confronts her fear by following her brother down the dark tunnel. The quest leads through a terrifying forest teeming with surreal images to a barren landscape where Jack stands paralysed in a circle of stones. As she puts her arms around him and hugs him back to life the landscape gradually loses its darkness and the stones turn into daisies. Tosin is immediately alert to the use of light and colour:

INTERVIEWER: Why is there a ring of stones around the brother?
TOSIN: I think it is . . . because as it gets softer and warmer it gets lighter and lighter.

Her choice of words is interesting. 'Softer' and 'warmer' are words that convey feeling and here she seems to be expressing an implicit understanding that the circle of stones is a metaphor for the transformation of feeling between the brother and sister. Rose's selfless act has quite literally softened Jack up, so why not place the ball and the book together against a brick wallpaper background that she perceives 'has no hard colours *on it'* and has been *'painted soft'*. Yet again, Tosin displays an intuitive understanding of Browne's intentions which suggest 'that the boy and girl are similar' and that Jack is not really as tough as he seems.

Cultural identity and linguistic development

During the interview Tosin tells me that she loves computer games and the way 'the pictures are done' makes her 'want to play'. This is an interesting observation as I have a real sense of her playing with this text and the play becoming even more imaginative when she is joined by others. The five others have not been chosen because they read as well as she does or have similar English-language experience; in fact, their profiles are deliberately diverse. In some educational settings the make-up of this group might be thought to inhibit Tosin's learning and prevent Mehmet and Manisha's English-language needs being prioritised. Despite the differences in language, literacy and culture, however, we have seen that this is an effective group and, by effective, I mean that every member has collaborated in making sense of this text and in constructing a shared meaning. This alone would endorse the make-up of this group but there is a further layer of effectiveness, one much subtler, that must be considered.

Siegler (2000) cites identity as one of the key factors affecting learning and describes it as 'a voraciously powerful theory one has about oneself'. Cummins (1996) devotes an entire book to exploring this theory in relation to second-language learners and draws on extensive evidence from educators and researchers across North America to show how schools affirm, ignore or devalue pupils' personal and cultural identities. McCarty's (1993) case study of a Navajo–English bilingual programme captures both the fragility of identity and the awesome power of institutions to act upon and shape the way pupils see themselves. If we want pupils to feel confident in their identities as learners, we must pay as much attention to content and context as we do to objectives. This is of course true for all pupils but especially those whose communities are viewed as inferior or deviant in mainstream society. An evaluation of effectiveness must, therefore, include this layer of identity because not to do so would ignore its centrality to learning.

Mehmet and Manisha are potentially the most vulnerable in this group in terms of access to content and context, having had less than six months' experience of spoken and written English. How they are enabled to engage with the reading curriculum is crucial as it will affect how they feel about themselves as learners and influence the kind of readers they become. They may be unable to read the written text of *The Tunnel* at this time but the great leveller in this group is that they can all see. Words may form a barrier but visual image is universal. The brief glimpses we have had of their interactive reading demonstrate an ability to decode symbolism, identify inter-textual links, construct a 'virtual text', understand feelings and behaviour and have an emotional engagement with the important human issues in the book. Returning to McCarty's metaphor of curriculum as a mirror through which children construct images of themselves, I feel sure that Mehmet and Manisha left this group with positive images of themselves as 'thinkers, learners and users of language'.

Tosin's visual alertness and sensitivity undoubtedly brought an added dimension to the group's interpretation of this polysemic text. She displayed an intuitive understanding of image, detail, light, colour, facial expression and body language as techniques the artist uses to convey ideas, emotions and relationships. But this is no one-way street. Just as she is helping other members of the group to pay attention to these techniques, they are helping her to see unnoticed images and to revisit and reconstruct her original thoughts. Although Tosin has much greater experience of speaking and reading English than Mehmet and Manisha, she too has a need to talk and negotiate meaning. The transcript of the discussion provides rich evidence of the group's capacity to expand learning by scaffolding both her thinking and that of one another through dialogue.

Sam, Mehmet, Manisha and Tosin draw on their experience of life and text to make sense of Browne's images and their experience of language to communicate this sense. Sam and Tosin are more experienced readers. Not only are they at ease being interviewed alone, but I suspect they enjoy having the undivided attention of an adult who is so obviously interested in their responses. From the outset it is clear that they understand and feel comfortable with this kind of literacy event in which the majority of questions are open-ended and the answers not pre-specified in the researcher's head. By contrast, Mehmet and Manisha do not initially display the same level of understanding and assurance but gradually become engaged as they begin to realise what is required in this kind of literacy event and to discover images that have meaning for them. Their levels of perception and interpretation fluctuate with each spread, but both have moments of responding to visual features with insight and empathy.

Cultural practices and learning to read

The same is true for the majority of the twenty-three pupils from different ethnic backgrounds that I interviewed or engaged in group discussions about Browne's books. There are, however, a very small minority of pupils across the age range who were less at ease with this more open kind of questioning and whose responses tended to be predominantly literal. Pupils like Funda (5), who so obviously found 'what' questions more comfortable than 'why' and had effective ways of diverting my questions or signalling to me that there should be no further probing. Whereas open-ended questions such as 'Tell me . . . ' offered many pupils the freedom and licence to go beyond the surface features and explore the aesthetic and affective dimensions of images, Funda stuck doggedly to the descriptive. She answered my questions by listing only what she could see. It was not that she was unwilling to answer my questions or unhappy about being interviewed, but I was left with the impression that Funda was simply confused. She did not understand what was required in this kind of exchange.

I discovered at the end of the day that Funda was in the lowest ability group for reading. She was described as having little confidence and being unwilling to take risks, rarely offering responses during individual and class book-sharing sessions. Nor did she opt to read in 'free choice' time. It would be all too easy to draw a correlation between her ability with written text and her analysis of visual text (and attach a deficit label) but I want to stand back at this point and take a wider view of the context in which she was developing her literacy. Funda was born in Britain and started her school four terms prior to the interview speaking Turkish, which is the language of her home. Neither parent is literate in English, but she has a sister in her late teens who speaks fluent English and takes responsibility for sharing the books that come home as part of the home/school reading scheme. Although I have no way of knowing how this book-sharing is conducted, Funda's responses to the interview questions suggested to me that she was more comfortable with a procedure that required her to retrieve information from the text with little or no opportunity for personal response or discussion. The literacy practices of the home are beyond the scope of this study so here I want to draw on research to help me understand Funda's interaction with the book and the situation.

Heath's (1983) ethnographic study of three communities in Carolina provides convincing evidence that children do not just acquire literacy, but learn different ways of being a reader and writer through involvement in social practices with adults and other children. The literacy traditions they are socialised into differ according to cultural context, as Gregory's studies also show (Gregory and Biarnès 1994). Gregory highlights the discontinuity between home and school literacy practices and its effect on some children's learning. Further evidence (Gregory 1997) suggests that discontinuity between home and community literacy experiences and those of the school may be typical for many linguistic minority children in Britain. The observation that words are privileged above pictures is particularly relevant to this study. Our preoccupation with the visual text may be completely at odds with the messages some children are getting about reading in their home community.

The influence of culture on interpretation has been explored by Mines in her study of three different groups of 6-year-olds reading *The Tunnel* (Mines 2000). Her analysis of the response of recent arrivals from Bangladesh, of second-generation Bangladeshi immigrants and of English children living in rural Sussex led her to conclude: 'how they looked at the pictures and what they saw was determined by the mental template that they applied to their reading, this being a largely cultural construction' (2000: 201).

Mines registered her surprise at how much this particular text enabled all children, including the recent arrivals, to draw upon their own cultural resources to make meaning and how hard they worked to fill in the gaps. This is consistent with my own findings. I am convinced that the universal themes of love, fear, conflict and reconciliation in *The Tunnel* act as reference points in the narrative mapping and, no matter how unfamiliar the territory becomes, readers can use them to get their bearings. (The transcripts of *Zoo*, however, suggest that the theme of animal rights is less universal and does not provide the same reference points for those whose cultural experience does not encompass this issue.) Although children's knowledge, understanding and values are culturally saturated, the extent to which this affects literary interpretation will always be mediated by each child's unique personality as well as the influence of their peers.

The teller and the told

One other factor nags away at me. I was alerted to it in Funda's transcript but became even more aware of its presence and influence on Eylem. He is 9 years old and, like Funda, second-generation Cypriot. Their profiles are similar in other ways: Turkish is the language spoken in their homes; neither set of parents is literate in English; and both children started school as emergent bilinguals. Meek (1988: 10) reminds us that:

To learn to read a book, as distinct from simply recognising the words on the page, a young reader has to become both the teller (picking up the author's view and voice) and the told (the recipient of the story, the interpreter).

Our study offered recurring evidence of children privileging 'the words on the page', which had an effect on their capacity to become both 'the teller' and 'the told'. In Eylem's case, he did not read the text but remembered words and phrases from the class reading which he drew on heavily. His teacher later confirmed my observation when she commented on his ability to 'quote from stories verbatim'. I encouraged him to look at the pictures but the transcript suggested a familiarity with the traditional, reading-comprehension-type question in which all that is involved is the retrieval of basic information from the written text. He did not move beyond this purely descriptive phase, even when the question was couched in exploratory language, so long as the actual text could provide an answer. The contrast between his facility with this passive kind of exercise and apparent inexperience with a more active, exploratory approach suggested to me that Eylem understood reading as a process of retrieval, one in which the meaning is fixed in words with little or no space for interpretation. Our focus on the visual image and the interplay between words and pictures was completely at odds with this understanding. He confirmed my hunch when he told me that the words and pictures tell the same story. Although he recognised the distinct roles of both media, words are accorded greater status because, without them, 'you won't be able to read the book. You'll still get some ideas from the pictures but it won't be that good when you read it.' The pictures seem to play a subsidiary role in terms of meaning ('because if you can't read the words the pictures give you an idea') but a very important one in maintaining interest ('in the end it will be boring because you ain't seen the pictures').

Final thoughts

Several years ago, I initiated a Key Stage 2 (ages 7–11) reading project in a number of schools. The aim was quite simple. I wanted to provide a safe, supportive environment in which pupils who had recently arrived in Britain not speaking English could develop both oracy and literacy while experiencing the sheer pleasure of sharing books. I wanted pupils to read and go on reading, so I chose books that would excite and motivate them. They were all picturebooks with themes that would appeal to older readers and images capable of being contemplated and explored. This was important as I intended to talk about the books with my apprentice readers even before we shared a language. Anthony Browne's books were favourites in this collection. He provided us with extraordinary images that generated a lot of looking and a great deal of conversation which, in the early days, was carried on through gesture, mime and exclamation rather than conventional words. If you had asked me then what these books were doing for my apprentices, I would have talked about relationships, mutual enjoyment and the importance of readerly-like behaviour. This response came from one who was starting out on a journey (although she didn't know it) and was unaware of the territory or the time it would take. The journey continues but this research has led to a significant place along the route where I have been engaged in reassessing and redefining my initial response, which was inadequate in recognising the potential of these complex visual texts.

Ask me now what these books can do for young bilingual learners and I will talk about emotional engagement and refer you back to Sam and Manisha, who use their experience of love and fear to make personal meaning of the text despite alternative cultural traditions. I will talk about intellectual challenge and the capacity of these books both to stimulate and provide ways of demonstrating thinking, especially for recent arrivals like Mehmet and Manisha who are not yet able to read the words. No reductive text could provoke such thought or provide them with the same opportunities for discussion, yet all too often the reductive text is their sole reading diet. I will talk of aesthetic analysis and how such detailed visual texts can overcome the barrier of words for those who do not yet speak or read English, providing more equal access to the world of story. And for those who have greater experience of spoken and written English, I will talk about the potential for accessing deeper layers of meaning through the interpretation of both word and image and the space between. Finally, I will talk about language learning and the power of these texts to inspire pupils to talk in a way that pushes their language to the outer limits, with the drive to communicate overcoming their natural fear of making mistakes. I am certain Sam is aware that his responses are riddled with syntactical errors but this does not prevent him from talking at length about his understanding and I want to leave the last word to him. Asked for his opinion of the book, he responded by saying that, 'when you read the story and see the pictures this makes you feel interested at the book' and then delivered his final verdict when he declared that *The Tunnel* was 'a real book'.

Chapter 7

Picturebooks and metaliteracy

Children talking about how they
read pictures

I think that stained-glass windows in church help you understand pictures too. Sometimes I go to church to look up at the stained glass windows, just look and try and tell the story, that's all I do. Because before you read a book you can understand a stained-glass window, because you just look. You can learn on a stained-glass window and then when it comes to a book you're ready and you can look at the pictures and know what's happening.

(Tamsin 8)

In *A History of Reading*, Manguel (1997: 104) mentions the similarities between the reading of pictures in the Biblia Pauperum (the first books with biblical images) and those in stained-glass windows: both allowed the non-literate to participate more fully and at their own pace in the interpretation of biblical stories – stories they had previously only had access to through someone else's reading. Even today, with so many images around us that the pleasure derived from this freedom is now so commonplace we take it almost for granted, we find that a child refers to these same stained-glass stories in order to describe how she looks at pictures.

Tamsin's explanation of how she 'read' pictures and the comments made by other children about the way in which they interpret image, and also what they say about how the author intends us to look, are clues to understanding how they make sense of pictorial narratives. These clues are usually based on children's previous book knowledge and on their experience with other types of media, from comics to computer games. This type of knowledge comes together with metacognitive skills when children answer questions about their expectations of a picturebook, its implied readership and their understanding of artistic techniques. It also reveals their perceptions of the complex relationship between word and image, one of the defining aspects of picturebooks, but also present in other types of media texts.

In this chapter, we will analyse some of the comments children made about reading visual texts in an attempt to understand the thought processes behind these skills. We shall discuss how the children described the artistic processes involved in making a picturebook and how they relate this process to their own creative experiences. Finally, we shall try to pull all these observations together in order to understand how children make sense of their own meaning-making processes and suggest ways that these metacognitive skills can be built on in order to help young learners become more critical and discerning readers.

'You can also read by pictures': how to read a picturebook

Not all the children were able to answer the question we asked about how they read pictures, perhaps because this was a new idea to them, or because they found it hard to articulate an answer. Generally, it was the more experienced readers or children of 9 and upwards who were able to describe the steps by which they approached a picture. This is a metacognitive ability which involves stepping back, an objectivisation of themselves as readers, something which is not easy to do even for adults.

The first distinction to be made is between the words and the illustrations. Greg (6), already a keen reader, was one of the few young children who was able to take this step back when asked what he looked at first in a picture: 'I look at the picture to give me a clue of what's happening. And then I read the story, the words.' Jim (7) looks first at the writing within the illustration: 'I look if they have speech bubbles and then I read the bit that it says, then read the writing and then look at the picture.' Joe's (10) description is perhaps the most accurate in terms of the eye going between the image and the text, not once, but several times: 'First I look at the picture just for a short while, then I read the text, then I take a longer look at the picture and see what's happening in it and see if there's anything going on.'

This distinction reveals the powerful attraction of the image and the fact that it is often easier to understand than the written text. But what happens when children look at a picture? Where do their eyes go first? Karen (7) demonstrated for the interviewer how her eyes rolled around the picture; other children described their eye movements in various ways. When asked how they read a picture, Corinna (10), Jason (9) and Erin (7) explained that they look first at the 'main parts', such as the characters and the 'things that stand out' or the actual objects and then they look at the background. Kevin (10) looks 'at the overall thing and then the detail'. Dave (8) revealed his scientific knowledge about how the eyes work: 'In your head you translate it from upside-down to the right way, 'cause when you see it, it's the other way.' Alice (9) said she first notices the usual things and then the unusual, like the 'normal' picture of Lily feeding the ducks and then the dinosaur on the other side of the canal. This way of looking, at the norm and then the exceptions, was also applied to *The Tunnel* and *Zoo* by other children. Another way of looking was to first follow the movement of the characters, as described by Eva (7): 'I think you look at the people that are walking, see where they're going. It tells you where they're leading you to in the book.'

As with the reading of text, the reading of images is not a simple left-to-right movement. The eyes tend to focus either on the largest identifiable object or on an object that has a particular interest for the viewer. When Jess (6) was asked what she looked at first in the spread in *Lily* with the vegetable stall, she said 'the bike, because I can ride a bike'. Looking is also affected by the narrative in terms of expectations: a few pages into *Lily*, the children were ready to find both the central characters, but also to search for the monster. So even if Lily was on the left-hand side of the spread, they would look for the monster first. In *Zoo* they learnt to expect the family on the left-hand side of the gutter and the animals on the right, and they were usually drawn first to the more colourful family side. In *The Tunnel* their eyes followed the sister and brother; as Sean (9) said, 'I look at what is actually happening, like the main characters, and then I look like round the edge to see if there's anything I missed, and then I look at the background.'

Older children are not used to having time to look at a book slowly. Because they read so fast, they sometimes missed details which they only saw when they were pointed out. As Joe (10) admitted: 'Well at first I didn't notice that all the humans didn't look like animals, I just thought they looked like normal people at first. The thing I first noticed was the family because they're the main characters, but then when I looked back I could see all the other people in the background and them looking like animals.' Kiefer (1993: 277) refers to studies of visual perception which found that 'children's eye movements within a pictorial plane are quite different from adults'. The reason for having 'many more and longer eye fixations' may be a learning function, not a sign of immaturity, and the result of this is that children notice more details than adults do.

'Working out things on the page': deductions

Metacognitive skills were also needed to explain the process by which one tried to make sense of the pictures. Only a few of the older children were able to give detailed descriptions of how they thought they did this. Talking about *Lily*, Carol (10), a struggling reader according to her performance at school, pointed out: 'It seems like you take ages on the book but you're actually looking at the picture and you're trying to know why, working out things on the page.' She goes on to say that what you start looking for in the book is the 'problem. Kind of like you want to know what's wrong with the dog.' Carol has already worked out that a reader forms expectations – about narrative patterns in this case – and looks out for them throughout the book.

Usually, the readers' deductive processes were implied through other comments about the book. For example, when Ruth (8) noticed the fairy-tale book on the cover and endpaper of *The Tunnel*, she thought they 'must tell us that whoever likes the book [is] the main person in the story'. A few pages later, she said she was looking for clues about how this person was feeling. So she is aware that the artist is using symbolic clues, which the viewer must interpret to understand a character and also to signal their importance in the narrative. Later, as she described the pictures of the forest, we can follow her thoughts quite accurately:

> Well one picture is nice and jolly and happy and just trees, and this picture is in darkness, forest, the trees there are very ugly, all swirls and squiggles. And you've got some weird trees at the back and they make you think why is that there, those vines? And someone must have been there, chopping wood. There's a rope. Someone must be climbing.

As she talks about the pictures, Ruth first contrasts their atmosphere, based on colour, light and pattern (Figure 7.1). She notices the background (weird trees) and then zooms back into the beanstalk and some of the most noticeable details such as the axe and the rope.

Many children told us that the process of reading a picture seems to involve first noticing the ordinary and expected; next there's the unexpected and extraordinary (there's always plenty of that with Browne and Kitamura); then asking questions, making deductions, proposing tentative hypotheses and then confirming or denying them as the reader moves on to something else, reads the verbal text or turns the

Figure 7.1 From *The Tunnel* by Anthony Browne

Source: Illustration from *The Tunnel* by Anthony Browne, copyright © 1989 Anthony Browne, reproduced by permission of Walker Books Ltd.

page. Tamsin's (8) account, for example, follows this process closely, though she also considers the main characters' actions, as well as detail and colour, as she tries to find the meaning in the pictures. She emphasises the effort this requires:

> I just look at it and I think, OK now, this is a picture of a stone boy and a little girl with her arms around him. What can that mean? Then you just think the boy's been turned to stone and the little girl's come to save him. That's what I think it is and then you see the stones turning to little flowers, so I think, OK now, this girl has saved her brother and the stones have turned into daisies and the background's changed colour too. So you just need to look really hard.

'Getting the words off of the pictures': the relationship between image and text

Valuing the contribution of the two signifying systems in a picturebook, the words and the pictures, also leads to insights into how children look at them, both at each system on its own and in conjunction. When we asked about the relative merits of word and image, pictures were usually declared more interesting because they were, of course, colourful and eye-catching. We followed up by asking the children whether the book would work if it just had pictures or if it just had words. Most children gave greater significance to the pictures and said that the book would not be as good without them, because the pictures help to show 'what's going on' and also 'what the characters look like, because some people can't read'. Several children thought that a good artist would need fewer words because it is all there in the pictures. As Denise (9) put it: 'The words are interesting because you can read instead of just trying to get the words off of the pictures.'

Most of the children expected picturebooks to have both words and pictures and found it no problem to 'make up' one or the other if missing (many had participated in these sort of exercises before: drawing pictures for words or making up words for pictures). However, they thought that getting the pictures 'right' was more important than getting the words right. To find out what's happened with just the pictures 'you have to use your head more' (Jason 9), whereas with just words 'you'd have to picture it all in your head, and you could see it would be a lot fatter book because there has to be more writing, describing and everything' (Dave 8). So images are translated into description and detail in a verbal text and are a more economic way of getting a message through, as Tamsin (8) pointed out: 'It would be really hard if he said [wrote] everything that was in *The Tunnel* so he just put in the pictures everything that was in there.'

Another revealing question was whether the words or the pictures told the same story. This proved difficult for many children who simply said 'yes'. However, many of them revised their answer either in the group discussions or in the re-interviews. Because the word/picture dynamics is different in each of the three picturebooks in this study, the pupils' responses were also different. In *Lily*, there is what Nikolajeva and Scott (2000) call a 'perspectival counterpoint' where words and pictures employ different perspectives to tell the story and involve both contradiction and ambiguity. Lily's story is told by the written text and Nicky's by the pictures. In *Zoo* the written text gives the narrator's point of view (one of the boys visiting the zoo) and the pictures tell the story of the animals; this could be described as a counterpoint in characterisation (humans/animals). Finally, in *The Tunnel*, the text and images tell a similar story except that the text is fairly bland and the pictures reveal much more.

With some prompting, the children who read *Lily* noticed that the words did not explain what was happening to Nicky and why he was frightened or mention the monsters which were only evident in the pictures. The pictures also provide 'the atmosphere' (Angus 9). Without the pictures, said Kevin (10), 'it would just be a happy book'. One of the children with learning difficulties pointed out that 'the pictures tell his [Nicky's] story and if he tells it the people wouldn't believe him'. On the other hand, Lauren (11) thought the words were needed 'to take the story along', to provide the narrative thread.

The responses to *Zoo* were similar because (again, with some prompting) most children realised the words and pictures were not telling the same story. Frank (5) noticed this at an elementary level: the words don't tell the same story as the pictures 'because when he said he had lots of food in the writing it didn't show in the picture. They look at the giraffes and the rhinos but they didn't say in the words.' Cristina (9) knew there was a distinction between the pictorial and verbal discourses even though she found it hard to express it: 'I think the pictures give more description about all the animals and the writing tells you a bit about the zoo, more of the zoo.' Older, more articulate children Lara (10) and Joe (10) really got to the heart of the matter. When asked which she preferred, Lara replied:

> The pictures, because the writing doesn't explain everything what you think. The writing only explains what the book is about and what is happening, but it doesn't explain what you feel and what they feel. So I like the pictures better because then you can think more stuff.

Joe also found the images more interesting because 'the pictures show what it's really like and what's going on with the animals'. He then refers to the perspectival counterpoint described by Nikolajeva and Scott (2001):

> I think they do tell the story in different ways, because the text is more like their [people visiting the zoo] point of view, but the pictures are more of the animals' point of view.

These responses contrast with *The Tunnel*, where both words and illustrations were felt necessary to understand the story. However, readers noticed that, although the words helped to 'guide' the reader through the book, the pictures created the sense of unease. This was particularly apparent in the spread in *The Tunnel* without any words, where Rose is running through the menacing forest. It was also one of the favourite images in the book for many children. Shanice (10) had to 'make up the story . . . it's making me think why the author put them [the various strange objects and figures] there'. Shanice also pointed out that, by looking at the pictures and making up your own story, 'you can understand more things than the writing'. Tamsin (8) summed up many of her peers' observations about the relationship between the visual and the verbal texts:

> Every book needs a bit of picture to make you understand. I mean if this book didn't really have much pictures except for the one in the front, you'd get lost a bit . . . if it was just writing you wouldn't really feel like you were in there because there was nothing to show you what it was really like. OK you could use your imagination, but if you want to know what the girl's point of view or the boy's point of view is you'd have to have pictures to see.

It is worth noting that at school Tamsin was considered a 'weak' reader, someone who had difficulties reading 'long' books, according to her teacher. However, as we can see here, her awareness of the reading process was far greater than any of her classmates and, indeed, of most children in the study. She had not seen *The Tunnel* before, but was familiar with other picturebooks and especially with fairy tales.

'He moved his imagination': the artistic process

The relationship between the words and the pictures leads to another element involved in the act of reading and viewing: the implied author/artist and his creative process.

The children's observations on the artistic processes involved in composing a picturebook not only indicate how they understand pictorial text, but also how they use metacognitive skills in doing so. In the following quote from 4-year-old Janet, she speculates about the steps Kitamura took to write and illustrate *Lily*:

> Well he first wrote the words and then he drew. He read them and then he drew what he thought might be what he wanted to draw and he looked at the pages. He had a first sketch there and then he looked at them and then he drew them with colours and put them in the book. I always draw people like that [and] if I can write them, I put words. I can write quite a lot of them.

The sequence, as Janet describes it, involves a lot of looking and thinking at various stages, as well as writing and drawing. The words come first and then an attempt at the drawing and finally colouring. She is also aware of the 'sketch' stage which implies the artist might make changes (there was only one other child who mentioned making a sketch first, 'in case he got it wrong'). In her last sentence Janet reflects on her own attempts at drawing, implying she is somewhat aware of the thinking, looking and revising involved in the process. The only difference is that she adds the words later because, at 4 years old, she is more confident about her drawing skills than her writing. This was reflected in her second drawing when, after finishing the pictures, she laboriously began to write a text above the drawing.

Throughout her two interviews, Janet attempted to explain her movements, talking about sequence and comparing the way she drew houses (square with triangle on top) with the way Kitamura draws them. She was also very articulate when describing her drawing of the tree monster with strikingly coloured squares above it, representing the warm colours of the curtains in Lily's room (Janet had told me she had similar curtains in her room and her favourite colour was purple), then a yellow square and a black square representing the lit and dark windows in the houses on Lily's walk. Although Janet struggled to talk about the pictures in the book, her sensitivity to Kitamura's use of colour (which unfortunately we cannot represent here) and pattern, is evident in the drawing. Her awareness of the steps involved in the process is also a recognition of the sophisticated cognitive skills which bridge writing and drawing when it is a creative act.

However, behind the children's comments one can also sometimes hear the cautionary voices of teachers or parents. Browne and Kitamura will be relieved to hear that 'he's very neat', 'he colours in nicely', 'he stays in the lines', and 'there are no mistakes'! This is Carol (10) (mentioned above as a struggling reader), talking about the way Kitamura has drawn the grass at different angles and the way she has been told to do it at school. Note the choice of vocabulary such as 'texture', which she may have picked up from the interviewer:

> I like the texture of the grass. When I was little I got told to never do it all different ways, so like I've already done that because I've been learned to do that . . . if I was an artist I wouldn't have done that because I've been learned from school when I was really little.

In general, comments on the artistic process can be divided into three groups: those that have to do with the actual techniques that the artist used; those that refer to the way in which he expressed his ideas; and those that show how the children understood his intentions. In the first group we find mention of specific paints and techniques, such as the possibility that Browne used a 'blow-pen' to spray the paint in one of the pictures, or that Browne used watercolours and Kitamura used crayons. It does not matter if these speculations are right or wrong, what really matters is that children are not looking at the illustration merely as a finished object but as the result of a process that begins with using a particular medium. Eisner is making a similar point in relation to drawing in his Foreword to Arnheim's *Thoughts on Art Education*: 'In the course of drawing, for example, the child must not only perceive the structural essence of what he wished to draw, which, Arnheim points out, is at the heart of skilled reasoning: the child must also find a way to represent that essence within the limits and possibilities of a medium' (1989: 4).

Children also regularly commented on the use of shadows, line and, perhaps most frequently, colour in the pictures. For example, Corinna (10) pointed out the importance of Browne using red for Rose's coat because of its reference to Little Red Riding Hood. Martin (7) said the same thing about Kitamura choosing yellow for Lily's tulips to stand out among the darker colours of the evening. Lara (10), an inexperienced reader commenting on *Zoo*, made many insightful references to Browne's use of colour.

> You can tell they [the animals] are upset because there is this dark one, not many colours, not bright beautiful colours, and it makes you think well . . . when it's people, it is happy, and it makes you feel oh we're happy, so we should be on the happy page. And the animals are really upset and are on the black page.

Other comments revealed what the children thought was going on in the artist's head as he drew. According to some children, first the artist has to 'imagine' the pictures in his head before he can draw them. Luke (5) thought that Browne writes the words for the story first and then thinks of a good picture to 'match' because 'words and pictures match exactly'. Sofia (8) believed that Browne drafts the written text first, makes a few changes and then draws pictures that match the text. Like others, she believed in the 'matching' of words and pictures because 'you wouldn't have a picture that says this, that doesn't match it, that doesn't quite make sense'. This thinking encapsulates the more literal engagement that some children had with Browne's work, in which words and pictures were perceived as telling the same story. Some of the older, more experienced readers like Lauren (11) had a more balanced view of how the artist went about his work: 'As I am reading it, the pictures link very well with the text, so he needed to know what was happening in both, both in the pictures and in the text.'

Pupils reading *Zoo* and *The Tunnel* were very aware that the author had to 'really think about it'. For example, as Erin (7) said, 'in a way the boys behave like monkeys and Browne chooses to draw monkeys rather than another animal'. In the group discussion, she also spoke of how Browne would have planned ahead carefully before doing it. Dan (8), who participated with Erin in the group discussion, agreed that Browne must have taken his camera to the zoo and then 'wanted to do something very, very careful with this book', and that even if he did make a mistake he would not 'give up'.

One question that children found hard to answer was what the artist had to know in order to do the illustrations. Many chose not to speculate but Carol's (10) reply condenses those who did. She spoke of the research Kitamura would have had to do before being able to create his story:

Well he needed to know a dog that looks like that and he needed to know a family that has a dog and how they kind of look after their dog and somebody that likes walking. You needed to interview somebody, to kind of know more about people and . . . how they kind of look after their dogs, or do they get scared and what do they do when they are scared and do you have any kids, do they walk the dog . . .

In other words, like Erin and Dan, there is a sense of the planning and time the work involves, the need to know your subject and then how you are going to set it down on paper.

This links to a third set of comments that imply an awareness of the artist's intentions behind the writing and drawing. Generally, it was considered that the artist had drawn in a particular style to make a picture 'more lively' or 'interesting' or 'funny' so 'people get excited and want to read on'. In some cases, this was linked to enjoyment, but in others it was linked to a commercial interest – creating a desire for reading would also make people 'buy it'. Sometimes their interpretation of the author's motives were linked to the story itself: one child thought Kitamura wrote *Lily* because he had a dog like Nicky (in fact, Kitamura got the idea for this story when he was living with a family who had a small girl he often took for walks in a pushchair). Others thought Browne wrote *The Tunnel* because he had a sister who was very different from him, or *Zoo* because he wanted people to go and see one.

Perhaps the questions that most revealed this awareness about intentions were those about the inclusion of the 'unusual' and this applied to all three books. Most readers suggested that the artists did it for the atmosphere, to make it look 'scary'. Several agreed that Browne and Kitamura draw in a way that makes you want to look carefully and not just turn over pages quickly. However, there were a few children who could only make literal sense of these features. One pupil kept insisting that Browne's 'brain must be off'! Finally, there were also those who said the artist put the things there 'because he wanted to' and as far as they were concerned, that was that.

Thinking, reading, looking and learning: conclusions

It is important to remember that these comments were made by children from different ages, as well as different socio-economic, cultural and linguistic backgrounds. It was impossible to do any further research into how each of these variables might affect viewing, but it is evident that they were all trying to make sense of the texts in front of them and most were able, to a degree, to express how they were actually doing this.

The children's answers reveal how the eye scans a picture, roaming over it, focusing on what they perceive are the salient features, then looking at background and other details. They also reveal how the eye moves between one part of the picture and another, piecing together the image like a puzzle. The eyes also move back and forth between the words and the images, leaning on each other for understanding, confirming or denying hypotheses about what is happening in the story. These movements correspond to some of the compositional elements described by Kress and van Leeuwen (1996) in their 'grammar of visual design', where, for example, the informational value of the left-hand area of an image is linked to what is already known or expected and the right-hand side is linked to the new or unexpected.

The children were aware of the thinking, looking, and planning required to achieve all this successfully and of the possibility of making and rectifying mistakes. They also revealed an ability to put themselves in the artist's head to imagine how he wanted the reader to react by creating images that inspired humour, fear and other emotions. The children were also able to go inside their own heads to describe what they were thinking and feeling as they read a picture (and also as they drew their own).

Their critical comments and observations suggest how these metacognitive skills can be developed and built on in order to help them become more critical and discerning readers. In the first place, their knowledge needs to be taken into account in the classroom. Once there is a space for them to articulate what they know and to discuss it with the teacher or their peers, they will feel more confident about their own skills and more interested in how the teacher can complement them. This can be done through looking at more picturebooks, comparing and contrasting them, as well as through children's own art work. Finally, children can be encouraged to bring their experience with other visual media to the classroom and use it to understand the processes of reception and creation and, in turn, reflect upon it, whether it be the latest computer games or ancient stained-glass windows.

A version of this chapter appears in M. Styles and E. Bearne (eds) (2002) *Art, Narrative and Childhood*, Stoke-on-Trent: Trentham Books.

Chapter 8

Thinking aloud

Looking at children drawing in response to picturebooks

Kate Noble

> Sometimes I practise when I draw. I draw a lot and it gets much better, I hardly scribble now, you see. I love drawing and colouring in 'cause it's really fun.
>
> (Polly 5)

Polly's comments show one young artist drawing, talking and 'thinking aloud' in response to a picturebook. Sedgwick and Sedgwick (1993: 29) assert that 'however it works, drawing is thinking aloud, a powerful route into knowledge.' Both quotes demonstrate the role of thinking in the creative process, but Polly also captures that unique pleasure that young children can derive from drawing. In this chapter I will look at how the children in this study drew in response to *Zoo*, *The Tunnel* and *Lily*. Through their drawings, we can see them 'thinking aloud' and begin to understand more about the metacognitive processes involved in creating visual texts.

Children can communicate what they see through their drawings and their drawings, in turn, reflect their responses to the visual stimuli they encounter. In *Art as Experience*, Dewey states that:

> Thinking directly in terms of colours, tones, images, is a different operation technically from thinking in words ... because the meaning of paintings and symphonies cannot be translated into words. .... There are values and meanings that can be expressed only by immediate visible and audible qualities, and to ask what they mean in the sense of something that can be put into words is to deny their distinctive existence.
>
> (1978: 73–74)

A visual experience demands a visual response true to its original form. From Rousseau onwards, we have seen an unprecedented interest in children's art, which has been both celebrated for its aesthetic qualities and explored as a tool for understanding cognitive development. Psychologists such as Arnheim (1966), Kellog (1979) and Gardner (1980) have demonstrated how children draw to make sense of the world around them. In simple terms, the toddler starts by drawing the world she knows and a waxy, circular scribble with two dots eventually becomes her mother's face. Early drawings form a bridge between the concrete world of experience (mummy) and the abstract world of symbols and signs (waxy scribble) and open the way into the other forms of symbolic representation such as reading and writing.

My involvement with the project began as a class teacher and art specialist. This chapter is both a description of my experiences working on *Zoo* with my own class of 4- and 5-year-olds and an analysis of the drawings of the other children in the study. As the only class teacher/researcher, my pupils had the advantage of being able to spend more time thinking about one picturebook. Our work formed a mini-project where the children were given the opportunity to look at and discuss the illustrations and text in great detail and make their own 'zoo' stories through play and art and craft. I was also able to watch them drawing. As well as working on *Zoo* at the time the researcher visited my classroom, we returned to it a few months later and spent further time discussing the text and drawing our responses.

Analysing the drawings

I have divided my analysis of the drawings into several sections, based on categories adapted from Davis (1993), Parsons (1987) and Lewis and Greene (1983). I start by looking at *literal* understanding, which constitutes a basic level of response, whereby the child draws people or events from the text to communicate story and content. Next I looked at the *overall effect* of the drawings, considering qualities such as the aesthetics of the image and a discussion of colour, tone, form and line. Finally, I looked at the *internal structure* of the drawing, examining the composition for balance and the relationship between objects or characters and their relative scale. I found that some of the most interesting *developmental differences* appear somewhere between overall effect and internal structure. (I will explore these differences later in the chapter, focusing in particular on one exceptional class of 10-year-olds.) Through their individual details many of the young artists move closer to what Parsons describes as the final autonomous stage of appreciation and judgement (see Chapter 1). A case study of an exceptionally gifted child, Yu, exemplifies some of these categories in more detail.

Literal responses

Children drawing in response to all three books showed literal understandings of their narrative content. The vast majority of children studying *Zoo* picked up on the central issue and drew animals trapped in cages. At all ages children highlighted the contrast between the worlds inside and outside the cages. In many of the drawings by the younger children an animal subject formed the focal point, often occupying a large part of the centre of the picture plane. Amy's drawing (Figure 8.1) was made in response to her first reading of *Zoo*. On a literal level her simple pen-and-ink sketch indicates that she knows that the story is about a family visit to the zoo. Both animal and humans are given equal status in the composition and occupy the same space.

The majority of drawings in response to *Lily* and *The Tunnel* also depicted people and events from the texts, communicating the children's understanding of the narrative. Many of the *Lily* drawings showed a child walking a dog, often placed within an urban scene and feature many of the strange monsters such as the snapping pillar-box, the river monster and the grinning tree (see Figure 8.2). Drawings inspired by *The Tunnel* picked up on the sibling relationship and focused on references to fairy tales and physical environmental features, such as the tunnel, the bedroom and the woods.

Figure 8.1 By Amy (age 4)

Figure 8.2 By Seamus (age 7)

Overall effect

The overall effect of each of the three books is very different. In Browne's books the illustrations are painstakingly drafted and contain meticulous detail of everything from the stripes on Dad's polo shirt to the stony pattern on the surface of the tunnel. Browne's almost photographic realism and skilful control of the composition give a solid overall effect which is heightened by sensitive use of colour. In *Lily*, Kitamura uses colour and line in a very different way. His pictorial style is more direct and cartoon-like with black pen lines encasing a wash of bright primary watercolours. In all three books colour, pattern and line communicate a strong sense of mood and atmosphere and open up many avenues for discussion. Looking at the drawings it does seem that the children have picked up on some of the different stylistic qualities of these two artists.

Will's (9) drawing evokes a disturbing overall effect and vividly characterises Dad from *Zoo* as the devil by using light, unstable pencil strokes; the big empty eyes and dark grimacing mouth form an eerie focal point (Figure 8.3). Will also captures Dad's brightly coloured shirt, which contrasts with the nightmarish features on his face. As a finishing touch Will captions the drawing, 'dad the devil are you scared?'

Figure 8.3 By Will (age 9)

Tony (10) drew one of the most articulate emotional responses to *Zoo*.[1] It is also worth noting that he was one of the children judged to be an inexperienced reader by his teacher and his interview was hesitant and uncertain. A black line down the centre of the page clearly divides the picture into two halves which stimulate very different responses. On the left-hand side he uses a faint pencil line to draw a small human figure and a pig. The figure appears behind long vertical bars whereas the pig is positioned outside the bars and is carefully coloured in a soft pink crayon. On the other side of the picture a large tree marks the division, negating the existence of any bars in this new world. A large hairy gorilla stands smiling underneath the tree in the centre of gentle, curving arcs of warm light coloured in yellow, blue and red. This side of the picture is coloured in bold, bright felt-tip and the overall effect is a potent image of containment versus freedom. Both Will and Tony have moved away from a literal representation of the story and added their own evocative details.

The younger children's drawings in the study were generally freer and less inhibited than the older pupils' in overall effect, and they often used the space more boldly. In response to *Zoo*, for example, Sara (4) (Figure 8.4) recreates the family, each member occupying equal space across the horizontal picture plane. Her lines are curvaceous and free, enclosed and protected by a large beaming sun in the left-hand corner, complete with a stretch of sky punctuated by one cloud and a flock of round-shaped birds. Her simple pen drawing is happy and spontaneous and the four smiling faces beam out at the viewer.

After reading *Lily*, Janet (4)* explored the expressive qualities of colour. The top left-hand half of her first picture is covered in a coloured stripe. The first section is made up of thinner strokes of purple, blue, red and brown before a square of intense black and then yellow. Cutting into the yellow square is a large green vertical form which echoes

Figure 8.4 By Sara (age 4)

the long neck of the sea creature in the river in Kitamura's story. The green form stands in a large purple square. Janet has worked with a great degree of care and control and the resulting image is both imaginative, original and highly symbolic. Her detailed explanation of the composition backs this up: she described the horizontal stripe of colour as representing her curtains, the black square acting as a dark window and the final yellow square showing light pouring through a window. Her second drawing* three months later is made with the same concentration, but now shows more interest in planning. Her drawing has become an exploration of forms laid out horizontally across the page, highlighted by a thick purple stripe of night sky along the top. Drawing this time in felt-tip, Janet again uses colour to articulate feelings but her drawing has become more realistic as she experiments with and re-creates the twisted shapes of Kitamura's lampposts, clock towers, buildings and trees.

Internal structure

Many of the drawings collected in the study show children beginning to experiment with structure to introduce new viewpoints. Christina (8) (Figure 8.5) starts by drawing a large orange tiger in the centre of the page and, having rubbed out her first attempt, tries hard to make her picture as realistic as possible. Although she has clearly had difficulties with the head, which is large and awkward, the hind legs and tail are drawn with greater accuracy, with the far leg placed behind the front leg in a convincing way. This thoughtful drafting corresponds with her interview when she talked about the way in which Browne positions a baboon to show it is sitting: 'I think the way he draws the baboon that's sitting down like a lion with his mouth open. He draws all

Figure 8.5 By Christina (age 8)

the fur first then he draws two legs and draws two more legs on the front to make it seem that it's sitting up.'

The tiger's tail and paws are carefully shaped, as is the butterfly fluttering outside the cage. The threatening grey felt-tip bars of the cage stretch vertically across the whole piece of paper and are reminiscent of the thick black lines around the animal pictures in *Zoo*. Although Christina has drawn green grass in the cage she makes a clear distinction between inside and outside by the position of the butterfly, shaping the grey felt-tip so as not to cover its pink wings. It is also interesting to note that she has continued these games in the top right-hand corner of her picture where she has written 'ZOO', doodling eyelashes and eye balls on the two 'O's. On a third line she has written, 'enjoy' a neat little joke of her own which demonstrates not only a real understanding of her drawings as means of communication, but also an understanding of the role and position of the viewer.

Several children drawing in response to *The Tunnel* depicted the boy turned into stone, one of the most haunting and compositionally sophisticated images in the book. As in the original drawing, Bobby (8) (Figure 8.6) has framed the image in a rectangular box, and the reader, peering in on the scene, empathises with the girl's sense of loss and isolation as she finds her brother 'still as stone' and sobs, 'Oh no . . . I'm too late.' Bobby has drawn in grey pencil except for a thin stripe of blue on the horizon blended into the grey clouds. The internal elements in the drawing have been placed with care: the jagged grass in the distance, the tree stumps and the circle

Figure 8.6 By Bobby (age 8)

of stones around the boy's feet. The figure has been redrawn several times, but Bobby has successfully depicted the boy frozen in motion, arm and leg outstretched to run away and, most chillingly of all, mouth and eyes wide open in fear.

Ashok (4) and Anne (9) chose the grinning tree from *Lily* as the central point in their composition, but a comparison of their drawings demonstrates the differences between the two ages. Ashok draws with great energy and his large green scribble tree is placed in the middle of the picture, complete with its menacing black mouth and dark eyes (Figure 8.7). The picture is as graphic and direct as might be expected in the drawing of a young child. In contrast Anne has drawn the tree as only part of the whole composition (Figure 8.8). Repeated rubbings out around the figure of Lily and the dog show that this young artist has placed considerable emphasis on 'getting it right'. Her colouring in is more accurate and controlled, and, unlike Ashok, she uses careful, solid blocks of colour. The arrangement of the internal elements is more worked out and more skilfully arranged and executed. However, her drawing lacks the direct aesthetic response of Ashok's tree. This deliberate planning brings us to an interesting point about developmental changes.

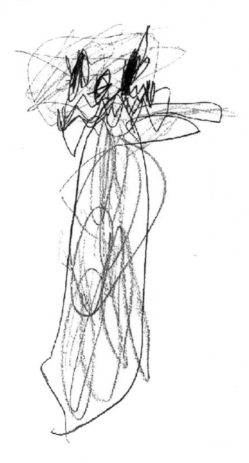

Figure 8.7 By Ashok (age 4)

Figure 8.8 By Anne (age 9)

Developmental differences: Polly 'switches her brain on'

In *Artful Scribbles,* Gardner's young son explains the difference between the drawings of older and younger children: 'As you get older, I think you look differently. You look more carefully at things. Also you think a lot, you plan before you actually make the drawing' (1980: 17). This notion of the role of thinking and planning in drawing comes through in several of the interviews and is evident in the pictures made by some of the older children, such as Christina, Bobby and Anne. However, we found that even younger children such as Polly and Janet were capable of engaging in the meta-cognitive processes involved in the creation of images. Here are more of Polly's (5) comments whilst drawing:[2]

> I'll just switch my brain on . . . that's the house in the distance that's why it's really small. . . . Now here I am going to use another green. Isn't grass two different shades of green? This is a lime shade of green . . .

Unfortunately, Polly's was the only transcript which captured a child talking aloud while actually drawing[3] but Erin's (7) comments to the interviewer also capture an awareness of the role of thinking and planning in the production of images, as well as showing her enjoyment of picturebooks:

ERIN: I really love his books.

INTERVIEWER: I want to know why you say that, Erin.

ERIN: Well he doesn't just say, 'I'll just write a story, I think I'll do it about this' and then he writes it. He actually thinks about it. Or he plans it ahead and then he really does good pictures and the pictures tell a different story, the same story only in a different way.

Erin's first drawing (Figure 8.9) uses bold colours and composition and is emotionally direct. However, by the time of the re-visit, her drawing had lost some of this earlier confidence, becoming more concerned with a moral message (like most of the older children) than from an emotional and aesthetic response towards a greater interest in the internal structure of the composition.

Davis (1993) explains this change in terms of 'U-shaped' development. In middle childhood (8–11) children reach the trough of 'literal' translation and are held back by the desire to capture the 'realness' of an object; they are no longer satisfied with a drawing which provides the essence or an impression of what they see. Benson (1986) also describes this period as an important time of conventionalism, a preoccupation with the rules of language and of graphic representation. The expressive qualities of the younger children's drawings are, perhaps, a direct result of a lack of restraints and rules. Gardner suggests another possible factor:

> Once writing mechanics and literary accomplishment have advanced sufficiently (as they ought to have by the age of 9 or 10), the possibility of achieving in words what was once attempted in drawings comes alive: the stage is set for the demise of graphic expression.
>
> (1980: 155)

Gardner suggests that the child's drawing is affected not only by the development of concrete operational thinking and increasing awareness of the self and its surroundings, but also by teaching methods which emphasise the primacy of the written word as a means of communication. Echoing Gardner, Davis fears that, 'Although artists thrive

Figure 8.9 By Erin (age 7)

and survive the literal stage, most individuals are lost in the trough of the U' (1993: 90). The desire for realism is impossible to achieve and only a few very gifted artists ever attain the degree of pictorial accuracy so craved in middle childhood. Most children are defeated by pictorial forms of representation, thus considering themselves unable to draw. This can be seen in the majority of the older children's drawings in the study which seem more constrained than those of the younger children.

The humanities project

As the U-shape model suggests, middle childhood does not necessarily have to herald 'the end' of aesthetic artistic response as long as children are given opportunities to continue to explore, accept and understand the uniquely expressive qualities of art and other aesthetic forms of communication. One class of 10-year-olds in the study proved it was possible to emerge from the 'U'. Working with an experienced and charismatic teacher, these pupils had taken part in an extended humanities project: over the course of the year they had examined the portrayal of refugees from the Second World War – and more recent conflicts – in a variety of media texts including photographs. The drawings they produced in response to *Zoo* were powerful and visually fluent, as their characters scream and glare out of the picture plane, demanding attention. Their interviews also showed that the children understood and used a wide variety of visual terms:

MAL: . . . she probably feels sorry for the animals . . .
INTERVIEWER: So how do the colours signal that?
MAL: 'Cos she's wearing that black and dark . . . dull and dark colours.
INTERVIEWER: So what does that mean? Black, dull, dark colours?
MAL: They're like . . . you usually wear black for funerals.
INTERVIEWER: Right. So you wear black for funerals. And what do black and purple
    represent?
MAL: Sad and sorryness.

They also discussed compositional devices such as the use of different borders around pictures:

BELINDA: It's like saying that like he probably says that the humans aren't really
    important, so he put like wavy lines round the picture. That the animals are
    more important than the humans so he's put like a straight border around the
    picture . . .
AIDEN: The animal pictures are all edgy and it's like you know, it gives the . . . really
    there's a tension . . .

This knowledge of picturing devices and techniques is also evident in their drawings. Sally (10) has attempted a complicated composition inspired by the close-up image of the caged gorilla in Browne's original text (Figure 8.10). She has drawn the cruciform bars of the cage so that they show up white against the grey fur of the gorilla and form a cross two-thirds up the vertical picture plane, deliberately positioning the gorilla's eyes on each side of the top section of the cross. This careful composition is strengthened by her clever use of colour. The drawing is executed entirely in graphite

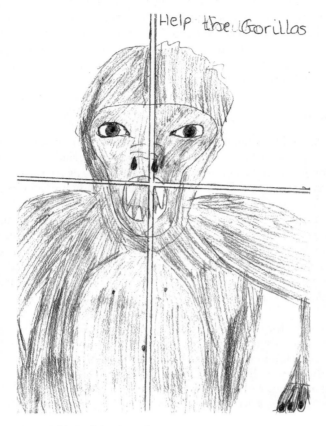

Help the Gorillas

Figure 8.10 By Sally (age 10)

pencil apart from the deep brown eyes and gaping red mouth which form the focal point of the picture and draw the viewer in.

In Belinda's (10) drawing (Figure 8.11) she experiments with the striped pattern of a tiger. Browne's style is characterised by his attention to the minuscule details of the daily world and many of the children's drawings echo this sensitivity to pattern and design; like Belinda, they experiment with stripes and marks on the animals' coats, playing with ideas about camouflage. A large number of children depict striped animals, tigers or zebras, which echo the bars of the cages, the black and white cover of the book and even the stripes on Dad's shirt. In Belinda's drawing the stripes have slipped off the tiger and metamorphosed into the cage itself, providing an interesting metaphor for the relationship between environment and animal. As it loses its stripes the tiger becomes unclassifiable to the human eye and the cage takes on a strange, organic and fluid quality of its own. This is cleverly juxtaposed by a lonely butterfly which has been positioned on the bare white paper underneath the cage. The issue of camouflage and the naturalness of the surroundings are the key to many of the drawings from this class and show an understanding of composition, content and message as well as the deeper philosophical and moral implications of the story.

Figure 8.11 By Belinda (age 10)

Many of the drawings by these pupils explored the moral dimension of *Zoo*. Some show a clear visual portrayal of human versus animal viewpoints and incorporate words into drawings to increase impact. One unsigned drawing (Figure 8.12) is divided into two parts named FREEDOM and ISOLATION. On the 'freedom' side of the page, a monkey swings upside-down on a banana tree, prophesying, 'no cage will spoil the world!' A smiling, colourful earth is drawn next to a person wearing clothes

Figure 8.12 Unsigned drawing

bearing slogans 'I hate zoos' and 'I hate animals in zoos'. This person says, 'it's great not to be in a cage'. The 'isolation' side shows a caged black-and-white earth with a mouth drooping downwards. Although the images in this drawing are strong and eloquent in their own right, it is interesting that the child felt the need to back up his or her moral view with the written word. This ties in with Gardner's point about the move from visual to verbal forms of communication.

All of the drawings by these older children contain striking individual details representative of the particular interests and motivations of the artist. They show the effects a gifted teacher and an in-depth analysis of visual image can have on the way children think, write and draw. As Gardner says, 'The capacity to consider various intellectual and social possibilities confers fresh powers on an individual's artistry' (1980: 213).

The *Zoo* project

As my class's understanding of *Zoo* developed, so too did the sophistication of their drawings and I can see many parallels between their work and the work of the 10-year-olds described above. This change took place in the context of a series of visual exercises and experiments which were designed to encourage the children to deepen their existing understanding by talking, looking and making. Their work also demonstrates the cognitive link between seeing, doing and knowing.

During our re-readings I talked to the children about Browne's pictures using direct questioning, and I also allowed the children to ask questions in return. One of the strongest compositional devices and the easiest for the children to see is the juxtaposition of the two worlds inside and outside the cages. We also talked about the way in which the artist uses the left (verso) and right-page (recto) spreads to illustrate the two different sides of the zoo debate. As our discussions about the book continued, many children began to place different emphasis on the relative size of animals to humans.

In addition to our focused work on *Zoo*, the class had wide experience of creating their own images, both from their imagination and in response to familiar objects, pictures and stories. Over the course of the year we carried out a series of experiments with colour, pattern, tone and form, which encouraged the children to develop their own visual vocabulary. They were also encouraged to draw their own stories, make books and use their own images as a starting point for writing. This particular class was also characterised by a wonderful capacity for being focused and having great concentration. Just as they were happy to sit for half an hour on the carpet analysing a picture or a book, a simple pencil exercise could occupy them for a whole afternoon. During class drawing sessions they were often so absorbed that they worked in total silence. Our return to *Zoo* enabled my class to use their newly acquired visual skills, having developed the confidence and control to produce drawings that were closer to their actual understanding.

Revisiting *Zoo*

After the initial in-depth study, I wasn't sure how the children would respond to *Zoo* several months later. When they came in from lunch many of them spotted the book resting on my board and a few started a discussion about which Browne book was their favourite. When I re-read *Zoo* with them I was conscious of a strange shift of power and felt that they were reading the story *to* me, often eager to interrupt my reading of the text with knowledgeable and confident observations and suggestions. During the initial sessions we had talked about the gorilla picture in some detail, although none of the children had drawn it afterwards. This time they were obsessed by it and one of the most striking observations was made by a normally silent child with special needs, Louis (4), who talked to the class about the compositional similarities between the gorilla picture and the family portraits at the start of the book (see Figure 3.2).

Lyle (4) was an exceptionally articulate child; in the class discussion he talked in depth about the visual symbolism in Browne's book, particularly the penultimate page which focuses on the gorilla's face. The children noticed how the page is split 'like the bars of a cage' and described the gorilla as 'looking like a king' and 'his eyes look like a person'. When I asked the class whether it reminded them of anything, Lyle responded, 'Jesus. Jesus died on a cross.' When asked why the artist had chosen to draw the gorilla like that he replied, 'Because God made Jesus and God made all the animals.' The children also compared the animals and people: 'The gorilla looks wiser, more like a person.' Lyle concluded, 'I think the animals are becoming wiser and the people are like animals.' His comments tie in with his own deeply religious home background. In *Art and Illusion* Gombrich writes: 'Whenever we receive a visual impression, we act by docketing it, filing it, grouping it in one way or another, even if the impression is only that of an inkblot or a fingerprint' (1962: 251).

Lyle has drawn on his own bank of visual experience, something all readers do in their own idiosyncratic ways when interpreting or responding to image. Although this particular child was frustrated by his attempts to communicate what he saw and understood visually, his verbal responses showed a proficiency in interpreting and understanding visual references and metaphors. This is a good example of what Kress is saying in *Before Writing* where he describes reading as a transformative action in which the reader 'makes sense of the signs provided to her or to him within a frame of reference in their own experience' (1997: 58). The reading process is multi-modal and, as we have seen, visual meaning can be communicated and interpreted in many different ways.

In *Zoo* the facial expressions and body language of the family and the animals are powerful communicators of the isolation and pointlessness felt by Mum and the apparent lack of concern of Dad and the boys. As we have noted elsewhere, many of the youngest children were able to talk about facial expressions and body language. My class and I discussed in detail how individual protagonists within the story were feeling. Initially, only a few of the children were able to articulate these feelings in their drawings, a finding backed up in research cited in Gardner (1980). However, on revisiting *Zoo*, I was intrigued to see that the children now had the confidence and skills to depict some of the more challenging and complicated images from the book. Many chose this time to draw the image of the gorilla within a cruciform frame. Louis (4) made a quite outstanding drawing of the family and the caged gorilla (Figure 8.13). Although his figures are still very immature and tadpole-like, he has deliberately drawn bemused frown lines on Dad's forehead. A strong white crucifix separates the gorilla from the family and his eyes have been skilfully placed on either side of the top section. Louis has also attempted to write the title of the book.

Figure 8.13 By Louis (age 4)

Many others made similar developmental leaps to achieve levels of expression and fluency unusual in such young children. The confidence evident in the discussion is also reflected in the children's drawings as they explore the theme of suffering on the cross – one of the most distinctive and poignant images of the western world – and relate it to the gorilla in the cage. The children were symbolically representing captivity and suffering in their drawings and communicating empathy for animals (and elsewhere for people, especially Mum). This finding runs contrary to beliefs about the egocentric perspective of the pre-operational young child.

The final drawings are by Jane (5), who made a quite remarkable leap between the two sessions. Her first drawing shows a literal understanding of the story and depicts a grinning elephant centred on the page inside a square box surrounded by a happy but androgynous 'tadpole' family (Figure 8.14). Her later drawing is an attempt at the gorilla's face seen through the crossing bars of the cage (Figure 8.15). Jane has made a deliberate decision about the composition and internal structure of her drawing and has halved the page horizontally and vertically with two thick bars in the shape of a cross. Her drawing focuses on the gorilla's eyes, placing each in a top quarter of the page. She works in graphite pencil to capture the texture of the gorilla's fur, hatching tiny lines in different sizes and directions, using darker, stronger lines on the bottom half of the face to emphasise the gentle sadness of the eyes. Her drawing explores not only Browne's dramatic composition and viewpoint, but also his realistic rendering of every tiny hair on the gorilla's face. In both drawings Jane uses the compositional devices of the cage to communicate entrapment. However, in the later drawing she is intrigued not only by the positioning of the humans to the animals, but also by the psychological dimension. The detail in the fur and the eyes reveals how important she understands the individual animals

Figure 8.14 By Jane (age 5)

to be. Her sophisticated composition creates drama and pathos articulated by skilful attention to texture and detail. By experimenting with and talking about artistic devices and conventions Jane has developed her visual knowledge and is now trying out these devices in her own work.

Figure 8.15 By Jane (age 5)

Final thoughts

Kellog (1979: 13) points out that 'children's hands and eyes must be active for intelligence to develop'. Looking at the drawings in this study has demonstrated to me that even the youngest children can interpret, comprehend and communicate the visual – far beyond what they might be assumed to know. The young artists in my class came to a deeper understanding through their visual explorations. What seems to happen when we draw is similar to the process that we experience through writing: by doing we come to understand.

Although many children draw spontaneously from a young age, adults have a role to play by allowing space for experimentation and practice. By focusing explicitly on external visual elements such as composition, line, form and colour, the teacher can develop children's capacities to internalise this visual language and, in so doing, come to understand and communicate through their pictures. These explorations should take place through looking at art, as well as developing children's graphic skills. Our study provided opportunities for children to explore what they saw through playing, talking, making and drawing, thus enabling them to demonstrate the sophisticated thinking of which they were capable. Drawing is a serious enterprise for young children; combining drawing with careful looking offers the intrinsic pleasures derived from all creative activities and the special way in which art nourishes 'the invisible realms of our mind' (Gombrich 1962: 239).

Vignette – 'it makes you feel you are trapped in a cage' (Yu 4)

Of all the drawings in the study, some of the most interesting in terms of overall effect, content and understanding are by Yu (4). She is a quiet and thoughtful child and, although both her reading and writing are advanced for her age, she said very little in the interviews or the class discussions. However, her drawings communicated a deep response to Zoo and an indication of some of her own preferences, feelings and experiences. In many of her early drawings the figure of Mum is drawn particularly carefully. As middle child of a young family of five children, her drawings perhaps indicate the importance and power of her own mother as primary carer.

Yu's early drawings reveal that she has understood the main themes in Zoo by depicting the family side by side with animals caged inside their enclosures. Yet she also shows a striking level of sensitivity to visual elements such as composition, design and characterisation. Yu's first drawing shows a giraffe and a large tree fenced in by a bold, three-barred gate (Figure 8.16). On the other side of the fence, to the right of the tree, stand Mum, Dad and the two boys who take up the last vertical quarter of the picture. Yu's composition shows an understanding of the contrast between the freedom of those outside the zoo and the unnaturalness of the animals' enclosures. The tree and the fence form a clear barrier between the animals and humans while a small, smiling bird sits on the fence next to the giraffe.

This distinction is reinforced by environmental details. A large sun, a few clouds and birds in the sky of the animal section form a marked contrast to the bars which separate them from the human protagonists. There even appears to be fruit on the giraffe's side of the tree and on the floor of its enclosure is a nondescript shape, reminiscent of the dirty cages in *Zoo*. Yu has taken greatest care over the figure of Mum, who is drawn bigger than the rest of the family with details such as her eyes which are drawn with lashes and tiny pupils. Yu skilfully controls the relationship between the different actors in her story by placing one in front of the other. Cox (1992) and others have discussed how very few young children achieve this partial hiding or occlusion in their pictures and will draw, for example, the whole object rather than partially obscuring a hidden object. Luquet used this example to demonstrate that 'children draw what they know rather than what they see' (quoted in Cox 1992: 88)

Later on the same day as the interview, Yu began her second picture, which is an example, not only of her widening understanding, but also of the way in which children continue to explore what they see through drawing. Sitting at a table with a group of other children, she began with an exploration of bubble writing which she placed in the top horizontal section of the picture. (I had noticed before how children enjoyed experimenting with typographic conventions and bubble writing is a good way of exploring both the shapes and conventions of text.) Next Yu started drawing an animal, a cheetah, which was then carefully contained in a cage, along with the bubble writing. As she drew in the bars of the cage she tried not to go over the lines on the cheetah before adding a few thin, dusty strokes of black dirt to the base of the cage. By now she had filled nearly the

Figure 8.16 By Yu (age 4)

(continued)

(continued)

whole piece of paper, so she reached for another piece on which she redrew the family. Again the tree forms a powerful divide, this time between the parents and the boys who are now squeezed into the left-hand vertical plane of the picture.

As with the first drawing, Yu reapplies carefully practised schema for her figure drawings. While the boys are treated in exactly the same way in both drawings and are nearly identical, once again it is the figure of Mum who receives the greatest attention: she is the largest character, occupying nearly half the picture plane. However, the figures of both Mum and Dad demonstrate changes in her schema. Mum is drawn in profile with her back to the children and her arms outstretched towards Dad to whom she is saying, 'Come back!' Drawing figures in profile is very unusual in young children's drawings as, once again, the child is required to draw what they see rather than what they know. A long, diagonal sweep of hair draws the character in towards the rest of the family. Mum's hands, arms and hair are emphasised, whereas on one of the boys the arms have been forgotten altogether. Dad's face is drawn in greater detail, his eyes are big and open and he has an angry, fuzzy mouth and expressive, upturned eyebrows, more reminiscent now of the father in *Zoo*. While Mum looks at Dad, Dad looks out of the picture towards the viewer. As in the book, he is fooling around and making silly noises, as do the children. Finally, Yu went back to the drawing of the cheetah and added a speech bubble for the animal, 'ha, ha ha'.

Three months later Yu drew again in response to *Zoo* after re-reading the book in the classroom (Figure 8.17). In this drawing, a large rhinoceros stands alone in the centre of the page in a dirty, barren enclosure. The cage has no bars and is bare except for the grey bricks of the top right-hand corner and a few mouldy, insipid green patches on the floor. The cage is dirty and scratched with graffiti. Yu has placed the viewer in the cage with the animal, a compositional device employed by Browne in *Zoo*. The most significant change in this later drawing is the facial expression of the animal. This time the eyes are slanted and angry, its mouth is open and teeth bared. The total effect is both unsettling and disturbing – similar to feelings evoked by the neglected, lonely orang-utan in *Zoo*.

In the final drawing after the second interview, Yu depicts a tiger and four birds (Figure 8.18). Three brown baby birds sit inside a nest perched on top of a palm tree while a much larger, rainbow-coloured bird flies towards the right-hand side of the page, pointing in the same direction as a dramatic, elongated tiger. Yu's positioning of the bars of the cage gives an ambiguity to her picture, as the reader is not entirely sure whether all the creatures are inside or outside the cage. Such indeterminacy is, of course, a feature of Browne's work.

Since Yu's first reading of *Zoo* she has spent time studying not only this book but other natural history books. In her later drawings the animals are more anatomically correct and individual for each animal type. The tiger is depicted in profile and is angry with a long, wavy mouth and upturned eyebrows. Yu is now working in felt tip and the bright blues of the sky and careful, multi-coloured pattern on the bird produce a powerful aesthetic response in the viewer.

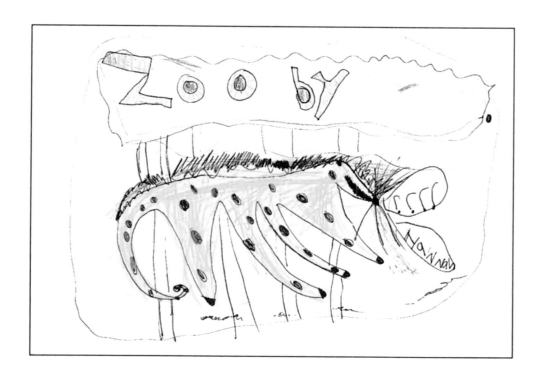

Plate 1 By Yu (age 4)

Plate 2 From *Zoo* by Anthony Browne

Plate 3 From *Zoo* by Anthony Browne

Plate 4 By Joe (age 10)

Plate 5 From *The Tunnel* by Anthony Browne

Source: Illustration from *The Tunnel* by Anthony Browne, copyright © 1989 Anthony Browne, reproduced by permission of Walker Books Ltd.

Plate 6 By Polly (age 5)

Plate 7 From *Lily Takes a Walk* by Satoshi Kitamura

Source: Illustration from *Lily Takes a Walk* by Satoshi Kitamura reprinted by permission of Catnip Publishing

Plate 8 By Charlie (age 9)

Figure 8.17 By Yu (age 4)

Figure 8.18 By Yu (age 4)

(continued)

(continued)

Yu is clearly a gifted artist and her mature understanding of the story is communicated through sophisticated, detailed drawings. She has begun to grasp some of the complex relationships between the actors in the story and her drawings show a striking degree of sensitivity to the emotional state of the main protagonists and the beginnings of characterisation. It is very unusual for such a young child to draw a figure in profile, to represent movement and to layer the composition by deliberately placing one object behind or in front of another. By continuing to provide her with opportunities to express herself visually, to draw what she sees, Yu will be able to communicate her considerable knowledge as well as adding to it. She is also able to express her powerful reactions to *Zoo*, strong feelings which she was unable to communicate in any other way.

Notes

1 Unfortunately this drawing is not included as it does not show up in black and white. (* indicates that the child's drawing could not be reproduced in black and white.)
2 Polly uses bold colour and line to represent Rose and Jack in the forest, the figure of the wolf in the tree, the tunnel and the siblings' mother shouting, 'Children' (written by the interviewer at Polly's request) from her house at the top of the hill.
3 When Kate planned her doctoral work soon after, she ensured that observing and taping the children while they drew in response to picturebooks was the main focus of her study.

Part II

Theoretical perspectives and new research on children responding to picturebooks

Theories and frameworks

Supporting research on visual literacy

This chapter revises the theory underpinning our research in the first edition where we considered what visual literacy could offer our understanding of picturebook reading through a review of the field. In this new version, we consider visual literacy again but we have fine-tuned our focus in order to look in more depth at theories, frameworks and approaches that are more closely linked to response to picturebooks.

Consideration of and literature about visual literacy has increased in the last ten years, with theoretical and empirical studies as well as practical approaches coming from different disciplines such as neuroscience, cognitive research, cultural and media studies, art history and psychology, as well as various perspectives within the arts, such as painting and film. This interest has also come from educationalists who have explored the potential of images for learning, especially via picturebooks, graphic novels and comics in the classroom. Given the advances in digital technology in the last two decades one would expect more of an impact of visual studies on official programmes of education but, with a few exceptions such as Australia,[1] it does not appear explicitly in the curriculum. Also, already in 1996 Kress and van Leeuwen had pointed to the dominance and power of visual language in many domains and were critical about that fact that this had not been understood by decision makers in education.

The original edition of this book contributed in a small way to bringing the concept of visual literacy to classrooms, judging from the reception the book has had in many countries, and we hope that this revised edition will go further in encouraging policy makers and teachers to include these ideas. It is important to note that we are not saying, nor did we ever say, that visual literacy should become another compulsory task in education or that the only way to enjoy picturebooks is through becoming visually literate. A child can enjoy a picturebook, of course, without sophisticated knowledge of visual literacy. However, what we also know for certain is that in order to expand or deepen engagement with a picturebook (or graphic novel, comic or any other visual art form, for that matter), some knowledge of terminology, of how visuals work (and how they work together with the words, in some cases), and of the processes of reading an image can be helpful in order to move readers beyond literal responses, to enrich the reading experience and intensify that initial pleasure. Examples of this abound in accounts of studies and projects involving picturebooks and readers, which we will be reviewing in this chapter and the next.

In our original edition we considered visual literacy in two different chapters, looking at it through the arts in the first instance and then at some of the processes involved in responses to visual texts, including those related to picturebooks. Our objective was to try to find theories and frameworks that would help us approach responses to visual texts and our study reflects the scarcity of suitable studies at the time. In this edition, we have brought together some of the material from these two chapters which we believe still have the potential to illuminate work in this area and we have also incorporated some references from our 2008 review of studies on response to multimodal texts as well as the most recent ones.

We have, however, moved on from the concern of some of the theorists with attempting to construct models of developmental response to visual images or to identify the phases viewers go through in their deepening responses to works of art. These models can be useful in some cases, but we are aware that they should be considered with caution in order to avoid generalisations or milestones that might lead to judging children's ability to read images.

The evolution of the concept of 'visual literacy'

The term 'visual literacy' was probably first coined by Debes in the late 1960s. His focus was on what a visually literate person could do: in other words: 'discriminate and interpret the visible actions, objects, symbols, natural or man-made, that he encounters in his environment' (Debes, cited in Avgerinou and Ericson 1997: 281) as well as the 'creative' application of these competencies for communication with others and appreciation of visual texts. The concept quickly gained currency in media studies, information technology, cultural studies and visual arts education. However, it remains a contentious term, squeezed into different shapes by different disciplines. Suhor and Little (1988: 470), for example, saw visual literacy as an 'aggregate concept' and no longer 'a coherent area of study but, at best, an ingenious orchestration of ideas'. Some writers favoured simple, 'common sense' definitions, such as Hortin (1982: 262), an educational technologist, who describes it as: 'the ability to understand and use images to think and learn in terms of images i.e. to think visually.' Sinatra (1986) considered the three essential components of visual literacy to be viewing, sensorimotor exploration and non-verbal representation. He believed that visual literacy is indispensable to thinking and defined it persuasively as 'the active reconstruction of past experiences with incoming visual information to obtain meaning' (p. 5). Others, such as Dondis (1973), another of the pioneers in this area, defined visual literacy as visual syntax comparable to linguistic grammar, using terms such as line, colour, shape, tone, dimensions and texture instead of verb, clause and sentence, etc.

In 1998, Raney warned us of the dangers of going too far down the road that might 'replicate the assumption of an autonomous model of literacy – that there is a fixed or "single code" to be learnt, that looking at things is a science, or that classifying and dissecting images will uncover their meanings' (1998: 39). Raney went on to suggest that notions like reading competence or decoding should be replaced with considering:

> [O]ur relationship to the visual world in terms of empowerment, choice, habit, passion or delight. . . . The driving force is prior expectations of meaning [which are] set up by the social fields in which an object is encountered . . . whether it is the frame of 'art', inclinations of gender, class identity or generation, or personal experience and associations.
>
> (1998: 39)

This view of visual literacy has its roots in structuralism (Saussure, Lévi-Strauss, Barthes, et al.), which suggested that far from coming to texts with an 'innocent eye',[2] the reader is 'a socialised being', a collection of 'subjectivities' responding to the visual world with a body and mind shaped by the realities in which he or she grew up' (Raney 1998: 39). This view fits comfortably within the idea of literacy as a plural – literacies (as opposed to the narrow view of literacy understood only as reading and writing) – and as a set of social practices (which involve cultural and ideological considerations). These ideas were pioneered by scholars such as Street (1984) in the UK and Heath (1983) in the USA (Heath herself straddles the disciplines of social anthropology, linguistics, English, education and, more recently, neuroscience). This view is particularly important in considering children's responses to multimodal texts, as it clear by now that their previous experiences with reading, viewing art and media, as well as their language, culture and gender, all influence their reactions to a picturebook. Raney therefore still provides, for us, one of the most all-encompassing and convincing definitions of visual literacy:

> [I]t is the history of thinking about what images and objects mean, how they are put together, how we respond to or interpret them, how they might function as modes of thought, and how they are seated within the societies which gave rise to them.
>
> (1998: 38)

Visual literacy and art

In his book *Visual Thinking* (1970), Arnheim was concerned with visual perception as a cognitive activity. He argued that artistic activity is a form of reasoning, in which perceiving and thinking are indivisibly intertwined: 'My contention is that the cognitive operations called thinking are not the privilege of mental processes above and beyond perception but the essential ingredients of perception itself.' Arnheim takes us back to Plato's belief in 'the wisdom of direct vision' and his equation of Socrates' blindness with 'losing the eye of the mind'. Arguing that the Greek philosophers first conceived the dichotomy of perceiving and reasoning, Arnheim reminds us that they never forgot that 'direct vision is the first and final source of wisdom' (1970: 7–13). In a later work, Arnheim (1989) described the process by which children gain their first 'intellectual concepts' through intelligent observation.

Langer had already discussed the power of the image and how it works on the human psyche back in the 1940s in her important work, *Philosophy in a New Key* (Langer 1990). However, few educationalists, other than those concerned in arts education and some psychologists, seem aware of what hard discipline is required in looking attentively at pictures. In *Iconology: Image, Text, Ideology*, Mitchell asserts: 'More clearly than any other use of the eyes, the wrestling with a work of visual art reveals how active a task of shape-building is involved in what goes by the simple names of "seeing" or "looking" (1986: 36). In a similar vein, writing in the foreword to Arnheim's *Thoughts on Art Education*, Eisner points out:

> The eye, as Arnheim tells us, is a part of the mind. For the mind to flourish, it needs context to reflect upon. The senses, as part of an inseparable cognitive whole, provide that context . . . The optimal development of mind requires

attention not only to intellectual processes but to intuitive ones as well. Children and adolescents should be encouraged to see the whole, not only the parts. Art can teach this . . . The gist of Arnheim's message is that vision itself is a function of intelligence, that perception is a cognitive event, that interpretation and meaning are an indivisible aspect of seeing, and that educational processes can thwart or foster such human abilities.

(Eisner in Arnheim 1989: 4–7)

Picturebook artists invite readers to do exactly this, to 'see the whole' through careful observation of the parts, encouraging the reader to move back and forth between the details and the big picture. As Salisbury and Styles put it, 'Today, the boundaries between the book arts, literature and commercial graphic art can be seen to be merging in the children's picturebook' (2013: 50). Browne makes this invitation explicit in his picturebook, *The Shape Game* (2004), where readers follow the family from *Zoo* into an art gallery and experience viewing and responding with them, through a variety of visual games and clues which work at both an intuitive and intellectual level.[3]

The work of Gardner and his Project Zero Team based at Harvard University produced much evidence and ground-breaking theories on arts education, including work on multiple intelligences and visual analysis. In his attempt to link human development and the artistic process, Gardner studied the moment in which children begin to understand and use symbolic systems. He thinks it probable that, by the ages of 3 or 4, children can experience 'discrete emotions', including those in response to a work of art, though they will not be able to articulate those emotions (emotional literacy and cognitive theories in relation to emotions and picturebooks will be referred to in more detail below).

Turning visual experience into language

There are many debates about whether spoken and written language can ever adequately take account of visual experience (Raney 1998). Kress has led the challenge against the dominance of verbal language over visual texts and is probably the most influential educational scholar in this field. Like Dondis, he is keen to develop 'an established theoretical framework within which visual forms of representation can be discussed' (Kress and van Leeuwen 1996: 20) and his work has reclaimed the language of syntax and applied it to visual texts. He argues persuasively that images can be the central medium of communication in any text and reminds us that ideology is always present. Kress points out that 'visual communication is always coded – it seems transparent only because we know the code already' (Kress and van Leeuwen 1996: 32). He shows us how we can read images by analysing visual grammar. His semiotic code of pictures uses the vocabulary of design – with terms like vectors representing action verbs, actors and reactors as nouns, colour and focus acting as locative prepositions, and contrasting, for example, rectangular forms as representational of the mechanical, logical, manmade [sic] constructions, with the more organic, natural disposition in curves and circles. The viewer, in turn, responds to the visual address produced by the image, but has some choice about how to respond.

In a fascinating article on art and language in middle childhood, Benson (1986) poses fundamental questions about whether spoken and written language are suitable ways of appreciating art:

> There are very complex questions which should prompt educational theorists to take a closer look at the pedagogical process of talking about pictures as a translational problem. . . . A primary feature of looking and seeing is silence. The look and the gaze are essentially non-verbal.
>
> (p. 134)

Benson goes on to suggest that the arts would not exist if all meanings could be adequately expressed by words. After analysing the metapictorial beliefs of young children, Benson wonders whether the 'ambiguity and multiple references' produced by art objects can result in 'the sort of intellectual tension that leads to a growth in understanding' (1986: 134–138). Clearly, the multiple meanings which complex picturebooks encourage the readers to explore, particularly through considering the interaction between pictures and words, open this possibility for growth, especially if the reading is accompanied by dialogue. While this then raises the issues of translating response into language it also suggests the potential of responding to picturebooks with visual language: drawing was one of the response strategies which was successfully employed in our original study and it set the precedent for other visual responses such as collage or photography which have been used in other studies involving picture-books (see Chapter 10).

Visual literacy and young children's development

Much of the initial literature on how young children read pictures has come from developmental psychology. The main focus of research in this field examines, usually under test conditions, how children respond to particular, often isolated images, or pictures in text-books. Because of its close focus on the cognitive, such research mostly fails to take account of the outstanding art work in many picturebooks which provokes affective as well as cognitive reactions in young readers, and also ignores the dynamic relationship between viewer and text which is so evident to those of us studying children's overall reactions to picturebooks. Because of this lack of under-standing of the picturebook as an object, we disagree with many of the premises of this type of research and we also question whether a 'developmental' model of response that is valid for all children can be constructed (just as the same is true for developmental models of any other type of children's abilities). However, we do acknowledge that some concepts from the work of Piaget and other theories of cog-nitive development, while not addressing visual learning directly, are still helpful in understanding how children learn.

Piaget, for example, links thinking with experience, that is, children act upon the world through their senses and develop hypotheses based on the consequences of their actions. He also showed that babies discovered predictable patterns and learned to anticipate, an important discovery for understanding both textual and visual stories. Sipe (1998) discusses this when he refers to the 'transmediation' of word and image in picturebooks:

Each new page opening presents us with a new set of words and new illustrations to factor into our construction of meaning. Reviewing and rereading will produce ever-new insights as we construct new connections and make modifications of our previous interpretations, in a Piagetian process of assimilation and accommodation. In other words, we assimilate new information and in the process we change our cognitive structures, accommodating them to the new information.

(p. 106)

This shows just how important picturebooks can be in contributing to children's development and some of the case studies summarised in Chapter 11 demonstrate this in detail.

The following example (an observation of Flora aged 17 months as she read *Peepo!* – taken from Arizpe's informal literacy journal of her children) shows how aspects of these cognitive theories can be applied to reading pictures.

I have always had misgivings about reading the Ahlbergs' *Peepo!* with a toddler. Although Flora enjoyed the story with its rollicking verse and repetitions and, of course, the peep-hole, I felt there was too much detail in the pictures for her to distinguish any of it clearly, except for the baby which constantly appears on the left-hand page. But my older daughter loved the book, so Flora must have seen it about a dozen times before the particular reading I will now describe. For some reason, it struck me that this time Flora was enjoying the book more fully and this was because she had made the connection between the baby on the left, the peep-hole, and the picture on the other side. Although it is hard to explain this intuition in words (especially as Flora could not talk at this stage), the evidence for thinking she had made a leap in understanding was her keen and prolonged scrutiny of the pictures after the reading. On the page where the baby is in a high chair, Flora pointed to the foot without a shoe. 'Where's the shoe?' I asked her, then turned the page with the peep-hole and showed her the missing shoe under the table. Flora's finger then went from the shoe under the table, back to the shoe-less foot and on to her own feet. She began pointing to the things she was familiar with on other pages, such as the bowl of porridge, cake and toy duck. I thought it was interesting that this awareness had occurred after Flora had spent two weeks in another house which was chaotic and full of objects and extended family, not unlike those in the book. It was as if this experience had helped Flora to distinguish individual objects amongst all the rest and connect them to the baby and herself.

This extract from Arizpe's journal of her children's reading shows how Piaget's 'pre-operational child' is dealing with the environment at a perceptual level and acting upon it, using both eyes and hands (literally grasping, turning pages, putting fingers through the holes and pointing). Flora had learnt to predict and anticipate there would be a baby, a peep-hole and a larger picture on every page and yet, as

Sipe noted, she was also gaining new information (about food, animals, objects) and connecting it to what she already knew. Flora's behaviour also gives an illustration of Nikolajeva and Scott's (2001) hermeneutic circle in action, and relates to Clark's first phase of understanding a visual work of art (see Chapter 1) in which the viewer engages with a text by getting a general impression of the whole and then goes on to the second stage, which is careful looking – something that needs to take time. Through my asking questions (about things which I knew she has experience of) and providing cues and prompts, we reached Flora's zone of proximal development and she was moving towards a new level of understanding.

In Chapter 1 we mentioned Clark's third phase of looking at art, the viewer connecting to her own experience (in this case, sitting on a high-chair watching family members going in and out of a cluttered room) and knowledge, shoes often get lost. This lead to a re-examination of the images, where Flora registered what she knew and was on the alert for other objects that she might have recognised; in this case, in the next reading she suddenly saw the little objects at the corner of the frame around the baby. It is difficult to say in what way Flora's everyday world was altered by looking at the pictures (Clark's final stage), but it is certain that the accumulation of knowledge from looking at this and many other picturebooks had an impact on how she viewed the world.

Emerging frameworks for exploring visual literacy and picturebooks

New perspectives from a variety of disciplines have contributed to exploring and illuminating the ways in which readers read images. These perspectives derive from theories related to sociocultural literacy practices, multiculturalism, multimodality and neuroscience and cognition. As we shall see in the next chapter, all of these have informed research on response to picturebooks, so in this section we wanted to briefly refer to these frameworks and the seminal ideas behind them.

We previously noted how the question of prior knowledge, understanding and exposure to visual texts came into play as we worked with children with a wide variety of experience of visual literacy, ranging at one extreme from a 5-year-old child recently arrived from another culture who did not yet speak English and who had little exposure to books, to confident, fluent readers of 11 with wide book knowledge who were already familiar with the artist's picturebooks. Some children therefore drew on sophisticated repertoires of multimodal reading and were familiar with literacy practices which centred on drawing meaning from texts while other inexperienced readers used what resources they had, making more naive, instinctive responses to the books. Readers tended to be fascinated rather than daunted or confused by the playful postmodern elements of intertextuality, intratextuality and metafiction. For all three books we also observed that the readers became involved with the characters, empathising with their feelings (such as Rose's night-time fears in *The Tunnel*) and that they were able to understand what a character thought and felt about others in what was a complex process (such as the mother's allusion in *Zoo* to her son's 'animal-like' behaviour compared to the animals behind the bars). All these observations can be explained and illuminated further by drawing on some of the more recent theories regarding reading and meaning-making.

From the work done on literacy as a social practice (Street 1984; New London Group 1996) we know that we all carry with us 'funds of knowledge' (Moll et al. 2005) which we apply when we learn and also when we read. Visual literacy is not an exception, it is also a set of practices that take place within, and which is determined by, a particular context, and these practices include knowledge and experience of a variety of different media which allow intertextual connections. Sipe was already drawing attention to the place of intertextuality in reader-response in 2000 (Sipe 2000) and more recently Mackey has argued that readers use these 'landmarks' to orient themselves in their reading (Mackey 2011). As we will see in Chapter 10, further research on response to picturebooks has confirmed that children's interpretative strategies involve intertextual references derived from their personal experiences and which enrich meaning-making.

From the numerous studies on multiculturalism or interculturalism and children's literature (e.g. Botelho and Rudman 2009; Short and Thomas 2011), further frameworks can be found for exploring both diversity in picturebooks and the influence of diverse literacy practices, which have implications when considering reader-response (Cai 2008) and especially the response to images (referring us back to Perkin's notion of 'multiconnectedness' mentioned in Chapter 1). Brooks and Browne (2012), for example, argue for a more 'culturally situated' reader response theory given that Rosenblatt only implicitly refers to the ethnic or cultural background of the reader (and all the values, practices, knowledge and experiences this implies).

> We intend not to depict the entire reading process, but rather the ways readers culturally position themselves when engaging with texts. We also demonstrate how various features and passages from a multicultural book call forth certain types of positioned responses. The theory explains why two racially or ethnically similar children might share similar or very different interpretations of a story.
>
> (p. 83)

Although they do not refer to picturebooks, these scholars build their theory of response from empirical research and identify cultural positionings that have to do with 'ethnic group', 'community', 'family' and 'peers' which emerge from what they call the reader's 'homeplace'. These positions are fluid and have to do with what the texts afford. Their theoretical framework offers those whose research is culturally-oriented a way of moving forward with reader-response theories.

Postmodern literary theory has contributed in a substantial manner to our understanding of the visual and of picturebooks in particular by providing terminology and definitions of the features of texts that work in less traditional ways. Although there are many different ways of understanding the 'postmodern', certainly the work on metafiction, intertextuality and non-linearity or fragmentation has helped to illuminate both words and images. While we mentioned the postmodern nature of Kitamura's and Browne's picturebooks in the first edition, these features of picturebooks have subsequently been highlighted and analysed in more depth. Among those who have applied postmodern frameworks are Bull and Anstey (2010) and both Sipe (2008a) and Pantaleo (2008). Dresang (1999) takes this theory further into what she calls 'radical change theory' while Allan (2012) identifies what she calls the 'postmodernesque', which focuses on the way in which picturebooks engage with discourses of postmodernity (p. 141).

The area of semiotics continues to inform our understanding of how texts work in multiple modes. The work of M. A. K. Halliday was used by Kiefer (1995) to categorise response, and the work of Kress, which expands on Halliday's theories, is often used to consider response to texts of the 'new media age', particularly to the elements of design (see also Walsh 2003, 2006). The modes and affordances of texts (Kress 2010 and Bearne 2009) have a particular relevance to the picturebook because it is such a versatile medium and can include a variety of features such as pop-ups, tabs, pockets and holes as collage, photography or computer-generated images. Painter, Martin and Unsworth (2013) use systemic-functional theory to extend accounts of the 'grammar' of the visual text and look at what demands it makes on the reader of multimodal texts. Albers (2008) advocates 'critical visual analysis' based on art, cultural studies and other disciplines and uses it to look in depth at the 'representational codes' (p. 191) transmitted to children by Caldecott prize-winning artists across the years. Callow and Zammit (2002) and Unsworth and Wheeler (2002) have extended work in this area in looking at electronic texts and how their elements not only create meaning but also digital possibilities which can be applied to responses to picturebooks.[4] The work of Mackey, for example, has brought in concepts of play, performance and tactility (2003) but it also considers the 'reading' behaviour of older pupils (2007 and 2011) and draws on media literacy and gaming theories, including ideas about embodiment and envisionment.

As we noted in the first edition of this book, the functions of the brain in processing symbolic representation is a fascinating and fast expanding field of study which is proving fruitful for understanding how visual literacy works. In research that also stresses the importance of play and art, Heath brings together findings from the fields of neuroscience, visual cognition, anthropology, and linguistics (2006). Through neurobiology scientists can explain

> recursive interactions between peripheral images and higher cortical centres that process symbolic representation. Collaborative work through art enables verbal explication and explanation about details, abstractions and process that lead to theory building dependent on propositional, procedural and dispositional knowledge.
>
> (Heath 2000: 121)

Heath argues that looking and talking about art is a higher brain function that has an effect on our emotions and on how we understand others (Heath 2000; Heath and Wolf 2012). According to Heath (2000), 'art is a particular form of play that ensures ample practice for learning to manage the mental work necessary to bring what is perceived to be disconnected into some kind of whole, however temporary and shifting' (p. 135). She argues that children's play and involvement in art prepare for this reconciliation and therefore support the 'development of language fluency and empathy for the perspectives of others' (p. 134). Importantly, she highlights that this apparently individual response actually depends on 'communal membership' because 'connections between perceptual and conceptual or linguistic representations [. . .] always will emerge in socially interactive situations that punctuate, underline, and enlarge individual understanding' (p. 138). Thus it becomes clear how important mediation and sharing are and establishes the potential for further research in this area.

The emotional aspect of reading has been taken up by other scholars such as Nikolajeva and Kümmerling-Meibauer who have considered the impact of neuroscience through cognitive poetics, in terms of what is expected of the reader, not only on children's literature in general but on picturebooks in particular. Nikolajeva, who uses cognitive literary theory to extend the work on picturebooks that began with Scott (2001) moving from the text to the cognitive effect of reading, emphasising aspects of affective engagement, such as mind-reading and empathy. Drawing on writers such as Wolf (2007), Carr (2010) and Vermeule (2010), as well as research on visual perception, Nikolajeva argues that visual stimuli play a more important part than verbal stimuli in affective interactions because visual knowledge is 'hard-wired in the brain' and therefore 'picturebooks present a whole new dimension of cognitive and affective challenges to novice readers' (2014: 99).

Furthermore, according to Nikolajeva, 'a visual image can evoke a wide range of emotions circumventing the relative precision of words' (2012: 278). She goes on to consider how multimodal literature might convey emotion to the implied reader through vicarious experience by activating long-term emotional memory. This explains why response is so closely linked to life experience and why 'text to life' and 'life to text' elements are – revealed in most of the studies reviewed here – almost always present in response. These and other ideas such as focalisation, 'mind-reading' and *emotion ekphrasis* which Nikolajeva applies to a range of fictional texts are particularly relevant to picturebooks and it is where visual literacy meets emotional literacy.

Kümmerling-Meibauer and Meibauer have also been developing a theory based on cognitive development and picturebooks (2013, 2015) because they argue that the relationship has not been explored fully, especially the ways in which 'language acquisition and literature acquisition interact, and how these interactions may be related to other cognitive processes, such as vision or emotional development' (2013: 144). Although neither Nikolajeva nor the Meibauers have worked directly with children, their ideas clearly have a lot to offer those who are engaged in empirical research.

These new ideas open the field to further studies that bring together visual literacy, picturebook theory and cognitive development. Although we could not supply details of all of the theories and frameworks we have referred to in this chapter, we hope we have provided a sense of the ideas that suggest exciting ways forward for researching visual literacy in relation to response to picturebooks. In the next chapter we will look at the ways in which the particular field of studies involving 'real' children responding to picturebooks has advanced in the last 10–15 years.

Notes

1 'Visual knowledge' is considered a key area in Australia's National Curriculum (Australia's National Curriculum (ACARA) 2013). *The Australian Curriculum* at http://www.australian-curriculum.edu.au/GeneralCapabilities/literacy/organising-elements/visual-knowledge.

2 In terms of the debate about the child's critical capacity in considering picturebooks, it is worth remembering the exchange between Nicholas Tucker and Brian Alderson about what a child's 'eye view' could contribute. Alderson pointed out that in terms of criteria to judge picturebooks, the 'proven appeal to children [. . .] will lead to judgements that have nothing

to do with illustrations as such' and he referred to Tucker's phrase 'the child's eye view' as 'that most dangerous of ideas' (quoted in Arizpe and Styles 2008: 364).

3 In the picturebooks created by Browne which appeared after the first edition of this book was published, he made even more explicit invitations to the reader to explore the world of art, not only in *The Shape Game* but also in *Willy's Pictures* and *Willy the Dreamer*. His other works continues to make frequent intertextual references to painting and other visual media.

4 For useful accounts of what it means to 'read the visual' in terms of multimodality and the multiliteracies that accompany it, see Anstey and Bull (2000) and, more recently, Serafini (2014), whose book is an excellent introduction to visual literacy, and looks at graphic novels as well as picturebooks. For a critique of multimodal theory, see Balzagette and Buckingham (2013).

Chapter 10

New research on children responding to picturebooks

In Chapter 9 we gave an account of the thinking around visual literacy which informed our original research and also pointed to some of the new work in this area that is influencing current approaches to picturebooks. In this chapter, we provide an overview of empirical research on response to picturebooks, most of which has been carried out since the first edition of our book was published, although we also refer to some seminal earlier studies. These studies tend to build on the work of pioneering and influential scholars in the field and reflect a wide range of perspectives, approaches and methods which reveal the wealth of possibilities for explorations involving readers and picturebooks.

Overview

Overall, some studies concentrate on what response tells us about the process of meaning-making; others are more interested in exploring the methods for obtaining response; and finally, the ones with a more educational intention look at how response can develop literary competence and literacy skills. We have tried to organise this review into sections that are related to the main focus of the different studies. However, in cases where the studies fit into more than one section, they may be referred to more than once.

In 2008, Sipe published an appraisal of both theory and research on response to picturebooks, focused on children from about 4 to 8 years old and in classroom situations (Sipe 2008a). He noted that these studies tend to be 'qualitative, descriptive and interpretive' (p. 381). Importantly, Sipe called for further research combining 'theoretically informed examinations of the visual features and text-picture relationships in specific picturebooks along with analyses of children's interpretations of those same picturebooks' (p. 387). Our own review went back to the 1970s and considered picturebooks within the wider area of multimodal texts and we looked at studies which took into account 'real' readers' responses. We noted how scholars were addressing not only multimodality but also multiliteracies, looking at previous reading experiences, intertextuality and cultural diversity, among others. We also noted the variety of ways in which response data was gathered and the different theories which were used to analyse and make sense of this data. Finally, we observed that much of this research was taking place in the classroom and having an impact on teaching in this context. We concluded that one of the challenges was for researchers to keep up with new technologies and adapt methodologies to work with them, and this was even before the appearance of digital picturebook apps!

Inevitably, this new review has its limitations. In the sections that follow, we have only been able to provide details about some of the major or – in our view – most significant studies since 2000, but we have attempted to at least reference as many others as possible to give an idea of how the field is developing in different directions. Despite our careful search, it is inevitable that we may have missed some publications and, given that new studies are constantly appearing, it is impossible for this review to ever be completely 'up to date'. We have also had to limit this chapter to work that has been published in English, despite the fact that much research on response has been carried out in other countries and languages.[1] It also proved impossible to include work done as part of postgraduate degrees, although Chapter 11 showcases three examples of innovative research from our universities (see also Appendix 7). It is also worth noting that, while this book focuses on picturebooks rather than other visual texts such as comics, graphic novels or illustrated books, the boundaries between these forms are often blurred and that there are now studies that look at response to these particular forms (e.g. Bromley 2000; Yannicopoulou 2004; Cedeira Serantes 2011; Pantaleo 2011a).

Pioneering and influential scholars in the field

As we mentioned in the Introduction, we built our original study on the pioneering work of Kiefer (1995) and on the few articles and chapters which looked at children's responses to picturebooks, in particular those of Madura, Lewis, Bromley, Watson and Styles. Although we were aware of a couple of Sipe's articles, at the time of our study we did not realise he was conducting similar research to ours on young children's responses to picturebooks, in his case read aloud by their teachers in the classroom. Sipe's theoretical ideas on emergent literacy learning were enriched by his observations and analysis of readers' responses and he always emphasised the importance of looking at responses to images as well as to words. As he concluded in one of his talks: 'The integration of visual and verbal sign systems is one of the most salient characteristics of picturebooks. Children's learning of illustration codes and conventions deserves more attention by researchers' (2011: 10). Sipe's influence in the field of children's literature and education has been widely acknowledged and we are sure that had it not been for his untimely death in 2011 he would have continued to produce work of significance (see the Special Commemorative Issue of *Children's Literature in Education* 42, 2012). It seems fitting, therefore, to begin this review by considering his work as a whole.

Sipe began his exploration of the field with his doctoral dissertation (1996) and refined his approach and typology in successive studies and publications. The book he published in 2008, *Storytime: Young Children's Literary Understanding in the Classroom*, brings together the fruits of this research. Here, Sipe combines frameworks from both the literary and pedagogical fields, and especially refers to the work of Rosenblatt, Britton and Bogdan, with the aim of developing 'a theory of literary understanding that is specific to contemporary young children, and that is grounded in their responses to literature' (2008a: 9). The response data was collected from five different studies with young children aged 5–7 and from a range of ethnic and social backgrounds (with a majority of less-privileged children from urban environments). Experienced teachers read aloud from picturebooks by a wide range of internationally renowned author/illustrators such as Maurice Sendak, Eric Carle, Anthony Browne, Chris Van Allsburg, Paul Galdone and David Wiesner. The children were encouraged to talk about the books during and after the readings which were carried out as part of the normal classroom activities and it is their marked engagement with the stories, especially their expressive engagement, that led to the development of his analytical categories, which will be discussed in more detail later in this chapter.

From the start, Sipe focused on children's responses to literature (1999) to find evidence of their literary understanding for both hermeneutic and aesthetic purposes, teasing out and identifying different types of responses such as personal, text-to-text and analytical. In two of his articles he describes the intertextual connections made by primary age children when reading versions of traditional tales (*The Gingerbread Boy* (2000) and *Rapunzel* (2001)). As he notes how images support understanding, he begins to move further towards exploring response to the visual, asking 'How do children use the connections to other visual texts to understand the composition, media, and semiotic significance of illustrations?' (Sipe 2000: 87).

This led to investigating more specific aspects of picturebooks, such as the 'page break', an aspect of the picturebook at the core of the 'drama of the turning page' (Bader 1976) and at the heart of the 'gap-filling' (Iser 1978) experience of reading. Sipe observed a class of second graders read Caldecott Medal and Honor winners and talked with an experienced teacher 'not about the words and pictures in the story, but about what has been omitted from the story' (Sipe and Brightman 2009: 93). Sipe and Brightman show how these discussions can develop with little interference from the teacher and how beneficial they are for 'high-level inference making' (2009: 93). This article includes both implications and acute questions for further research and also for teaching, both of which show just how much potential even this one aspect of a picturebook has for both these areas.

Sipe's research often concentrated on overlooked angles of enquiry, for example, with McGuire he looked at response to endpapers (Sipe and McGuire 2006a) and also at negative comments made by children about picturebooks (Sipe and McGuire 2006b). The researchers identified six categories for explaining responses that express resistance or opposition, ranging from not liking a new version of a story they already knew to finding characters or events too painful to consider. Their categories are significant as they help us realise that children can reject picturebooks as much as they can love them but that this provides an opportunity for discussing, for example, different perspectives or authorial decisions. Sipe (2008a) also identifies helpful categories for the 'basic literary impulses' that guide children's responses: the 'hermeneutic impulse' or the desire to 'grasp the meaning of the narrative'; the 'personalising impulse' to forge connections with life experiences; and the 'aesthetic impulse' which involves 'surrendering' to the power of the text (Sipe 2008a: 189–192).

Finally, always with an eye on the pedagogical side, Sipe also looked at mediation, describing the ways in which the teachers' enabling and scaffolding contributed to the children's understanding. He identifies five conceptual categories for adult talk and highlights the crucial importance of asking inviting questions and encouraging the role of peers as enablers.

Another scholar whose work has run parallel to ours since 2002 is Pantaleo. Like Sipe, with whom she also collaborated, her work is prolific and influential within the field especially in relation to education. Pantaleo has worked with teachers and pupils across primary classrooms using numerous picturebooks and has looked at the creative responses emerging from different forms of activities as well as applying various theories such as Rosenblatt's transactional theory and Dresang's Radical Change Theory (Dresang 1999; Pantaleo 2004a, 2009a). She has focused on young student's understanding of the postmodern aspects of picturebooks such as meta-fiction (2002, 2004a, 2004b, 2005), intertextuality (2012a), as well as their effect on readers, for example, on their narrative competence (2009b, 2010) and artwork (2012b). Pantaleo has explored collaborative talk (2011b), writing (Pantaleo and Bomphray 2011) and creating multimodal texts and artifacts that involve under-standing of colour and other visual elements of art and design (2012b; 2012c). She has written about response to particular features of picturebooks and graphic novels such as colour (2012b), typography (2012d) and panelling (2013). Pantaleo's extensive body of work has built up a detailed picture of the transaction between readers and the word-image relationship which has implications not only for literacy and pedagogy but also for advancing our understanding about how picturebooks and graphic novels work. Pantaleo's studies provide solid evidence for the ways in which complex picturebooks and graphic novels can help students develop as readers, writers and imaginative thinkers and therefore, alongside Sipe, provides a leading voice in those calling for the necessity of teaching elements of visual art and design in parallel with using these texts in the classroom.

Both Pantaleo and Sipe's work is behind that of a whole generation of scholars who have produced important research with implications for teaching. Working with Dutch children, Van der Pol built on Sipe's research to examine their implicit knowledge of structures and conventions of picturebooks and what it means to be a competent reader of fiction, arguing for the importance of having literary conversations (rather than simply asking for text to life and life to text connections) in order to deepen children's understanding of features such as character and irony (Van der Pol 2012). Serafini, whose book on visual literacy (2014) provides an excellent intro-duction for teachers to this area, writes about his discovery, as a young teacher, of picturebooks and of how Sipe's work influenced his thinking about his students' responses (2002). Since then, Serafini has also written about response to postmodern picturebooks (2005), to historical fiction picturebooks (Youngs and Serafini 2013) and about developing interpretive responses (Serafini and Ladd 2008) as well as analytical approaches (Youngs and Serafini 2013). What Serafini brings to the field is a clear sense of the importance of the semiotic resources in a picturebook which allow interpretation: 'To ignore the perceptual and structural aspects of visual images and multimodal texts in favor of a socio-cultural perspective would limit readers' interpretive repertoire and forego relevant perspectives for making sense of images and multimodal texts' (Youngs and Serafini 2013: 196).

Chapters and articles on response to picturebooks have appeared in three volumes edited by Evans (Evans 1998, 2009a and 2015a), the most recent of which addresses 'challenging and controversial picturebooks'. Evans herself has also written about the responses of a group of children with whom she has been working for several years; her work consistently shows the potential of picturebooks to draw out children's ideas about challenging topics such as art (2009b) the meaning of life (2011) immigration (2015b).

As for the work by Arizpe and Styles which followed the original study, both of us continued to focus on the postmodern aspect of picturebooks and response (Arizpe and Styles 2008 and Arizpe 2009, 2010). Styles then produced *Children's Pictrebooks: The art of visual storytelling* with Salisbury as lead author (2012) that took a historical and thematic approach to picturebooks and was as interested in published and developing illustrators as in children's responses to picturebooks (2012), while Arizpe went on to do more empirical work on response to wordless picturebooks with children from diverse backgrounds in the 'Visual Journeys' project which will be detailed further below (Arizpe, Colomer and Martínez-Roldán 2014).

Research on response to the specific features of a picturebook

Some studies have concentrated on children's responses to the special features that define picturebooks as a genre. Given that it is the interaction between the words and the pictures that defines a picturebook, most studies consider what children make of this interaction and in particular, whether these semiotic systems are telling the same story (or not). In our original study we found that when the children noticed that words and pictures were not telling the same story, they were fascinated by the differences (Arizpe and Styles 2003). Many other researchers have observed the process that Sipe called 'transmediation' (1998), also referred to in Chapter 9, where the continuous shifts between the meaning from words and images build the readers' understanding.

Research using wordless picturebooks has also served to highlight how children perceive the relationship between words and pictures when the former are 'missing' and also to provide further insights into the process of visual meaning-making (Crawford and Hade 2000). Many studies involve readings and retellings of this type of picturebook to address the wide range of cognitive skills involved in this process, although Arizpe's review of these studies also showed that some of them tend to see the picturebook as a functional medium for collecting data and ignore its aesthetic qualities (2013 and 2014).

Many scholars have explored the way in which the visual features expand understanding of the more traditional elements that normally appear in picturebooks. For example, Sipe and Ghiso (2005) and later Prior, Willson and Martínez (2012) analyse the inferences about characters that children made based on the images. However, most researchers have been excited by the more unusual features that define a picturebook as 'postmodern' and especially those that include a variety of peritextual features and that subvert traditionally written stories where the illustration simply mirrors the text.[2] Arizpe and Styles were among the first to highlight evidence that children can deal with the complexities afforded by contemporary picturebooks and this has also been confirmed through other studies that focus on postmodern features, in particular, Pantaleo who tends to explore both central and peritextual features in her studies. Studies that consider other features which have a significant role in postmodern picturebooks include children responding to endpapers (Sipe and McGuire 2006a), page breaks (Sipe and Brightman 2009), frames (Pantaleo 2014 and Smith 2009) and typography (Pantaleo 2012d).

In a study with a slightly different approach, McClay (2000) compared the responses of adults and children to the non-linear narrative and the ambiguities of David Macaulay's *Black and White* and showed that children tend to have fewer problems than adults when it comes to interpreting postmodern features. While researchers such as Sipe (2008a), McGuire, Belfatti and Ghiso (2008) and Swagerty (2009) stress the importance of mediation and discussion to increase understanding of postmodern picturebooks, they also show that young children can deal with the complex processes of interpreting and comprehending these texts, a process where dialogue and contested interpretations among peers have a crucial role. This literary competence has also led researchers to argue for using postmodern picturebooks even with children who are not completely fluent in the language of the text or who may be from a different cultural background and details of studies that focus on this aspect can be seen below.

Research on response to specific themes

There are many studies that explore response to difficult or sensitive issues through picturebooks and there is certainly not a shortage of challenging topics, ranging from depression (Pantaleo 2015) to criminal justice (Oslick 2013) and migration (Arizpe, Colomer and Martínez-Roldán; McAdam et al. 2014). While teachers often shy away from discussing some of these topics with children, researchers are curious to find out how children react to them. In some cases, this research is carried out with groups of readers who have had particular experience of these issues, which is why some of the research mentioned here overlaps with the next section.

A group of studies that also comes under this section is composed of those which use picturebooks based on fairytales or traditional stories including versions which may be challenging in some way (Sipe 2001, Sipe and Brightman 2005). Campagnaro (2015) for example, looked at cognitive and aesthetic development through response to some of the symbolic elements of the visual texts. McGilp (2014) uses versions from different cultures to explore multicultural and language learning. Although not based exclusively on fairytales, Ghosh (2015) considered response to the portrayal of wolves in 'polysemic' picturebooks and shows how readers bring their knowledge of traditional tales to their reading but also their willingness to engage with irony and ambiguity. In a study where children also responded to a wolf character but using a wordless picturebook, Mourão (2015) shows how young children base their interpretations on cultural expectations which also come into the collaboratively written stories they created.

Whether the topics are considered controversial or not, most studies look at ways in which the reading about a particular theme can lead to improving understanding in some way. This applies particularly to themes around multiculturalism given the intention is to try to increase awareness of diversity, multilinguality and, generally, understanding of the 'Other'. Not surprisingly, given the debates around migration, racism and fundamentalism, these studies have increased in the last 15 years and most researchers would agree with Sipe that 'interpreting stories allows children to become more knowledgeable and tolerant of cultures and customs that are not their own' (Sipe 2011: 10). Brooks and Browne (2012), however, show that the process is interactive, that is, the text invites particular cultural positioning but the reader's culture also shapes the response. This leads us into the next section which first considers research with readers with particular needs and then readers from diverse cultural or ethnic backgrounds.

Research with specific readers to develop particular competences

Studies usually select a particular group of readers, either with specific special needs or with a common context or background, with the aim of finding out more about their literary understanding, their literacy skills or the personal experience they bring to their reading and in order to develop particular competences. The studies in this section often also include a selection of picturebooks with themes or features that support both the investigation and the development of strategies to support intervention in some form.

There are studies with readers with special needs, such as deaf children (Williams and McLean 1997) or children with ADHD (Leonard, Lorch, Milich and Hagans 2009) (for a case study involving autism, see Chapter 11) and most provide evidence to show that response to picturebooks is a good tool for exploring concepts and attitudes supporting language and literacy development or the social skills of these groups of children. One scholar who has looked to picturebooks for developing personal and social skills is Lysaker who considers how children develop understanding of the self as reader and also of their 'social imagination' through looking at the narratives they produce from wordless picturebooks (Lysaker 2006 and Lysaker and Miller 2013). However, some of these studies adopt a more psychological approach which means the research is not so much interested in response to picturebooks as aesthetic objects, as in the re-tellings that occur in controlled situations.

While we cannot extend this review to research on responses by older readers, it is worth mentioning that there have also been studies involving pre-service teachers and teachers (McClay 2000; Anstey 2002; Short 2004; Johnston and Bainbridge 2013; van Renen 2011; Marshall 2015). There is also little in-depth research involving adolescent readers responding to picturebooks, although the potential for their literacy and literary learning has been recognised for some time (e.g. Lott 2001). Interestingly, we did not come across any published studies of parents responding to picturebooks either.

Many studies now include an interest in the development of visual literacy. This means that although talk, re-tellings and other forms of oral communication are the most common form of response, we can now see that drawing, performance and other creative responses are incorporated, not only with the aim of obtaining more data on meaning-making but also to develop these forms of creativity themselves.

It is therefore not surprising that using picturebooks for language learning is one of the fastest growing areas of research. Studies concentrate either on teaching English as a foreign language or on teaching English to new arrivals. Enever and Schmidt-Schonbein (2006) and Bland (2013) have looked at the potential of picturebooks to teach English in Germany as has Mourão in Portugal (e.g. Mourão 2012). These studies reveal positive findings in the field of language learning but they also take pains to point out that this learning cannot be separated from the aesthetic and emotional effect of reading. One example which shows just how tightly these are interlinked is the in-depth case study of the linguistic and emotional development that occurs through a bilingual child's reading by Arizpe and Blatt (2011).

The largest group of studies involving readers with certain characteristics seems to be concerned with addressing diversity, either from a more linguistic interest (bilinguality, multilinguality, language learning) or a more cultural interest. Brooks and Browne (2012), for example, look at both through the 'ways literary interpretations are influenced by readers' ethnic backgrounds as well as the cultural milieu embedded in the stories they read' (76). In our review (2008), we had already noted early studies that involved diverse readers and picturebooks, building on Gregory's work from 1994. We concluded that this research provided evidence that 'children from culturally diverse backgrounds bring their own experiences to the texts and may have difficulties with intertextual references or culturally specific features; however, their comments can be just as insightful as any of their peers' (Arizpe and Styles 2008: 369).

Further studies have showed how children use their cultural 'funds of knowledge' to make sense of picturebooks, even those with complex, postmodern features (e.g. Arizpe 2009, 2010; Martínez-Roldán and Newcomer 2011). In Denmark, Møller Daugaard and Blok Johansen also looked at multilingual children responding to a Danish postmodern picturebook and especially its metafictional features (2014). Their findings led them to propose that 'multilingual children should be offered postmodern picture books along with other types of books – precisely because of the potential that lies in the apparent difficulty of such books'(2013, 18). Working with multilingual children and multicultural fairy tale picturebooks, McGilp (2014) aimed to validate the children's first language and culture in the classroom. In the United States, several studies make use of culturally relevant picturebooks to work with minority ethnic groups. Artistic responses to picturebooks helped bilingual/bicultural Latino children increase their 'literate comprehension' in Carger's study (2004). Hudelson, Smith and Hawes (2005) and Lohfink and Loya (2010) used bilingual books with a similar group of children and found children attended to the issue of language and bilingualism, made cultural connections and developed their literacy skills. This type of research also looks to helping readers understand their own cultural identity and that of others (see also McGonigal and Arizpe 2007). On the other hand, Lysaker and Sedberry (2015) describe how the retellings of picturebooks by two boys with no exposure to culturally different peers, allowed them to engage vicariously and empathetically with unfamiliar experiences. Finally, a study on response to picturebooks in Colombia, shows how racial prejudice can appear in children's understandings and can therefore become the subject of discussion (Cuperman 2013).

Arizpe's work with children from diverse backgrounds (2009) led to the 'Visual Journeys' project which attempted to look at response more globally and is one of the most ambitious so far in terms of its international multi-site nature. The inquiry involved groups of immigrant students responding to David Wiesner's *Flotsam* (Arizpe and McAdam 2011; Walsh, Cranitch and Maras 2012) and Shaun Tan's *The Arrival* (Martínez-Roldán and Newcomer 2011; Arizpe, Colomer and Martínez-Roldán 2014) and examined literary and visual meaning-making as well as how these books encouraged a better understanding of migration and promoted intercultural understanding. A further development from this study was working to increase awareness of issues around forced migration through response to picturebooks within a classroom based project (McAdam et al. 2014).

Methodologies

It is worth noting that almost all empirical research with picturebooks is based on the Reader-Response theories of Iser (1978) and Rosenblatt (1978, 1982). While other theories are brought to bear on the response, especially given the visual aspect of the texts, the view of reading as a transaction between the text and the reader (Rosenblatt) where response-inviting structures in the text encourage readers to 'fill the gaps' (Iser) is still at the core of most studies. However, the more recent visual literacy and picturebook theories that we mentioned in Chapter 9 are beginning to influence empirical research and what has been changing is the methodology for obtaining response to picturebooks. The range of methods is perhaps one of the most exciting aspects of picturebook research because it has demonstrated a variety of possible pathways to explore response as well as the creativity that can be encouraged in responding to picturebooks.

Earlier methods were based on talk (from semi-structured interviews to literature circles) and this continues to be part of most studies, however, since the original publication of this book, visual and other types of response are now almost an expected part of research. These methods remind us that we are dealing with picturebooks which are multimodal artefacts and are also as a way of encouraging the development of 'new literacies' (Anstey and Bull 2009). The methods used in most studies to obtain readers' responses are sometimes difficult to distinguish from teaching strategies and many acknowledge the important role of mediation.

The research based on oral responses usually references the 'book talk' recommended by Chambers (1993) and his seminal request 'Tell me'. These studies typically employ different types of questions, prompts or instructions, including retellings, and they range from discussions which were almost completely unguided (McClay 2000) to discussions in the classroom that follow a particular teacher's lesson plan. In some studies, the oral response is based on page by page 'storybook picture walk' (Paris and Paris 2001) or 'Walk-throughs' (Arizpe 2010, 2014; McAdam et al. 2014; Möller Daugaard and Blok Johansen 2014), where the researcher and the reader(s) take time to look carefully at each spread. When wordless picturebooks are involved, readers are often asked to retell the story in their own words or create captions or speech bubbles (Mourão 2015).

Like Noble/Rabey (in Arizpe and Styles 2003), many researchers have elicited response via drawing or artwork. This works particularly well with young children who find it hard to express themselves for some reason or for children who are not yet able to write. Another important reason for having a visual response is that words can't necessarily sum up the aesthetic experience of looking at a picturebook. Written responses often are a part of work done in the classroom (Pantaleo and Bomphray 2011). Drama and performance have been employed by Mackey (2003) and Adomat (2010). Carger (2004) used painting and clay sculpture. Carger observes the benefits for language learners of responding via art:

> When given the opportunity to use art, I consistently found the students to be focused and on task, often chatting informally about the book or technique at hand. They glided from topic to topic, made intertextual comments, and engaged in authentic conversations. For these young English Language Learners, the benefit of engaging art activities connected with literature was multifaceted.
>
> (p. 288)

The Visual Journeys project used visual strategies, in particular annotations (Farrell, Arizpe and McAdam 2010) and photography (Arizpe and McAdam 2011) as well as drawing a graphic narrative (Arizpe, Colomer and Martínez-Roldán 2014). In McAdam et al. (2014) these visual methodologies were linked to critical pedagogies around intercultural understanding and proved both successful and enjoyable for the students involved.

The next step in the research process is the analysis and in this field a variety of interesting ways of examining the qualitative data have been used. The analysis will depend on the researcher's aim. Many tend to start from an interpretative paradigm and use some version of Grounded Theory (Strauss and Corbin 1998), coding through close examination of the response, usually dividing it into 'conversational turns', to create categories and a typology. Others look for emergent or generative themes and discourse patterns (Freire 2008; Erickson 1986; Gee 2005). However, others have used analytical elements from linguistics and semiotics (Kiefer 1995, Walsh 2003) or socio-cultural literacy theories (Martínez-Roldán and Newcomer 2011; Arizpe et al. 2014).

As Sipe points out, citing Martínez and Roser (2003), one of the drawbacks of grounded theory is the difficulty of applying typologies across other studies, so, as they suggest, Sipe attempted to replicate his own 'system' across his different studies. While this has made his typology one of the strongest yet, it should be noted it was only used for a particular age range[3] and it is less certain that the conditions would be the same even when working with the same age range in other cultural contexts. Nevertheless, his typology continues to be referred to, proving that at least some of the categories work across studies (e.g. Braid and Finch 2015).

The emergence of new theoretical frameworks like cognitive criticism, as well as the use of new analysis software and the interdisciplinary nature of research collaborations, will begin to have an impact on research on response. One potential option would be to see how the more culturally oriented theories fit in with the recent research on cognitive criticism. The work on digital picturebooks (or picturebook apps) will also require new ways of looking at the transaction between text and reader and of obtaining response (Mackey provides a glimpse of this in Chapter 12). The considerable amount of research, as evidenced in this book, is now also something that must be taken into account and built on in any new study. There is also now a wider interest in international publications and issues around translation which opens the possibilities of looking at response to both words and images in other languages (e.g. McGilp 2014). Finally, the influence of marketing, consumerism and ideology could be more fully considered by scholars in the field.

For every aesthetically engaging picturebook, there are potential studies on readers' responses, studies that could be carried out considering a number of theoretical frameworks and methodological approaches. This means that care must be taken in the selection of the text and in the decisions made regarding the research process. The three case studies in the next chapter illustrate how postgraduate students' thoughtful and innovative qualitative research can continue to add to the evidence for reading and working with picturebooks. The process and the challenges will be taken up in Chapter 13 where we also look at some of the dos and don'ts involved in carrying out this type of investigation.

Notes

1 For example, many of the members of the GRETEL Research Team and the students of the Master's Programme of the Autonomous University of Barcelona have carried out research with picturebooks in Spanish, both in Spain and in Latin America.
2 For more on 'postmodern' picturebooks, see Nikola-Lisa 1994, Watson and Styles 1996, Lewis 1990 and the essays in Sipe and Pantaleo 2008.
3 In fact, in an email correspondence between Sipe and Arizpe, Sipe queried the use of his categories for the older readers (11–13) in the Visual Journeys project.

Chapter 11

New case studies of children responding to picturebooks

Since 2003, a popular module on children responding to picturebooks has been included in the Cambridge Master's course, Critical Approaches to Children's Literature. In Glasgow, the MEd in Children's Literature and Literacies also supports students who choose to write their dissertation on this topic. Several PhD theses have reader response to picturebooks at their core at both universities. Clearly, the range of publications on children reading pictures in the last ten years combined with our own enthusiasm for the topic has rubbed off on those we have taught. In this chapter we look at three varied examples of the research undertaken by students working on our Master's or doctoral programmes[1] who have shared our ambition to find out more about children's interpretations of picturebooks.

Our initial research revealed that we often learned more from group discussions and inviting drawings from children than from conventional semi-structured interviews. Since then our students have convinced us that there are many other means of providing evidence of children's responses to picturebooks by using a variety of data collection methods, including annotating copies of spreads from a picturebook, adding text to blank speech bubbles, games with simple puppets of key characters and dramatic play based on picturebooks.

Indeed, it is encouraging to find that our results of fifteen years ago are largely borne out by more recent student researchers and we believe their results deserve a wider public. To that end, we have selected examples that show children of various ages and abilities engaging with three different picturebooks. Each researcher has selected a focus based on their choice of picturebook, the age of the children[2] they were working with and their own particular interests. As in our original research, we were impressed by the commitment of the children to the task and the insightfulness of many of their responses. We hope the examples which follow give a flavour of the quality of scholarship going on in our universities and schools relating to children's responses to picturebooks. Only minor editing, agreed by all, was concerned.

Case 1: Susan Tan[3]

We begin with an extract from a study by Susan Tan, who was working with three 9-years-olds using Maurice Sendak's *We Are All in the Dumps with Jack and Guy* (*Dumps*) (1993). We chose the following extract from a much longer piece of work because (i) it shows the emotional impact of a complex picturebook on young readers; (ii) it demonstrates how much information about children's responses to a text can be provided by asking them to draw; (iii) it is a good example of how well chosen questions and a discerning teacher can elicit profound reactions in young readers; and (iv) it shows how children of this age, while alert to some of the harsh realities of life, need to look for elements of hope in what they read, especially relating to family life.

Dumps, among other things, is about homelessness. Susan began by drawing attention to the plain brown endpapers with the texture of cardboard, which you might expect children to link with cardboard shelters of the homeless. Here is Max responding to the request, 'Tell me about the endpapers', after two readings of this picturebook:

MAX: Just the material, like it's a bit like card, but then it's like rough, sandpapery card surface. So maybe it's a mix of sandpaper and card. [. . .]

INTERVIEWER: Do you think it connects to the story at all?

MAX: Not really. It just might be . . . it just feels, it just feels weird, so it might be the type of area . . . that it's like that, maybe it's rough . . . like . . . like, their lives. Rough like their lives.

First of all, it's worth noting that Max needs time to say something important. He begins with a negative, 'Not really', but then you can almost hear him thinking aloud as he goes beyond an interpretation of the endpapers as similar to the cardboard boxes Jack and Guy live in to make a metaphorical connection between the roughness of the paper and the harshness of the children's lives. Here is Susan's account.

Many critiques levelled at *Dumps* argue that it is too graphic for children, yet my participants demonstrated an immediate awareness of the impoverished world Sendak had created, lending credence to Sendak's own claim that 'the children know' (Sendak 1998). When asked what sort of place this was, Oscar simply replied, 'a dump'. Similarly, as they looked at the cover in the group reading, all three children agreed that the book was about homeless children seeking shelter. The participants demonstrated that they were aware of, and willing to engage with, what Lewis (2001) terms 'ecology' within picturebooks – the environment and 'ecosystems' created by picturebooks themselves, as well as the series of relationships created by the 'reading event' as children encounter texts (p. 46). As they acknowledged the realities of homelessness, the children demonstrated a deep understanding of what Lewis identifies as the 'social and cultural contexts' in which 'language and literacy [are] always embedded' (p. 47). Commenting on one character in Sendak's spread, Max remarked:

MAX: That guy's looking a bit sneaky, like a detective, maybe that was his job before.

INTERVIEWER: So you think he doesn't have a job now?

MAX: Yeah, that's probably why he's homeless.

From the material fact of the children's homelessness, the students then became what Margaret Meek (1988) terms 'the teller and the told' (p. 25), deriving narratives from the images about the children's lives on the streets and demonstrating an awareness of what such lives might entail. Max remarked, as Jack and Guy are being flown through the heavens: 'I wonder why there are all those little angel things up there? . . . I bet it's all of their friends who have died.' In this acknowledgment of death and the assumption that Jack and Guy have had friends, presumably other street children, who have died, Max not only tapped eerily into one of the references on this spread – where Sendak pays tribute to the late James Marshall – but demonstrated an all-too accurate under-standing of the realities of poverty and homelessness.

But most 9-year-olds can't face too much harsh reality. Max was not the only child to invent a happy ending for *Dumps*. Each expressed mixed responses. In separate interviews, both Max and Cora labelled the end of *Dumps* as a 'sort-of happy ending'. When asked why, Cora explained that, 'now Jack and Guy are being nice to the little boy, and the little boy is really happy now that he's got a friend or something', but '*they're still like homeless, and they still haven't got much clothes* (our emphasis)'. Similarly, Max felt it was 'sort-of happy, because the boy actually has people to be with, *but it's still not that happy because they don't actually have a house still. It's like happy, but not happy* (our emphasis)'. Oscar, who was particularly focused on ideas of family and home, even distinguished between 'home' and the physical site of a 'house' when asked what constituted a happy ending, explaining that the ending was 'good' because 'they're home and they are happy again,' but not good '*because they haven't got a house . . . like, they live somewhere, but they don't have a place to live in* (our emphasis)'.

After their interviews, I asked the participants to draw a response to the book. All the children decided to include a happy ending in their drawings. Cora drew a vibrant and colourful house in an illustration complete with all three characters, text and a speech-bubble. (Note the positive colours, the pretty butterfly and flowers against a vivid sky, the bright sun, the kisses round the 'We are happy now' statement. The importance of 'We've got a home' is emphasised by a speech bubble, three exclamation marks and a couple of kisses! The smiling children's arms are raised in a positive salute.)

Compared to Cora's, Oscar's illustration of a home is sparse, and did not include Jack, Guy or the little boy. However, in his description of the seemingly simple draw-ing – featuring a house with three windows and labelled 'home sweet home', Oscar revealed a great deal of thought behind the drawing.

OSCAR: It's the future and they buy a house, and the moon's smiling.
INTERVIEWER: And the pictures in the windows?
OSCAR: That's the stairs, and a spare room.
INTERVIEWER: And what about these spots of green on the house?
OSCAR: Mould that they need to clean up.

With his emphasis on 'stairs' and his choice to include a 'spare room', Oscar created a world of plenty, a home in which all are provided for and extra space abounds. Even further, with his inclusion of 'mould' above the windowsills, Oscar created a detailed world of domestic routine, implying longevity, stability and domestic owner-ship in this tiny detail of a household-chore. But Oscar's greatest domestic focus was revealed when asked about the figure in one of the windows, a silhouette whom he identified as 'Jack's dad: the one with the hat'.

Figure 11.1 Cora's happy ending

When asked if anyone took care of Jack and Guy, the whole group demonstrated a fascinating unwillingness to consider that children might live without parents. Max decided that 'they look like they're about teenagers or adults', thus old enough to live on their own. Similarly, while Cora posited that they were 'about old enough to look after themselves', she amended that 'they [had] a dad or something to look after them', even though he was not shown or ever present. Oscar, however, not only maintained that Jack, Guy and the little boy had parents, but took great pains to 'find' them in the text. When asked who takes care of Jack and Guy, Oscar promptly flipped the book to the beginning and systematically went through and 'identified' parents for all of the children. On one spread, Oscar found the little boy's mom, and on another, found a pair of feet that could belong to his dad. He found parents for Guy in a similar fashion, and pointed out a man who 'could be Jack's dad because they've got the same hat'. Continuing to construct Sendak's storybook world, 'telling' the story even as it was 'told' (1998: 25) to him, Oscar created a detailed narrative of family, and extended that narrative into his own illustration (Meek 1988). Lessening the harshness of the street-world, he gave Jack, Guy and the little boy parents, and envisioned a happy ending where they could live in their 'home' – still together amongst their community, but this time in a house, 'a place to live in'.

We Are All in the Dumps with Jack and Guy is a complex text, which most adult readers would find demanding. It was no surprise, then, that the children interviewed, who only saw the book twice, responded with confusion over certain aspects of the story – often needing to 'work out' what was happening. Yet, while the children's understandings of the complete textual and narrative details may have varied, each child communicated a strong emotional and moral reaction to the book,

Figure 11.2 Oscar's happy ending

not only understanding its social message, but going further to engage deeply with its moral questions and complexities. Drawing from the text, from their knowledge of the outside world, and from their own experiences, the children parsed out the intricacies of Sendak's human narrative. However, at the same time, each participant demonstrated a fascinating limit to their ability or desire to fully comprehend the implications of Jack and Guy's social situation. As the children were presented with a cruel and ugly world, and, for the most part, understood this world, they simultaneously worked in the spaces left open by the 'playful picturebook' (Lewis 2001: 81), utilising the open-ended nature of counterpoint visual and textual interaction to create their own narratives. Children were given parents, characters were given histories, and moments in-between and beyond the pages of the story were drawn out in vibrant detail. Faced with a text that many call too adult for children to comprehend, the participants embraced most of its gritty intricacies, claiming Sendak's world and story for their own.

Case 2: Kim Deakin[4]

Kim Deakin's research focused on an 8-year-old autistic boy, Danny,[5] who attended Richmond Hill Special School where she was his teacher. Danny was a great enthusiast for reading and Kim was surprised one day to find him writing and drawing on a picturebook, behaviour that was unusual for him. When she questioned him gently, his excitement was almost palpable. Here is her account of Danny's encounter with Polly Dunbar's *Penguin*, a delightful picturebook that explores for young readers what it means to understand another person.

As I turned the page Danny jumped up and down bellowing at the top of his voice, 'SAY SOMETHING!' Laughing and pointing to the page of a picturebook he had drawn all over, he continued, 'Sorry, Kim, Danny, Kim look, LOOK! EATS, LION EAT'S BEN/DANNY!'

This study examines Danny's exploration of Dunbar's picturebook and how he used the ambiguities and nuances of the illustrations to give him the time and space to bring his own experiences to the text. The empathy displayed for a fictional character provided a rare glimpse into Danny's altered perspective on the world. Nikolajeva explains how the interplay between illustrations and words in picturebooks can provide a tool for children to glean an understanding of human emotions from fictional characters, but cautions that 'mind-reading normally develops at the age of five and is slower or even totally impeded in autistic children' (2012: 275). Likewise, Martin suggests that 'The tools of friendship, such as reciprocity, sympathy, and empathy, are a formidable challenge for a child with autism' (2009: 110).

I began with these questions to help me unravel some of the possibilities:

- How does the interplay between words and images in *Penguin* help Danny explore human emotions?
- How does Danny bring his own experiences to the text?

I felt for this research I required a methodology that would provide a way of recording observations that would ensure validity and robustness. I turned, therefore, to research methods used in early years settings, such as child initiated, free-play, as they better reflected the cognitive and developmental stage Danny displayed.

Reifel draws on research by Paley in which stories, whether through literature or fantasy play, help children to 'interpret and explain [their] feelings about reality' (cited in Reifel 2007: 31). Following Reifel's model, I proposed to capture Danny's engagement with Dunbar's picturebook by facilitating three focused but child-led sessions over a two week period, supplemented by observing spontaneous responses that presented themselves during normal classroom activities. The story hinges on Ben's unhappiness with the unresponsive behaviour of Penguin, until one day Penguin does something extraordinary.

The lack of a setting or background for *Penguin* offers an uncluttered white space which Nikolajeva and Scott suggest 'reflect the child's limited experience of the world' (2001: 63). This minimalistic effect means the reader has no distractions from the images of emotional connection (or disconnection) between the characters.

As Serafini points out, 'the positioning of objects and characters determines their importance and how viewers react to them'(2009: 21). Hence, a dual perspective is created between the reader and the characters, enabling the former to enter the imaginary situation and exchange places or to watch subjectively the interplay between the characters as they act out the scenario.

In Figure 11.3, the emotional tension between the characters is demonstrated by their physical distance and gaping white space, while the gutter provides a physical barrier which emphasises how disconnected they are. Ben gets increasingly frustrated by Penguin's lack of response to his friendly overtures. As his fury hits a crescendo, an enormous speech bubble dominates the centre of the spread, signalling a significant turn in the plot as the face of a disgruntled looking lion creeps in, perhaps a metaphor for an authority figure. However, Penguin becomes the unlikely hero by siding with Ben and biting Lion on the nose (Figure 11.4).

Ben ignored Penguin.   **Penguin ignored Ben.**

Figure 11.3 Penguin and Ben

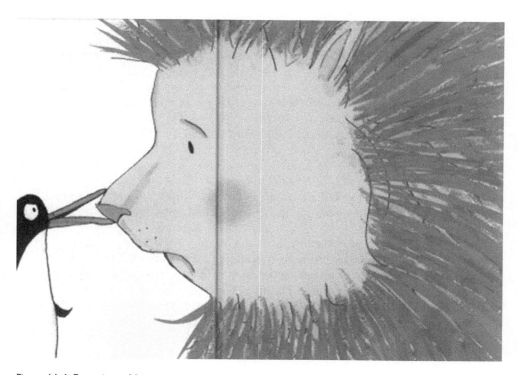

Figure 11.4 Penguin and Lion

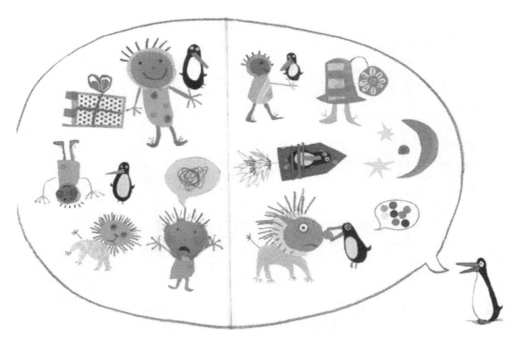

Figure 11.5 'And Penguin said . . . '

The twist at the end of the story is shown by the text, '*And Penguin said . . .* ' (Figure 11.5), where a huge pictorial speech bubble projected from Penguin's open beak empowers emergent readers to re-tell the story supported by the sequential illustrations and through the 'voice' of Penguin. As a consequence Ben is finally able to understand that Penguin, although non-verbal, has become the friend he so desperately wanted at the beginning of the story.

In this picturebook, Dunbar has created a welcoming space for children to explore their own emotions through the perspectives of fictional characters.

Each element of Danny's communication observed throughout the study was recorded following Reifel's (2007) model to create a 'text' of actions: non-verbal and verbal responses, supplemented by photographs, mark-making and drawings. This enabled me to analyse the effect of the devices Dunbar employed such as space and drama, gaze and perspective, use of language and typography.

Danny's clandestine mark-making in the picturebook suggest that his connection with Dunbar's characters and scenarios were intrinsically linked with his own experience so that he was able to enter a fictional world that explored some of the reality of his own life. Danny retrieved information from both word and image; he memorised words, often repeating the refrain, *Penguin said nothing,* and his mark-making gave indications of how he was feeling. For example, Danny's response to Ben's tantrum sequence can be seen to have triggered a powerful memory of his own.

Ben got upset.

Figure 11.6 Danny's response to Ben's tantrum (1)

A whirl of looping lines obliterates the words, *Penguin said nothing* (Figures 11.6 and 11.7). Here we can see the picturebook providing Danny with a vehicle through which he could pause and reflect and show common purpose with the characters – all at his own pace.

Danny also demonstrates self-referentiality, through mark-making (Figure 11.8). Danny's 'tadpole', which he confirmed as a representation of himself by naming it, is placed in-between the physical gaps of Penguin and the action of Ben being eaten by the Lion – literally positioning himself within the fictional scenario. When asked 'who's that?' he jumped up and down with excitement, 'IT'S DANNY, IT'S DANNY! LION EATS BEN. EATS DANNY!' Danny felt the need to physically fill

Figure 11.7 Danny's response to Ben's tantrum (2)

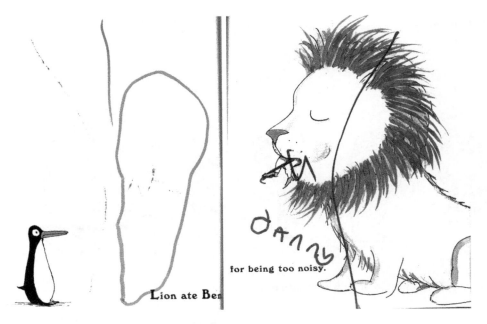

Figure 11.8 Danny puts himself into the story

the gap. Indeed, I would suggest Danny's altered perspective required him to have a literal reference point through his drawings. The zigzag line across the half-eaten Ben and a strong vertical line across Lion perhaps indicate that Danny reckons he is next in line to be eaten, or even acting as protector of Penguin. On subsequent readings when asked 'who is that?' his commentary confirms he has adopted Ben's role, but interestingly has also begun to understand Penguin's alternative perspective:

> Picture, blue, Danny.
> Put Ben in the lion.
> Danny in the lion.
> Watch out penguin!

The impact of Dunbar's drama of being eaten by a lion intrigued Danny and his marks (Figure 11.9) tracked the process of him being swallowed from mouth to tail, his signature and comments confirming self-referentaility:

> Lion's eaten.
> Lion's he's eaten Ben.
> He's eaten Danny.

Valuable insight into how Danny identified himself with Ben's character and how he eventually replaced him was revealed further in his blue and orange felt-pen drawing

Figure 11.9 Danny suggests that he is eaten by Lion

(see Figure 11.10). Unlike previous marks made across Dunbar's illustrations, where he seemed content to stand beside Ben, this drawing highlights a shift in perspective and for a time Danny appeared to create a double personality, a mix of himself and Ben. Danny began drawing in the middle of the page using blue loops for Penguin's face and body with flippers on the left. Unhappy with his first attempt he placed the toy penguin firmly upside-down and changed to an orange pen. With almost palpable concentration he drew the feet at the top followed by body, head and features, finally adding flippers.

Deciding on blue, which, interestingly, he had used throughout the picturebook, following Dunbar's choice for depicting an imaginary lion (signifying perhaps his understanding of the difference between real and imaginary worlds), he then produced a much more sophisticated schematic representation of a human body; upside-down, with clearly defined legs but no arms. Remarkably, he then drew two faces, one noticeably smiling, enjoying the fun of being upside-down and the other looking on, more serious.

When asked 'Who's that?' he named each face, revealing himself to be the happy boy playing alongside Penguin. This both altered the action in the story, providing an alternative scenario of Penguin joining in and playing, but also clearly showed Danny swapping roles with the unhappy Ben.

Danny confirmed himself firmly within this fictional world later during an ICT lesson. Here (Figure 11.12) purely from memory, he added detail to his orange 'tadpole' drawing, representing Lion's mane and beautifully captured the self-satisfied smile

Figure 11.10 Danny's drawing of himself and Penguin

as in Dunbar's illustration. Dunbar's words, 'Lion ate Ben for being too noisy' were paraphrased below the picture, indicating Danny was now replicating Ben's fate.

Can a picturebook then, as Paley suggests (2005: 15), be the catalyst to provide a vehicle for a child with autism to explore, investigate and reproduce human emotions? Or perhaps, as Kress and Van Leeuwen (2006) suggest, the 'emotive immediacy' that visual images provide ' . . . allows the viewer to scrutinize the represented characters as though they were specimens in a display case' (2006: 43). The answer was an overwhelming yes. By instinct, Danny spontaneously demonstrated Paley's assertion (2005: 57)

Figure 11.11 Faces by Danny

lion eat danny

Figure 11.12 Lion eat Danny

that 'the more complex the thought the greater is the child's need to view its meaning through play', accurately mirroring Ben's facial expressions and gestures as he explored difficult human emotions in a safe environment, giving him the opportunity to enact and understand attempted reciprocal communication. This further enhanced his understanding of both Ben's and his own puzzling attempts at communication. The futility of Ben's efforts at reciprocal communication were evident to Danny through Dunbar's presentation of differing vectors between the characters. As Ben only looked directly out towards the beholder once it offered Danny the opportunity, as Nodelman (2008: 20) suggests, to become more objective and realise that Ben 'is not seeing everything'. Penguin, however, gazes out from the book at least ten times demanding attention, to which Danny responded on one occasion, 'Silly Penguin. Says nothing'.

In subsequent readings Danny enjoyed emulating Ben's 'dizzy dance' but commented 'Penguin didn't dance'. Although he continued to mimic Ben's actions throughout the tantrum scene, Danny developed a more objective perspective giving him insights into how Penguin may have felt being subjected to that level of anger.

On one memorable occasion, silence descended in the classroom as the adults witnessed Danny suspended in reflection (Figure 11.13). Hogan reminds us of the ambiguous nature of understanding 'precisely' (2011: 4) what someone is imagining in response to a story but this pivotal moment appeared to nudge Danny into creating a surprise of his own. He had moved from his introspective, autistic perspective, through Ben's egocentric frustrations, then experimented with Penguin's more selfless, altruistic behaviour. Pausing, tracking and commenting on the action, 'Penguin bit lion', he suddenly assumed the heroic role of Penguin and with great glee, bit Lion's nose.

Could it be, as Paley believes, that stories not only allow children to explore complex human emotions within a safe fantasy world but also enable them to transfer that knowledge to the real world? Dunbar certainly invited children to take ownership

Figure 11.13 Danny with Lion

of her picturebook and Danny demonstrated the capacity to respond by projecting emotions onto inanimate toys. All the more extraordinary as Wolfberg comments that children with autism 'rarely produce pretend play by . . . activating dolls as agents' (1999: 3). Many readers enjoy exploring a fantasy world to escape reality but, paradoxically, Danny, with his altered perspective on life, entered a fictional world to explore reality. Dunbar's picturebook serves this function for children who are at the faltering beginnings of trying to fathom how relationships work, to learn that they may yet be able to understand themselves and others. Real life is full of emotionally charged situations and other children's reactions are often fleeting and unpredictable. Picturebook scenarios provide the luxury of space and time to explore, imagine, wonder, think and reflect.

For Danny, the empathetic lessons learnt seem to have become embedded, giving him a promising new perspective when communicating with his peers. Three weeks after my study, Danny, whose normal approach to children new to him often proved unwelcome (such as putting his face much too close to the new child, smelling their skin, touching their mouths, eyes, hair, etc.), was observed smiling as he approached a non-verbal child. Paraphrasing *Penguin*, Danny was heard to say:

Who's that?
That's Sam.
Say hello, say hello to Danny.
No, Sam says nothing.
Sam doesn't talk.
Ahhhh poor Sam.

Figure 11.14 Danny bites Lion's nose

Case 3: Jennifer Farrar[6]

Jennifer Farrar's MEd research project explored some of the links between the aims of critical literacy practices in an early years classroom and the effects of the meta-fictive devices used in postmodern picturebooks, such as David Wiesner's *The Three Pigs*. Guided and informed by an understanding that seeks to position the text as a constructed object, Jennifer considered what younger learners' responses to Wiesner's text might reveal about their ability to adopt a critical, analytical stance. Using a variety of data collection methods, including literature circles, pupils' written or drawn responses and verbal annotations of their own work, Jennifer suggests that metafictive devices can provide readers with access to a critical metalanguage by provoking discussions about how and why texts are assembled. This study also demonstrates how picturebooks might be able to inspire or encourage sophisticated critical literacy practices in the early years, both as powerful pedagogic tools offering readers ways of making meaning from the multiple texts that surround them, and enabling young children to question and challenge the status quo in the pursuit of equality and social justice (O'Brien and Comber 2001: 153). Inspired by Pantaleo's enquiry into Wiesner's *The Three Pigs* with a similar age group of 5-year-olds (2002), Jennifer set about conducting her own study.

As well as making reference to the decision-making powers of authors, I also repeatedly referred to David Wiesner by name to draw pupils' attention to the existence of the 'human' at the end of the pen. If children can 'internalise the interactive behaviour of the adult who is reading the story' (Morrow and Gambrell cited Pantaleo 2002: 72) then I wondered whether the pupils would notice and replicate my focus on the 'decisions that authors make' (Kamler and Comber 1997). I am aware that the use of such an interventionist approach could be interpreted as an attempt to 'put words into children's mouths' (O'Brien 2001: 167). Yet, like O'Brien, I have undertaken this research in the belief that teachers should make it possible for learners to inquire into and, if necessary, challenge the positions taken by texts 'as well as the sorts of readers . . . they produce in the process' (p. 167).

My general research question was to ask whether picturebooks containing meta-fictive devices might act as sites for critical literacy and whether this could be detected from pupils' responses? My analytical approach was informed by the correlation between Luke and Freebody's decoding and meaning-making resources (1997) and some of the Halliday-inspired categories employed by Farrell, Arizpe and McAdam (2010) to analyse pupils' annotated spreads.

A sweep through the data recorded during the literature circle sessions suggested that many pupils tended to relate to the text as subject; that is, their comments were linked to narrative development, characters' feelings, the identification of an interesting illustrative detail or anticipating key aspects of the plot.

[At this point in the Wiesner text, the pigs' paper aeroplane has crash-landed.]

ALL: Uh-oh!

LEWIS: They crash!

FINN: The wolf looks surprised because he didn't think he was going to get all crunk-led up.

ABBIE: It's like an ocean.

ANDREW: The wolf looks like he is in the story now.

LOTTIE: I can see the wolf there . . .

JF: You can still see that the wolf is still in the old story. He hasn't learned to jump out, has he?

ANDREW: That pig looks like . . . you can't see the white furry bits . . .

ABBIE: (laughing) Look at his eyes!

ANDREW: L . . . and the paw looks different.

JUDY: I think he's got off the aeroplane and got all dizzy.

This extract is representative of many of the group discussions: the pupils are not perturbed by the 'seemingly chaotic narrative' of the picturebook (Goldstone 2004: 199) and meaning emerges out of this chaos as a result of both individual and shared reading experiences. Andrew, for example, appears focused on discovering links – or inconsistencies – between the 'old' story world where the wolf remains, and the 'new' world the three pigs jump into; Judy seems to build on Abbie's comment about the pig's wonky eyes by providing a reason for them: ' . . . he's got off the aeroplane and got all dizzy'; while Finn also suggests a hypothesis for the wolf's surprised expression.

The nature of these comments seems to confirm Farrell, Arizpe and McAdam's description of meaning-making as a process, where, during the first stage, readers attempt to anchor or 'situate the characters and actions' (2010). Their work suggests that pupils may need to respond to the text-as-subject before being able to move onto more critically focused text-as-object comments. Similarly, Smith describes the stages of the meaning-making process as the accumulation of 'layers of resonance', which,

Figure 11.15 The pigs crash land (Wiesner 2001)

once in place, provide the 'playground in which meaning is constructed' (2005: 8). By depicting meaning-making as a many-layered process, both studies seem to suggest the value of re-reading texts, to allow pupils more opportunities to consider the texts from different perspectives.

I attempted to frame my approach to the text as an enquiry into the decisions made by Wiesner, following examples provided by O'Brien and Comber (2001). For example, when discussing the different ways the pigs are drawn in the different story worlds, Abbie incorporated my approach into her answer: 'Maybe David Wiesner wants us to think you can get the same story but paint it, do it differently.' Her comment also reveals an understanding of authorial intent and its impact on the reader. During a different group discussion about Wiesner's use of white space, Lucy said:

> Because David Wiesner wanted the . . . there's some pictures to show that they know, to let the people who are reading the book, to let them know they are flying away and there is going to be no more writing.

Lucy's initial use of 'Because David Wiesner . . .' is evidence of her willingness to adopt new ways of talking about texts, but as her change of direction mid-sentence reveals, she was uncertain about how to best express her ideas. Helen's experience was similar:

JF: Why has David Wiesner done that? [Had the wolf blow the pig out of the story.]
HELEN: In all the other stories, people don't come out of the story and maybe just to make it more interesting he has done it.

Helen's answer indicates that she wanted to compare *The Three Pigs* to other texts she knows, showing an awareness of generic conventions and the possibility of alternative versions, but she struggled to articulate her ideas. Previous studies have found that students' expressive potential may be hobbled by their lack of visual grammar or metalanguage, leading to short, non-specific comments such as Helen's, 'he wants to make it more interesting', which may fail to convey the extent of a student's deeper understanding.

Despite their unfamiliarity with the approach, these examples reveal that some pupils did begin to respond to the text-as-object status by attempting to replicate some of it – including some aspects of the metalanguage I had modelled – in their answers or comments. This supports the idea that pupils will 'take on the ways with words, or the ways with reading, that the classroom promotes' (Smith 2005: 23). As a further example, the following response occurred during a discussion about the double-page spread that shows the pigs facing a plethora of story choices. They walk between the pages of different stories, laid out as strings of story boards, which stretch off into the distance, suggesting their breadth and possibility:

JF: Why is David Wiesner trying to show us that there are loads of stories and loads of different decisions?

RACHEL: Because we could choose . . . we could pretend that they are in another story.

By linking Wiesner's depiction of multiple story possibilities with the reader's ability to choose between them, Rachel alludes to the processes of selection and synthesis that are 'fundamental' to making meaning (Rosenblatt 1986: 123). Similarly, her use of 'pretend' suggests an understanding of the nature of the relationship between the reader and the fictional text: that the reader must adopt a stance towards the material they encounter (Rosenblatt 1986: 124). Although it is impossible to tell if Rachel would have offered such a response without prompting, it seems reasonable to suggest that either my own stance or Wiesner's text offered her the possibility of a scaffold or a structure upon which to build (McClay 2000: 100). Of course, some of my Wiesner-focused questions prompted different sorts of answers:

Figure 11.16 The pigs sniff out new stories (Wiesner 2001)

JF: Why has David Wiesner done that? Why has he blown the pig out of the story?
IONA: I'm going to catch him! [lots of giggling; pupils pretend to catch the pig in their hands.]

While all of the exchanges, including the above, were interesting and enjoyable, some of the more insightful text-as-object focused comments were clearly prompted by Wiesner's use of metafictive features. In particular, students responded enthusiastically to the contradictory nature of the verbal/visual relationship (Anstey 2002: 447; Pantaleo 2004b: 231). In the following extract, John refers to the disparity between the written text (which claims the wolf has eaten the pig) and the visual (which shows the pig exiting the story frame) leaving the perplexed wolf looking around hopelessly for his lunch:

JF: Why does it make you laugh?
JOHN: Because they have said two different things about it.
JF: Who has said different things about it? What do you mean?
JOHN: So they have said one thing and then another thing about the same thing.
JF: So you mean that the words tell you one thing and the pictures tell you another?
JOHN: They tell you different things.
JF: So which one is the real story then? How do you make a story if one thing is telling you one thing and another thing tells you something else?
JOHN: You put both in.

Figure 11.17 Breaking boundaries (Wiesner 2001)

John responded by deconstructing what has occurred – the contradiction of the written and visual elements – in order to pinpoint what made it so amusing. In addition, his comment 'you put both in' offers an insight into the 'inner conversation' (Walsh cited in Farrell, Arizpe and McAdam 2010) that took place when he encountered – and made meaning from – a metafictive device of this type.

Similarly, Rachel's response to the same device provides a snapshot of her thought processes, showing how she seemed to struggle to decide which mode to place most 'trust' in:

JF: How do you make sense of it [the fact that the words say one thing and the pictures another]?

RACHEL: Because the words are right and the pictures are not. No, the picture's right and the words are not.

JF: How do you decide?

RACHEL: Because I know he didn't eat it up because the picture looks like [he's] blowing and [the pig's] going 'hey, you blew me right out of the story!'

JF: So if you are reading this . . . how do you know if the words are right or the pictures are right?

RACHEL: Because I made up my mind and I know what it is.

ANNIE: This is just a different version of The Three Pigs.

From this exchange, it seems Rachel's instinctive reaction was to privilege the written over the visual without question, perhaps because this is in keeping with schooled literacies (Meek 1988), but she changed her mind after consulting the text. Her re-consideration of which mode to prioritise is interesting because it suggests the 'ecological', interdependent nature of the relationship between words and images in picturebooks, where a consideration of both is necessary for meaning (Lewis cited in Pantaleo 2011c: 63). In addition, it hints at the power of metafictive devices – such as the indeterminacy created by contradictory words and pictures – to provoke or 'prod' readers into paying closer attention or to read the text differently from normal.

By discussing how they made sense of the conflicting words and pictures in Wiesner's text, both John and Rachel seem to describe something of the transaction between reader and text (Rosenblatt 1986). John's recommendation that any conflict between words and images could be resolved by 'imagining it in your head' suggests an awareness of the way readers utilise their personal context or knowledge in order to make meaning from the ideas presented by the text (Rosenblatt 1986). Similarly, Rachel's response seems to refer to the individual nature of the meaning-making process. Despite her initial confusion, she was quickly emphatic about the validity of her own interpretation, as her repeated use of 'I know' and 'I made up my mind' suggests. In a sense, by emphasising the power of her version, Rachel obliquely alludes to the multiple interpretations that are possible from every textual encounter (Anstey 2002), a point that is succinctly reinforced by Annie's comment about the existence of alternative versions: 'This is just a different version of The Three Pigs.'

I hoped to gain insights into children's creation of meaning from images by asking pupils to describe the decisions they had made as authors. Would there be any evidence that Wiesner's use of metafictive devices had enabled pupils to respond to the text as an object? Would the pupils be able to sustain the text-as-object focus by considering their own texts as artefacts, and from a critical distance? Finally, from this, could I suggest that pupils had engaged with critical literacy practices?

My initial analysis of the ten pupils' 'stories about their stories' provided a bewildering array of data. Wary of the generalisations that could result from an attempt to assign their responses to categories (Lichtman 2012), particularly when referring to such a small sample size, I read the students' own texts and transcripts in search of 'text-as-object' type responses, as I had done previously. Additionally, I used Pantaleo's list of metafictive devices (2004b) to help interpret the children's work, with the wider aim of establishing links to critical literacy practices. In the next section, I attempt to show how they may be linked back to the text or to an example of a critical literacy practice.

Wiesner's use of metafictive devices in *The Three Pigs* seems to have inspired some of the children. His 'jumping out of the story' technique was used to great effect across a variety of imaginative situations: Lottie's Goldilocks hopped out to safely avoid the wrath of the returning bears; Nicole's bored princess was able to jump out of her story into a more exciting location while William's characters used it both to escape from peril and to stage a comeback. Similarly to Wiesner's use, where the pigs jump out of the traditional *Three Pigs* narrative in order to avoid the attentions of the predatory wolf, the pupils also disrupted traditional narrative time and space relationships (Pantaleo 2004) in order to bring about an escape or rescue of some sort. It is hard to tell if the pupils were attracted to the technique because it allowed them to 'hyperlink' parts of different stories together, or because it created an emergency exit for characters facing peril. The fact that they incorporated it into their texts shows the ease with which they can absorb aspects of the texts that surround them. In addition, having characters 'jump out of a story' draws attention to the fact that the text *is* a story – an artefact replete with limits or boundaries – that, as Wiesner's example demonstrates, can be transgressed and redrawn, only differently (Biesta 2005).

Wiesner's text appears to have inspired other forms of transgression, such as Helen's mermaid, who was bored by her life because she 'knew everything' about it. Instead she wanted to wear a bikini and go surfing in a different part of the 'very deep sea'. Unlike Rachel, Helen's narrative doesn't transgress its temporal or spatial limits. Instead, her text seems to challenge the boundaries of traditional character types. Her use of a bored mermaid is interesting and could perhaps be interpreted as a comment on gender roles and the representation of female characters, yet her treatment of the father/king figure is also significant. Helen described how her king differed from the other storybook kings she knew because he agreed to the surfing, provided the bikini and told the mermaid to be careful: 'In all the other stories, the kings don't want the mermaids to go off but I wanted it to be different so I made a different decision.' From Helen's explanation, it is clear that she is aware of the author's role as decision maker and the transformative power this entails, which I interpret as a text-as-object response. By interrupting her knowledge of taken-for-granted assumptions about kings (as inflexible and domineering), she created a character who listens ('[he's] a person she goes to talk to') and takes his daughter's feelings into account ('the king knew that she really wanted to go on an adventure'). Yet, to return to the earlier point about the importance of metalanguage (Callow 2008), the critical potential Helen shows appears to be curtailed by her lack of vocabulary for talking about texts. When asked why she wanted to make her text different from 'all the other stories' she referred to, she replied: 'Because if things are different it is really nice.' As Arizpe and Styles (2003) suggest, greater knowledge of a technical vocabulary could help pupils like Helen to articulate their responses with greater clarity.

Of course, it is not possible to tell if the authorial decisions Helen took were inspired by examples from Wiesner's text, yet by asking her to explain them it is possible to trace aspects of the picturebook's influence. For example, she seems impressed by Wiesner's decision to tell the tale of *The Three Pigs* in a way that 'shatters readers' expectations' (Goldstone 2004: 197), instead of revisiting familiar material. She compared the versions of the story she already knew unfavourably with Wiesner's: 'In my story [the versions she has at home] . . . they just run to the next house and it is always the same.' Interestingly, Helen's interest in Wiesner's techniques can be traced back to the smaller group sessions, when she reacted with approval and enthusiasm to the way that Wiesner's characters could jump in and out of different stories: 'I had never thought of it before and it's quite a good idea.'

A third and final example comes from William, whose story of the feud between a pig, a wolf and a mouse uses the 'jumping out of the story' technique. As his text is predominantly image-based, asking William to comment on it was useful as it enabled me to interpret his own interpretation of the text, rather than simply relying on the results of my own analysis. The value of asking pupils to express and explain the thinking behind their text was underscored by the fact that William was able to point out his use of contesting discourses (Anstey 2002), a feature I had overlooked, presumably due to my adult tendency to privilege the written word and to skip and scan over visual texts, despite my best intentions.

Figure 11.18 William explained that his words and images told different stories

JF: [reads from text] 'The mouse got eaten up by the pig and the wolf.' Why did you decide to have that happen?

WILLIAM: Because it's like the story you read but it wasn't actually real because he . . . blowed it out of the story.

JF: So who blew it out of the story?

WILLIAM: The wolf and the pig.

JF: So your words tell us he gets eaten up but does he really?

WILLIAM: No.

JF: Oh, I see, so your pictures are telling us . . .

WILLIAM: . . . like that they were blown out of the story.

JF: So your pictures are different from the words?

WILLIAM: Yes.

JF: That's interesting. Why did you decide to do that?

WILLIAM: Because . . . you get to see different stories.

Although William's answers are brief, they also provide evidence of how he appears to have internalised and reconstructed Wiesner's use of contradictory words and pictures. Like Watson (1993), I felt astonished by William's insight and annoyed at my failure to immediately recognise what he was doing. By asking him to justify the decisions he had made as an author, I was inviting him to reflect on his own work and hoped that I was creating the means for him to express his thoughts about reading and the production of meaning.

Despite these ambiguities, and the impossibility of separating the power and influence of the metafictive devices from the impact of my role as a facilitator, some of the responses discussed here seem to indicate that pupils were willing to tolerate an approach with a 'critical edge' (O'Brien 1994), shown by their willingness to wonder or speculate about why texts have been created in a particular way. As Comber has noted, young children come to school with sophisticated analytical skills: the task for teachers is to help develop them (2001: 171).

I would like to tentatively conclude that postmodern picturebooks have the potential to function as sites of critical literacy practice as Wiesner's text appears to meet many of the qualities identified by Pantaleo (2004) and Anstey (2002): it is consciously constructed to challenge the reader; its unusual layout and design forces the reader to access the text in a non-linear way; the use of contesting discourses require a heightened level of reader interaction and make multiple readings possible while its non-sequential nature creates ambiguity and indeterminacy (2002: 448).

In common with other studies using metafictive picturebooks, I conclude that texts such as *The Three Pigs* can help to develop new literacies (Anstey 2002: 456; Pantaleo 2004), perhaps because they provide a platform for talking about texts and how they are structured. Many researchers in this field have emphasised the importance of metalanguage to critical analysis (Comber 2001; Arizpe and Styles 2003; Callow 2008) and texts such as Wiesner's provoke the need for such a vocabulary by drawing attention to the act of authoring. When Goldstone notes that postmodern picturebooks do not 'blanket the reader with their stories' (2004: 201), her use of 'blanket' is apt because – to extend the metaphor – the reader is not entirely covered up or smothered by the world of the story: there are 'limbs' visible and not everything is tucked in snugly. In texts such as *The Three Pigs* we see the edges and may be prompted to ask what they are, why they exist and who decided where they should be.

In agreement with other studies into the critical potential of learners in the early years, I conclude that approaching a text as an object of enquiry, rather than focusing on its subject or content, can provide pupils with the room to distance themselves from texts and view them critically (O'Brien 1994). Additionally, asking pupils to verbally annotate the decisions they have made while constructing their own stories appears to be a useful way of encouraging more classroom talk and thinking about how texts work and how language is used and manipulated by every user, including the pupils themselves.

Running parallel to this could be a similar project with teachers or parents, to introduce (or reacquaint) them with the metafictive devices that postmodern picturebooks contain. Not only would this help to anchor and develop a shared metalanguage both in the classroom and at home, but it might also help to convince adult co-readers that reading picturebooks counts as 'work'.

Notes

1 The 'students' have, of course, all given their permission for these extracts to be used and brief biographical details are given.
2 Although our examples are of children aged 5–9, we could have chosen equally interesting research with young people from 10–15 years.
3 After gaining an MPhil and excellent PhD from Cambridge University, Susan returned to USA. She is a Postdoctoral Teaching Fellow at the University of Massachusetts, Boston. She received the 2015 Gish Jen Fellowship for Emerging Writers at The Writers Room of Boston.
4 Kim Deakin gained an MEd from Cambridge University in 2014. Kim was Literacy Co-ordinator at Richmond Hill Special School in Luton. Her Headteacher, Jill Miller, encouraged her to work in the creative way that is evident in this chapter. Kim has since moved to Somerset.
5 Please note that at the request of Danny Wilkinson, his parents and the school, their actual names are given.
6 Jennifer Farrar is an ESRC-funded, final year PhD candidate from the University of Glasgow. Her PhD, which builds on the project described here, explores how parents and their young children respond to the metafictive devices used in a set of picturebooks, including Wiesner's *The Three Pigs*. Jennifer has worked as a journalist and teaches English at secondary level. Her interest in critical literacy's role in the early years stage has been sparked by her experiences as a parent of young children.

Chapter 12

Digital picturebooks

Margaret Mackey

PART I

Nancy is 3. She and I frequently read picturebooks, mostly on paper but sometimes digitally. On this occasion, she has requested that we look at the iPad version of *Spot the Dot* (Carter 2011), although I have given her the option of exploring the paper pop-up edition of the same title (Carter 2013). We settle in a chair together and open the app. A green screen appears, with black letters across it. A man voices the words on the screen: 'Spot the red dot.' The 'o' in 'dot' fills in with red. The screen now features a variety of colours and shapes. A line of circles crosses the top of the screen, and when Nancy finds and taps the red dot, it moves to occupy the left-hand circle in this line. As we progress, the format does not change but the bright clutter of the screen becomes more complex, and spotting the requisite dot becomes more challenging. Even when I help, Nancy takes full credit for filling up the line of dots across the top of the screen.

This scene represents many of the most-loved aspects of a classic combination of child, adult, lap and picturebook. Nancy and I are snuggled up together; our hands dance over the screen in a choreography of joint discovery. Our eyes look outward in the same direction, perusing the screen very intently. Our conversation is focused on the images in front of us. If I compare this scenario to its sister act featuring the paper pop-up version of the same concept book, I notice at least two points in favour of the digital version: it often lasts longer than an encounter with the paper edition, and Nancy gets to interact in more robust ways with the screen dots than the paper dots because I am constantly monitoring her handling of the fragile pop-up extravaganza of the paper edition.

Even with my pop-up paper book, for which another name is 'movable', the most obvious point of contrast between the two versions is that one set of dots is fixed and the other is in motion. Furthermore, that mobile set is moving in two different ways. The dots themselves can be dragged across the screen, even by the tentative touch of 3-year-old fingers. The text is also movable in that it can be instantiated on a variety of screens and does not reside permanently on any one of them. This element of words in motion constitutes one main theme of my chapter. The second motif, to which I will return late in the chapter, is the issue of the autonomy of the child reader. With *Spot the Dot*, Nancy is happy to locate a paper dot, but her pride in dragging a digital dot across the screen to its proper home is a palpable response to a more extended and visible reward.

Picturebook choreographies

I begin my consideration of digital picturebooks with this little scenario of child, adult and two versions of a picturebook because I want to eliminate some shibboleths from the very beginning. What matters is the core relationship between child, adult and text. Too many people seem to have a reflex reaction that the digital somehow interferes with both the real and the idealised virtues of that child/adult/picturebook encounter. There may be many cases where the digital edition is inferior to the paper version but where a text makes intelligent use of the digital affordances and an adult co-reader is on hand (as we say), I am not sure there is any inherent reason why this default assumption should apply.

Guy Merchant has made a detailed study of young children's interactions with iPad stories. He describes the ways in which 'multiple actions and interactions are woven together in a complex choreography of events' (2014: 135). Paying careful attention to the tablet as a material object, he extracts a typology of hand movements relating to tablet use: stabilising movements – holding, or balancing on the knees or other surface; control movements – general tapping, precision tapping, swiping, and thumb pressing; and deictic movements – pointing, nodding, and other gestures directed towards the screen contents (2014: 124). I would add dragging to this list, but otherwise I am intrigued by the way his analysis directs our attention to the tactile demands of working with the virtual (and it is worth noticing that his scenario also includes a helping adult). A contrasting list of the hand movements needed to control a paper book would be very instructive; it would include pointing and tapping and stabilising, but would also incorporate the tally of gross and fine motor actions needed to manage orientation, page turns, and the like.

With *Spot the Dot*, the paper version came later, and may thus be perceived as an adaptation of the iPad edition. A comparison of the two renditions of this title provides some details to flesh out Merchant's list of reader activities with a specific consideration of two versions of the same text.

The visual cacophony of the electronic version is cleverly controlled by the instruction screen inserted before each mini-game: against a bright screen, four black words are displayed, saying 'Spot the [insert colour] dot'. The 'o' in 'dot' then infills with the requisite colour, always a vivid contrast to the background shade on the screen. Readers must touch the coloured 'o' to start the sequence, as a friendly voice-over instructs them. Screens full of dots and other shapes must be scanned to find the right dot. An unassuming musical soundtrack enhances the experience. Upon replay, the dots shift their location, though the particular game for any given colour remains the same.

Two years after the appearance of this app, Carter published a conventional pop-up book of the same title. Some pages pop, others involve lifting flaps or moving tabs, but the general challenge remains the same: find the dot of the right colour in a bright and busy background of conflicting dots.

Instead of alternating screens between instructions and challenge, Carter uses the left-hand page of each opening for the unchanged words: 'Spot the [insert colour] dot.' In this edition, however, the background of the page matches the colour being sought. The book contains fewer colours, but it plays comparable variations on the search, using two pages apiece of lift-the-flap, pull-the tab, and turn-the-wheel. The final opening is a double-page pop-up explosion of dots. In this case, the instructions are written in white on a black background, weaving their way through the dots, and there is a joke more witty and intelligent than anything on the app version (spoiler alert): the white dot is actually the full stop that concludes the sentence of instructions.

In this case, both versions of *Spot the Dot* are appealing, and make excellent use of the affordances of their format. It is not surprising that Nancy likes them both.

Two digital alphabets

How to define a digital picturebook in relation to an app remains a fuzzy question. It may be helpful to investigate two digital alphabets for young children. One app very popular with 3-year-olds and their parents inhabits the borderline territory between app and book, and could be defined either way. The second example tends towards the 'book' end of the digital spectrum, but what it really manifests is the kind of dismal didacticism that mars much material for the young on any platform.

Endless Alphabet

Endless Alphabet (Originator 2013) displays many of the attributes of a conventional concept book, but its born-digital qualities are more immediately obvious. Its relationship to its picturebook cousin, the alphabet book, is complex.

Endless Alphabet allows users to 'page' through a sequence of words compiled on a set of moving virtual flashcards, and to select one by tapping. The chosen word flashes on the screen and a voice reads it aloud. Then a group of animated monsters rages right through the letters and sends them flying all over the screen. Readers must glide each letter back to its correct place in the word, represented by an outline. As you drag the letter with your finger, it repeats its sound, in many cases developing teeth and a tongue for clearer articulation (these embellishments disappear once the letter is fitted into its slot). Once the letters are all in the correct order, the word is spoken again. An animation demonstrates its meaning, followed by a voice-over definition. One of Nancy's favorite words is 'DEMOLISH' and the meaning is given as follows: 'When you demolish something, you break it on purpose.' The animation involves a tall tower of bricks and a monster who knocks it down with great relish. The animation and definition section is repeatable.

Many of these features might be expected in an alphabet book: the full set of words listed in alphabetical order, some kind of illustration, a definition. But the activity and the interactivity set this delightful app apart. Dragging the letters, children are in a position to consider some of the work that letters do, as they hear each sound and observe that the letter has its own place in the word, and that in some words certain letters appear more than once. Once children master the simple tasks their fingers need to perform, they can control many other aspects of the app: which word is chosen, how many times they watch the animation, and so forth. The voice-over supplies all the reading aloud required.

The app gamifies letter learning, but there are no scores and no tests, and the replication of the word-building exercises feels like play rather than drill. The potential for repetition allows for a certain degree of reflection on the way words work, but nobody would call the overall impact of this app contemplative. The letters and words are in constant motion.

The Animal Alphabet Picture Book for Toddlers

An exercise in digital comparison makes it clear, however, that more than 0s and 1s are required to develop as captivating and clever a production as *Endless Alphabet*. That digital concept books can be every bit as dreary as their worst paper cousins was proven to me as soon as I googled 'digital alphabet picturebooks,' and acquired an item listed on the first screen: *The Animal Alphabet Picture Book for Toddlers* (Harper 2013). This text is billed as 'The Essential Kindle Learning Tool for Every Young Child,' so I loaded it onto my (admittedly old) Kindle and took a look.

Harper sets his priorities clearly at the outset of this book, earnestly addressing parents:

> This edition was created to help stimulate the minds of very young children by using the power of mental imagery combined with the alphabet. It really is one of the first steps to learning but to achieve the best results, parental participation is essential.
>
> I would advise you to use this as a tool before bedtime and monitor how well your child recalls the information the following evening and so on.
>
> (2013: n.p.)

My elderly Kindle shows only black and white images, so it is fair to assume this volume would seem less drab when colour is available. However, since it is marketed explicitly for Kindle use, it does not seem too much to expect that the words and images might be sized (if not actively *designed*) so that related material could appear on a single Kindle screen rather than taking as many as three clicks to show a single page. I used it on the recommended default font setting, so it really seems reasonable that it should conform to the affordances of the display frame.

Essentially, and not surprisingly, the content comprises 26 animal images along with the relevant letter of the alphabet. The letter information is at the top left-hand side: 'A is for Antelope'; the picture is in the centre of the screen, unless it is too large, in which case readers must click to a subsequent screen. Under the picture is a line of image credits and the underlined phrase, 'Click here to continue' in a font as large as the letter line at the top (n.d., Locations 35–39). If the picture is too large, these two lines of information can take a third screen before advancing to the next letter.

After a run-through of the alphabet, the book moves on to quizzes. The thought of such soul-destroying drill being part of an unfortunate toddler's nightly routine is distressing ('Time for your bedtime alphabet test, little Timmy!'); the waste of the affordances that a digital text could make available is also troubling. Nothing about this dreary production is worth anybody's time and attention.

The world is very full indeed of alphabet books for small children and some paper versions are as terrible as this Kindle travesty. But the fact that I turned it up so easily and acquired it with the expenditure of just $3.04 (Canadian dollars – the price has since risen) and the investment of less than a moment's purchasing activity on my Kindle is a sobering reminder that nothing about digital productions is inherently up-to-date or dynamic.

The Animal Alphabet Picture Book is premised on the assumption that the parent is essential to inform and test the young learner. *Endless Alphabet*, on the other hand, deliberately empowers its youthful users. I have watched many 2-year-olds manipulate it independently; the only physical or conceptual skill required is the ability to tap on a selected word and then the knowledge and capacity to drag a vociferous letter to its matching outline shape on the screen. Subsequent learning is highly scaffolded by the design of the app.

Such autonomy can lead children astray, of course. Nancy used to drag letters to the words of *Endless Alphabet* in fairly random order, but she is now very systematic about inserting them in order: right to left. When I showed her that words are organised left to right, she assembled a single word in that array, and then returned to her own structure. No doubt she will survive this misapprehension just as children stop producing mirror writing, but it is a reminder that not every childish assumption, no matter how rationally and intelligently based in observation of the materials in front of them, is actually correct.

The other hazard of child autonomy in relation to *Endless Alphabet* is that parents may seize the opportunity to disappear from the exchange altogether. One complaint about apps is that they do not foster the human exchange of conversation that is what really teaches the young. A *New York Times* article asks a key question: 'Is e-reading to your toddler story time, or simply screen time?' (Quenqua 2014: n.p.). The quality of the surrounding conversation is a vital part of the experience, either with paper or with digital materials. Yet even this important consideration is not an absolute. I will return to the potential for apps to empower independent use at the end of this chapter.

Digital and paper

In striking contrast to the digital book's potential for a kind of 'live action', a paper alphabet book manifests what de Kerckhove calls the pre-eminent quality of paper words (pop-ups aside): their stillness. De Kerckhove calls a book

> a resting place for words. It sounds trite, but in fact the printed page is the only place where words do have a rest. Everywhere else, they are moving: when you speak, when you see them on a screen, when you see them on the Net, words are moving. But a book is a restful place. The printed word is, and always was, still.
>
> (1997: 107)

There is a substantial cognitive and pedagogical challenge to be faced in sorting out the educational virtues of repetition versus stillness. And an entire epistemological and ontological discussion could probably be fuelled by the question of whether images embody the same inherent dichotomy as de Kerckhove attributes to words. But there is no question that motion is a component of the digital. *Endless Alphabet* could fairly be re-titled *Endlessly Moving Alphabet*. Any paper alphabet book is fixed – the letters and pictures stay in the same place on the page; the pages are bound in a singular relationship with each other. Even the pop-up dots in Carter's 'movable' paper book are always to be found in the same place on the popping page. *Endless Alphabet* is not open to genuine negotiation with readers; the words on the screen are displayed in a fixed order; the reader cannot subvert the orthodox spelling of the word by dragging the letters to a different home; the little animation never changes its pre-ordained demonstration and definition. Yet it is never still.

Even the duller *Animal Alphabet Picture Book* does not fix its words in a particular place; they evaporate at the press of the Kindle page-turn button, and can only be retrieved by an elaborate search process or by working through every intervening page in strict order. A word printed on paper has the significant capacity to be *there* – on a specific page, where I can flick back and find it again. It is always in the same place, and does not need to displace other words in order to be the focus of my attention. Its relation to the other words is of a 'both/and' nature, and may be described as featuring a 'next-to' or 'far-from' location. In an electronic book, it is very much a case of 'either/or': I am looking at the antelope *or* the bear. I must evaporate one to look at the other.

Alert readers, of course, will have noticed my false dichotomy in the previous paragraphs. It is not a zero-sum game; there is no need for readers to pick *either* repetition *or* stillness. Fortunate children will experience both qualities in their different texts, and will develop tacit repertoires concerning their distinctive virtues. Adult caregivers can enhance children's experiences with both formats by pointing out their characteristic affordances.

Nevertheless, *Endless Alphabet* will change how many readers (not necessarily just children) look at a static book-based alphabet. Just like its earlier predecessors, film and television, this new medium will have some of its most significant impact on paper books in how it alters the perspectives that readers bring to their experience with the book.

And caregivers may need to pay extra attention to ensuring that young children actually do gain experience with the still words of paper. As smartphones and tablets become more ubiquitous, more and more children will be able to take at least occasional access to moving words and images for granted. Provision must be made for access to books; they do not automatically ride on the incidental coat-tails of daily adult life the way a smartphone increasingly does. An intriguing report from the National Literacy Trust at the end of 2014 suggests that lower-income children (those labeled C2 and D or E) have greater access to touch-screens and reduced access to paper, compared to those from upper socio-economic levels (AB).

Compared with their AB peers:

- Twice as many children from DE households look at or read stories on a touch screen for longer than they look at or read printed stories (29.5% vs. 17.4%) . . . .
- Slightly more children from C2 and DE households use a touch screen in a typical week than those from AB and C1 households (31.9% vs. 27.0%) . . . .
- More children from DE households use technology more for educational activities than for entertainment (43.2% vs. 30.4%).

(Formby 2014: 9)

Digital ontologies and the young child

Mary, aged 4, lives in a small community in a rural part of Canada. Her parents have smartphones and she is as adept as the next privileged Western child in turning up photographs and videos of herself; as a consequence she knows about tapping and swiping. However, she was not familiar with the possibilities presented by apps designed for children. It was interesting to watch her interact with *Endless Alphabet* and also with the *Sesame Street* classic, *There's a Monster at the End of This Book*

(Stone and Smollin 2013), a story whose engaging and subversive qualities have transferred very effectively to a digital version.

The idea of words breaking down into letters for the child user to reassemble was a new notion to Mary, but it did not take her long to work out the necessity of shape sorting and matching that allowed her to collect the letters back into the right order. She was less attuned to the definition and its corresponding animation. The whole exercise seemed to be fairly abstract to her, though she was clearly intrigued and delighted. But we are talking about a single session; I have no doubt that a very small number of further encounters would expand her responses.

With *There's a Monster at the End of This Book*, she instantly took on board the ethos of the story: that readers should reject Grover's urging not to turn the page because it will bring everyone closer to the eponymous monster. Mary tapped the screen with relish, no matter how eloquently Grover begged her to desist or how ingeniously he tied up or hammered down the page so it would resist turning. Little flashes of light on his knots and nails invite young readers to touch the screen to dissolve his constructions. Mary swiftly grasped the nature of her role in this story.

A few weeks after my encounter with Mary, I showed the digital version of *There's a Monster at the End of This Book* (this time on an iPad screen) to Nancy. Mary had recognised Grover but she did not appear to have extensive knowledge of his background. Nancy, however, brought a large intertextual repertoire of *Sesame Street* experience to her experience of this digital book. She watches YouTube extracts from the television programme on her parents' iPad, and that screen version of Grover is probably the most familiar to her. There are also *Sesame Street* books in her house, she has gone through several sticker books, and the family owns a set of small *Sesame Street* plastic characters that includes Grover.

Nancy refused outright to dismantle Grover's ropes and planks. 'Grover said not to,' she protested. We stalled on an early page of the story as she dug her heels in and would not tap the screen. Instead, she agreed to read the book version (Stone and Smollin 1999/1971) as an alternative. The paper Grover had far less totemic authority over Nancy's actions. I offered her a peep at the last page to see if there really was a monster but she refused. She readily disobeyed paper Grover's requests and turned the pages; she even giggled. When we returned to the digital version, she was more willing to contradict all his instructions.

Prior to this experience, I had not given a single thought to the significance of intertextuality and ontological authority in the toddler's relationship with paper and screen pages. Nancy's initial response to the digital screen version of Grover caused me to reconsider the nature of her understanding of how Grover exists in the world. Clearly paper Grover broke the spell of authority that she associated with screen Grover. It seemed as if the iPad version of this lovable monster was more 'real' because he was simply an interactive incarnation of the video Grover with whom she was already very familiar.

Issues of primacy are extremely important in our era of adaptation, commodification, and re-working. The first version of a character that you meet may automatically claim to be the authoritative persona, at least in your own mind and for your own purposes. Sometimes a more complete and better-rounded incarnation that you meet later will overtake that first version. Or one telling of a story may completely capture your heart and attention and dominate your mental pantheon of versions from that point onwards. And it may be that an interactive character takes over from a still character. There are many ways for a single version to captivate a child's imagination.

These decisions are often very private and often taken for granted rather than deeply considered. In Nancy's case, seeing Grover on a paper page seems to have broken the spell of 'Grover-ness' that caused her to connect the app character to the video character in seamless ways. As we bring up children in an era of extreme proliferation of versions, it behoves us to pay attention to their priorities, and also to their potential for intertextual misapprehension and misunderstanding.

PART II

The unstill word and its potential

There used to be a beer advertisement that described its product as 'reaching the parts that other beers cannot reach'. A feature of a word still on a page is that its portability is limited to what can be physically carried; a digital word in motion may indeed reach parts and places not reachable by the tangible book.

At the nontrivial local level, in the West at least, the ubiquity of the smartphone permits access to a story even when a caregiver has not provided for waiting times by bringing a paper book along. Globally, digital platforms allow children's materials to piggyback on adult platforms in ways that have significant consequences.

Two different multilingual online libraries demonstrate some of the potential for digital picturebooks to expand their footprint in the world.

Unite for Literacy

'Unite for Literacy' is an American site that offers simple and brightly coloured books with English text that can be narrated aloud in a total of eighteen other languages (though the words on the page remain English). Their mission is to provide easily accessible books in what they term 'book deserts', geographic areas where a majority of homes have fewer than 100 books in total in the household. Their map of such book deserts is confined to the United States (surprisingly large swathes of the country are included), but it is not difficult to imagine that such book deserts occur in very large areas of the world, and of course the website is accessible worldwide as well. Sponsors are invited from private, public and civic sectors to help with the funding of ever more books.

The books thus created are short and bright, with simple sentences about topics likely to be meaningful to young children. To take a representative example, *What Colors Do You Eat?* (Hartman 2013) contains ten double-spread openings, including the title page. The right-hand page contains a line such as 'I eat red tomatoes' in a bold sans serif font. The left-hand page incorporates a vivid close-up photograph of the relevant food. Pages are turned by clicking a triangular arrow on the right side of the right-hand page. The voiceover narration must be activated separately for each page by clicking on the familiar megaphone icon at the bottom of the screen. English is the default and remains in place throughout; each of the eighteen supplementary languages can be imported separately, but there is room for only two options on the screen at a time, English and one other.

Changing the voiceover option and turning the page are the only two elements of interactivity in this simple text; its mobility lies more in the portability of the screens that access it. Nevertheless, its potential for making a powerful intervention in the lives of some children is manifest.

The International Children's Digital Library (ICDL)

The International Children's Digital Library (ICDL) describes itself as

> a research project funded primarily by the National Science Foundation (NSF), the Institute for Museum and Library Services (IMLS), and Microsoft Research to create a digital library of outstanding children's books from all over the world . . . . The materials in the collection, all presented in the original languages in which they were published, reflect similarities and differences in cultures, societies, interests, and lifestyles of peoples around the world. At the end of the initial research period, it is anticipated that the ICDL collection will include approximately 10,000 materials in at least 100 languages.
>
> (http://en.childrenslibrary.org/help/faqs.shtml#A1)

The site presents many hundreds of digital facsimiles of books published in a wide variety of languages. The initial array of a book, after you click on its cover, is a graphic of its entire spread of pages. The readable close-up text is displayed one page at a time, and readers simply click on a page to move on to the next. The long list of titles can be searched via a wide variety of often very sophisticated indices. Not every book on this site is a picturebook, but picturebooks are well represented. The first screen I checked of books aimed at children aged 3 to 5 turned up books in Danish, Mongolian, English, German, Portuguese and Persian/Farsi (http://www.childrenslibrary.org/icdl/SimpleSearchCategory?ids=84&langid=&pnum=1&cnum=1&text=&lang=English&ilang=English).

This large and polyglot library is as near to every child in the world as the closest site of Internet access. Although the words on the page are as still as it is possible for a digital word to be (they still vanish on a click), they are mobile in the larger sense of travelling the globe. Their ready availability becomes part of the global repertoire that fosters literacy in many languages.

A pedagogy of interactivity

A Western concern about interactive digital picturebooks is that parents will use them as babysitters, depriving children of the productive conversation that arises out of laptime with paper books. When everyone in the child's community is illiterate, that capacity of the tablet screen to function effectively without adult scaffolding takes on a different resonance.

Chang, Tilahun, and Breazeal (2014) present an account of a project in two remote Ethiopian villages. Forty-one solar-charged touchscreen tablets, loaded with more than 325 apps fostering literacy development (including picturebooks), were given to children aged 5 to 11. These communities are so isolated that books, paper and pencils were unknown to them (Wolf et al., 2014: 7). With no adult intervention, the children of one village collectively took one day to deduce how to turn on the tablets; the other group took two days. By the end of the first month at least one person had looked at every one of the apps (Wolf et al. 2014: 15). The most popular was TinkRbook, an app that 'represents a new kind of interactive story that supports and invites children to "tinker" with text and graphics to explore how these changes impact the narrative . . . an interactively reinforced association links the written word, the spoken word, and the graphical depiction of the concept' (Wolf et al. 2014: 13). The words and images *move* when a user gestures; that motility permits a responsiveness to child users that can short-circuit some elements of the role of adult intervention. At the same time, its very flexibility is designed to attract the attention of adults who are not literate themselves, and to recruit parents back into that essential conversation with the child, even if they are insecure in their own literacy skills (Isaacson 2014: 4). Isaacson suggests that tablets may work similarly in less isolated pockets of poverty and deprivation in the West; he points to the American South.

This example of interactivity is channeled towards developing literacy in areas where it was previously completely unknown. The early accounts of its success demonstrate the potential for new ways of becoming literate. They also suggest new ways of thinking about how the dynamic power of literacy can be productively packaged and transported. The 'box of books' approach that has played such a huge role over the whole of the previous era may be on its way to obsolescence.

PART III

Conclusions

We are still in the very early stages of digital forms of story. My chapter offers only a brief overview of a few highlights. Yet it is possible to see a theme in the experiences of Nancy, in her media-rich environment, Mary, with her more restricted access to digital pleasures, and the children of Ethiopia, who have had no prior experience of recorded text of any kind. The movable digital words and images invite the probing index finger of even a very young child, and the road from limited experience to at least a preliminary form of autonomous interpretation is a very short one.

At the same time, we need to remember the hypothetical child in this chapter, poor little Timmy with his bedtime alphabet drill. Nothing is inherent in the fact of digitisation. Dreadful content and dysfunctional scaffolding practices are not eliminated by the introduction of electronic reading.

We need also, at least for the foreseeable future, to bear in mind the difference between the moving page and the still page. No matter how revolutionary the potential for emancipation in the movable text, we should hold fast to the essential virtues of stillness until we are utterly certain that what replaces paper has improved on it. Parents appear to be in the conservative corner with regard to this issue: a 2013 Pew Research poll showed that 81 per cent of parents thought it very important and a further 13 per cent thought it somewhat important that their children should read paper books (Zickuhr 2013: n.p.). But Formby's finding that lower-income parents are moving more swiftly to providing access to electronic gadgets for their children is a reminder that (as usual) we are dealing with a very complex phenomenon.

A dispassionate observer would probably find value in the idea that children should have exposure to both formats, and it seems likely that many children will achieve just that kind of balance. But in a time of radical flux, nothing remains certain for long. The role of words and pictures that move in response to any of a variety of forms of reader action will continue to evolve, and it will remain important for us to attend to the significance of that evolution. Careful research that makes room for the experiences of children and their caregivers remains as vital in the digital realm as in the world of paper books. We have much to learn.

Chapter 13

Moving forward on response to picturebooks

Implications for research and pedagogy

In this final chapter we summarise some of the main findings from our original research as well as adding those from the last 10–15 years which have confirmed and supplemented these initial findings. We also provide some guidelines for those who want to carry out research on response to picturebooks, based on extensive experience with our own studies and those of our students. Finally, we refer briefly to the implications for pedagogy and further research.

Summary of findings

In this section we attempt to provide a concise picture of the evidence that supports the importance of children reading and responding to picturebooks. We start with a list of the most salient findings from our original study:

- Children as young as 4 were very good at analysing the visual features of texts.
- Most children were deeply engaged by the texts and keen to discuss the moral, social, spiritual and environmental issues they raised.
- Analysing visual text, and the relationship between word and image, made demands on higher order reading skills (inference, viewpoint, etc.).
- There was no clear correlation between reading ability (as identified by the class teacher) and the ability to analyse visual texts.
- As well as learning through looking, we had clear evidence of children learning through talking, and the importance of enabling questions was underlined.
- There were many similarities between the responses of children in schools with completely different catchment areas.
- The younger children's drawings often showed understandings they were unable to articulate.
- While we were aware of development in children's ability to interpret visual texts, the trajectory by age was not always clear cut.
- Our findings confirmed our original belief that careful looking and constructive dialogue enables children (including those who are very young or do not speak English fluently or do not read print confidently) to make worthwhile judgements about pictures which are often profound, complex and richly interconnected with other ideas or symbolic systems.

- The children in our study learned effectively because they found the activity they engaged in to be worthwhile. Children can become more visually literate and operate at a much higher level if they are taught how to look, confirming Avgerinou and Ericson's argument that 'higher order visual literacy skills do not develop unless they are identified and "taught"' (1997: 280).

Five years later, in our review of research on response to multimodal texts, we found most of these findings supported by the work of others (Arizpe and Styles 2008). We think it is worth reminding our readers about these similarities despite the differences in terms of texts, population and methodologies. Once again, the first thing to come through for many researchers was the excitement and pleasure of engaging with picturebooks and the emotional bonds forged with the texts. Some of the other findings we highlight again here as they stress the importance of:

- using well-crafted picturebooks that have the potential to "teach" readers both literary and literacy skills as the reader/viewer is encouraged to engage deeply and this can lead to critical thinking and meaningful learning;
- having time to look closely at images and do re-readings;
- valuing the intertextual knowledge and visual literacy practices that children bring to their meaning-making from outside the school context;
- providing meta-language to discuss the visual features of picturebooks as well as some reference to how pictures and text interact;
- asking about and discussing cultural references in picturebooks;
- considering the role of the mediator in the interaction between children and picturebooks;
- encouraging in-depth interpretation and understanding through talk and collaborative discussion.

As we saw in Chapters 9 and 10, the work of Kiefer, Sipe, Pantaleo, as well as our own, has provided some of the initial paths that others have followed and taken forward in new directions based on new picturebook and visual literacy theories. The increasing number of studies, with wide differences in intention and methods, mean that the results can no longer be reduced to a series of succinct bullet points. However, we would like to list the areas where research on response has made, or is beginning to make an impact, and we look forward to reading about further investigation in these areas:

- cognitive development
- critical thinking
- language acquisition
- emotional literacy
- visual literacy
- literary learning
- second/additional language learning
- social and cultural awareness.

Carrying out a well-crafted study

Anthony Browne had this to say in his afterword to the first edition:

> When I first read *Children Reading Pictures* I found it intensely moving. I was deeply touched by the children's response to *Zoo* and *The Tunnel*, and equally impressed by the gentle and subtle questions of the interviewers. The children's sophisticated reactions didn't surprise me as I've known for some time how we often undervalue the abilities of children to see and understand. They were able to pick up on themes and ideas that I hadn't expressed in the text, only in the pictures, and proved wonderful readers of visual metaphors. This book, I think, proves beyond doubt children's innate ability to derive true meaning from pictures.

We were delighted that Browne found the evidence of the children's responses to his picturebooks stirring and inspiring. Since then we have worked at our respective universities with numerous Master's and doctoral students and classroom teachers who were eager to learn more about how children interpret picturebooks by setting up their own research studies, often based on our model. We are now, therefore, very aware not only of the benefits of such research but also some of the pitfalls to which we alert readers in this chapter. We can also assert with confidence that a well-crafted research design linked to a well-chosen picturebook, an open mind, careful observation and the ability to listen to what the children have to say can lead to worthwhile results, some of which are documented in Chapter 11.

Before we consider some pointers for a successful study, it is important to distinguish between research that simply 'uses' picturebooks as a convenient medium for gathering data about comprehension and storying and research that takes proper account of the aesthetic qualities of a picturebook with particular characteristics that impact on the reader in many complex ways. As Nodelman argues, it is also fundamental to think about what the work is for and what it might accomplish (2010: 18), and we would add that simply recording the 'interesting' things that children say, without having a strong theoretical framework to carry out in-depth analysis, does little to contribute to our understanding.

In all cases, issues of ethics regarding the reader must be considered as well as the crucial role of the mediator in this process, whether it is a researcher or a teacher. Effort should be made to avoid the pitfall of overgeneralisation from limited data noted by Nodelman. This can lead to the neglect of the picturebook itself, or to a contrived context or to research that fails to fully incorporate the children's voices. Finally, as Nodelman adds, it is important that the researcher be aware of the 'unspoken and taken-for-granted assumptions about both children and literature' and engage in 'self-critical thinking' which has 'the best chance of producing knowledge that is, if not generalisable, nevertheless usefully shareable' (2010: 17–18).

The picturebooks

Choosing a picturebook that has the potential for rich exploration is essential. Those that are multi-layered or display interesting tensions between word and image or have postmodern features or are aesthetically challenging often work best. As supervisors of such research, we were sometimes faced with the dilemma of not wishing to dampen the enthusiasm of a student (many of the 'students' we mention are in fact teachers) keen to use a particular picturebook but aware that it was unlikely to elicit a lively response in the children. On most occasions we were right and wished we had been firmer about steering the student to another book. Those fairly new to appreciation of visual literacy often take some time to see the potential of picturebooks and they may need solid support and several good examples to help novice researchers choose well for themselves.

Having selected a suitable picturebook, the next requirement is to analyse it insightfully and to do so they would be wise to engage in critical reading by more experienced researchers. On our Master's course at Cambridge, we set students the task of producing and then presenting to the whole group a PowerPoint analysing the key elements of the picturebook intended for use with children before the full research design is attempted. Although the students find this demanding, it makes them give serious attention to what is most important about their book and what they want to find out from the children.

The next issue to be grappled with is *deciding on a focus likely to be of interest to the age group concerned*, as no researcher would ever be able to probe all the possibilities in a picturebook. Once this has been determined, then decisions need to be made about which pages or spreads offer most potential. In our experience, most students begin by being too ambitious and have to learn to be more realistic about what can be managed in a short session.

Eliciting response

Our experience shows that where interviews take place, and how they are set up, can make a huge difference. Researchers need to consider important details such as where interviewer and interviewee sit, whether to share a book with a child or have one each, as well as avoiding noisy and distracting classrooms or problems that can be associated with the informality of working in children's homes.

If the decision was made to talk to children about their responses using semi-structured interviews, either individually or in pairs, or to conduct group discussions, the most frequent problems we encountered related to devising too many questions, often lacking focus and clarity, or questions which were too demanding (or too bland) for the age group with which they were working. A quick rule of thumb suggests that children younger than 7 will find about ten well-constructed questions an ideal number, whereas 10+ can manage up to twenty, the upper limit.

Apart from stamina and maintaining interest, another reason for not starting out with too many questions is that, depending on how the child responds, supplementary questions are likely to be asked. These can't always be prepared in advance so listening carefully to what the child has to say is essential. In terms of timing, half an hour is more than enough for under 7 year olds, and an hour is the maximum time you might spend with 10+. In our experience children aged 6 and under work better in pairs as being interviewed individually by an unfamiliar adult is too daunting for most young children.

The crucial role of good questions in eliciting quality responses from the children was highlighted again and again in our discussions. In interview situations children often think there are right answers they need to supply and strive to give the researcher/teacher the answers they think s/he wants. Children need to be reassured there are no right or wrong answers and that the researcher is simply interested in their views of the picturebook. The questions need to be carefully constructed and this is where a pilot study is beneficial so that they can be tried out on small numbers first and improved when necessary. Even so, children often needed a few easy questions, to which they gave straightforward answers, before getting into their stride. The simplest is often best: 'Tell me about this page.' 'Do you think Rosie might know she is being followed by a fox?' 'What makes you think that?' 'What' seems to be more comfortable than 'why?'

Most of our questions for the first edition of this book required children to probe the visual text analytically. Unlike the National Curriculum tests for reading print in England and Wales, which have a high percentage of information retrieval questions, we concentrated on questions that required children to use inference and deduction. Some of our personal response questions were demanding: 'Did the cover make you want to read *Zoo*?' (Why or why not?) 'What do you find interesting about the gorilla picture?' 'Would you describe *Zoo* as funny or serious?' (Why?)

A typical example of a question requiring inference would be 'Why do you think Anthony Browne showed a hamster on the title page before the story begins, when it's a book about going to the zoo?' Other questions focused on explaining textual evidence. For example: 'Did you notice anything special about the way Anthony Browne used colour/body language/perspective in *Zoo*?'

Although the younger readers found our questions taxing, the overall response to all three texts in our original study was very positive and the children appeared to find the experience interesting and the questions inviting. They also seemed to respond well to the fact that, when they volunteered information, we would often encourage them to probe more deeply. The rigour of the analysis and the amount of time devoted to considering a single picturebook appeared to surprise the children, but they also seemed to enjoy rising to the challenge. By the time they had the group discussion at the end of the day, instead of understandable reactions such as boredom or 'we've done this already', on most occasions children were eager to contribute, especially when we made it clear we wanted to move on from the earlier interviews. Like Kiefer's respondents in *The Potential of Picturebooks* (1995: 24) we found that 'children in all settings displayed an enthusiastic willingness to immerse themselves in the contents of their picture books'; however, we would not agree so wholeheartedly that 'verbal language seemed to give them the tools to understand these complex art objects', as some young children were only able to show their response visually.

In the interviews, all the researchers asked the same prescribed questions, though we took a fair amount of licence in asking supplementary questions when replies opened up interesting channels of discussion. In what follows, the first interview question was scripted; after that further questions were devised by interviewers on the spot, if it seemed worthwhile to pursue a line of enquiry. The following examples are typical of how we responded to the children to help them keep probing the meaning.

Sometimes all that was required was a simple 'Why?' or 'Is there anything else you would like to say?'

INTERVIEWER: Do you think Anthony Browne is a good artist?
CHLOE (8): Yes, yes.
INTERVIEWER: Why?
CHLOE: Because he like thinks about the animals, then he like puts all the detail in them. And like because he's all serious, he puts horns up there [picture of Dad where the clouds behind him look like horns, a visual metaphor for the devilish way he is behaving]. It's clouds, and like he gets all the detail in the floors [a reference to Browne's hyper-real style and famous attention to detail in wooden floors, brick walls, etc.].
INTERVIEWER: What do you think Anthony Browne wants us to imagine in that picture?
SIMONE (10): Erm . . . to imagine that you're there so you can see everything.
INTERVIEWER: Now is it just about seeing everything or . . . ?
SIMONE: He makes us feel like you're in her shoes to make you feel how she's scared or you're in his shoes [the brother's] making her scared.

Other times the researchers asked thoughtful questions which meshed with what children appeared to be trying to express. Sometimes the questions had no effect and, despite our hunches that children were on the point of breakthrough, they remained clammed up. In this extract the interviewer wants to know whether Erin understands that Browne is suggesting that pets are often kept in captivity as well as more exotic animals in a zoo. She suspects that Erin understands this connection, as she has noticed many other subtle things about the book. But on this occasion, her questions do not elicit any further understanding from Erin.

INTERVIEWER: Why does Anthony Browne show us a picture of a hamster in a cage?
ERIN (7): Well a hamster is an animal and at the zoo you see animals.
INTERVIEWER: Is there any other reason for choosing the hamster?
ERIN: They're also in zoos and got funny cages.
INTERVIEWER: So why might he have chosen to put a hamster in a cage?
ERIN: I don't know.

At other times, the questions seemed to release previously unarticulated ideas. Without the supplementary questions, much of the children's knowledge and understanding would have remained unknown to us. In the extract that follows, the interviewer finds out by further questioning, not only that Paul feels empathy for the orang-utan's unhappiness, but that he also associates it with being caged and reads the animal's body language correctly.

INTERVIEWER: Why do you think we are not shown the orang-utan's face?
PAUL (5): Because he's sad?
INTERVIEWER: Why do you think he's sad?
PAUL: Because he's trapped in a cage.
INTERVIEWER: How does Anthony Browne show us that he's sad?
PAUL: Because he's trapped.

INTERVIEWER: How do you know that?
PAUL: Because there's a cage there [pointing].
INTERVIEWER: Is there any other way that Anthony Browne shows us that he's sad?
PAUL: Because he's sitting against the wall and won't show his face.

We have already mentioned the importance of having a clear focus for any line of questioning. However, some of the worst examples of picturebook research is when the interviewer concentrates so much on their particular emphasis that they fail to notice the children's replies show a different line of interest. You always need to be alert to how the children are responding and expect the unexpected.

Beyond the questions

In the previous chapters we have attempted to show *the possibilities and importance of obtaining data other than oral data, such as drawing and other forms of artwork and activities.* Finally, there is the issue of how best to analyse the data. We refer the reader back to earlier examples, especially Chapter 10. Categories used to analyse the data usually arise from the data itself and are based on a variety of theories, from linguistics to literary criticism, grounded theory and aesthetics. Another aspect of this type of research which needs a closer look is the way data has been classified and analysed. Many studies are not clear enough about how this was done and, in some cases, little account seems to be taken of other researchers' attempts to categorise response. We hope this book will go some way towards helping new researchers link their work to what others have already achieved, thus developing our knowledge of this burgeoning field.

Implications for pedagogy

Whether it is language or literacy skills, literary understanding or the exploration of curricular topics, it is clear that picturebooks have much to offer in terms of pedagogy. Many teachers are now turning to picturebooks for teaching but many others are still unsure about how to use them in the classroom and are uncomfortable about working with the images. It almost goes without saying that teachers need to be familiar with a wide range of picturebooks (and, ideally, including international examples) and have some knowledge of how they work before offering them to their pupils.

It is also the case that the pressures of the curriculum limit the time that can be spent with picturebooks and policies insist on a focus (and assessments) based on the written word. As some teachers have pointed out to us, it is all very well to look and talk about picturebooks with one child or small group, but what happens when there are 30 children in a classroom (and not enough copies to go round). There is not space in this book to explore using picturebooks in the classroom in any detail, but we hope that there are enough ideas and examples to give teachers a sense of what to aim for.

We would also urge teachers to read some of the studies mentioned in this book, such as those by Sipe, Pantaleo, and Serafini, who have worked alongside teachers and show not only what can be done in large classrooms but also how much teachers can contribute to the study (see also McAdam et al. 2014 for an account of the project 'Journeys from Images to Words', which attempted to address some of the concerns of teachers in using picturebooks).

Regarding teaching, what we found most important in our initial study, and what has also been highlighted in others that followed, are two essential points: first, that the picturebook is valued not only as a vehicle for learning but also as an aesthetic and cultural object; and second, that the children's responses are also valued and given space to emerge and develop. Whole class 'read alouds', projectors, 'big books' and the Internet (online picturebook archives) can help access the texts, and small group tasks allow children more in-depth discussion and collaborative learning. Allowing children to experience the text in a variety of ways, some more guided and some more independently, over different periods of time means there is opportunity for deep response to develop.

The children themselves can also be relied on to take the activities further if the teacher is enthusiastic and listens to what the children have to say. As Kiefer notes: 'When teachers gave children encouragement, opportunity and time to respond to picture books beyond the group read-aloud or individual reading sessions, children often chose a variety of ways to extend their initial reactions to books' (1993: 271). When a teacher has some training in art, or at least in understanding how images work, it can make a huge difference both to the quality of the children's own artwork and their ability to interpret visual text. The more picturebooks children are exposed to and the more experienced the teacher (or mediator), the more the children's critical sense of narrative and image will increase and be able to extend into further learning of literature, language and art.

Lane Smith's *It's a Book!* (2011) shows so much better than words alone something of the sheer joy of reading picturebooks. No gadgets required, just the child, the book and the story. It was our love of this dazzling and versatile genre, and our interest in its young audience, that made us undertake the research in the first place, and our devotion has not wavered in the intervening years. One of the great pleasures of teaching children's literature is watching a class (of students or children or teachers) new to picturebooks begin to appreciate the richness of these texts and to note the intellectual, aesthetic and emotional engagement start to happen. In addition, working with developing illustrators[1] as we have also done (though not discussed in this book), we have been privileged to see the process in action and been struck by the sheer inventiveness of the up-and-coming practitioners, as well as those already established. There is hardly a topic that has not been explored by picturebooks – from the most searing and challenging issues of our day (see Evans 2015a), to the reassuring and amusing for the very young. Of course, there are some publications that are bland or predictable; it is to the large quantity of rewarding, exciting, innovative and superbly illustrated picturebooks we want to draw readers' attention.[2]

We hope that the material presented here has inspired our readers to find out more about picturebooks, about how words and images interact in this unique artefact and how children understand and respond to them. We have attempted to show just how many exciting avenues for explorations there are; in fact, there are as many possibilities are there are good picturebooks. We conclude, therefore, by highlighting the pleasure of reading picturebooks, something we should not forget in all this talk of research! The delight a child takes from a picturebook is what is most important and should be encouraged. We do not want to suggest it should be interfered with through too many questions! We will leave the last word to Dave, aged 8: 'The pictures look so good. You just want to read it.'

Notes

1 We have had the pleasure of working for many years with Martin Salisbury and Pam Smy and their students taking the MA in Illustrated Books for Children at Anglia Ruskin University.
2 See Salisbury's *Play Pen: New Children's Book Illustration* (2007) and Salisbury and Styles' *Children's Picturebooks: The Art of Visual Storytelling* (2012) for suggestions of outstanding picturebooks.

Appendices

APPENDIX I

Questionnaire

Questions to be asked orally by teacher:

1 I like to read picturebooks now.
2 I used to like to read picturebooks.
3 I like to look at books on my own.
4 I like to talk about books with my friends and family.
5 Where do you do most of your reading (home/school)?
6 What types of books do you read most at home?

- finding out books
- stories
- magazines
- poetry
- comics
- picturebooks
- computer manuals
- other.

7 Do you prefer books, television and video, or computer games?
8 What videos do you watch?
9 What programmes do you watch on television?
10 What computer games do you play?
11 Have you read books by (chosen author: Anthony Browne/Satoshi Kitamura, other)?
12 My favourite picturebooks are:

PUPIL RESPONSE SHEET:

NAME: _____ AGE: _____

1. 🙂 😐 🙁 _____

2. 🙂 😐 🙁 _____

3. 🙂 😐 🙁 _____

4. 🙂 😐 🙁 _____

5. HOME   SCHOOL

6.
   FINDING OUT BOOKS   COMICS

   STORIES   PICTUREBOOKS

   MAGAZINES   COMPUTER MANUALS

   POETRY   OTHER

7. BOOKS   T.V. AND VIDEO   COMPUTER GAMES

8.

9.

10.

11. YES   NO   NOT SURE

12.

APPENDIX 2

Interview questions for Lily Takes a Walk

1 Does the cover make you want to read the book? Why? What does the cover make you think the book is going to be about and why?

2 What does the title page suggest to you?

3 [*first picture*] What are the expressions on Nicky's and Lily's faces? Why do you think they are different?

4 [*snake*] What's happening here? What are they looking at? Who's thinking that [*written text*]?

5 [*tree*] How do you think Nicky is feeling? Why?

6 [*shopping*] Tell me about this picture.

7 [*lampposts*] Would you like to be on this street on your own? Why/why not? Why doesn't Nicky look at the Dog Star like Lily? Why are the steps wobbly-looking? How does Satoshi Kitamura use colour in this picture?

8 [*Mrs Hall*] Who is Lily looking at? Where is Mrs Hall? What is Nicky barking at? Why do you think Lily and Nicky always seem to be looking in different directions?

9 [*bats*] Tell me about this picture. Where did that man come from? What else do you notice?

10 [*canal monster*] Tell me about this picture. What is Nicky doing? How do you know he is shaking? Do you notice anything that has appeared in the other pictures? Have you seen these in other books by Satoshi Kitamura?

11 [*dustbin monsters*] What sort of expression do you think Lily has on her face now? Where do you think she lives? Why? What sort of monsters are these?

12 [*supper*] What do you think Lily tells her Mum and Dad? Do you think Lily noticed any of the monsters? What do you think Nicky would like to tell Mum and Dad? How do you know? Tell me about these [*speech bubbles*]? What did Satoshi Kitamura need to know in order to draw this picture?

13 [*bedroom*] Tell me about this picture before and after lifting the flap. What's in Nicky's head now? Did Nicky imagine the monsters? Did Nicky imagine the mice? What do the mice want the ladder for?

14 [*bedroom*] Did you notice any other ladders in the other pictures/other Satoshi Kitamura books? Why do you think they are there? How does this picture of Lily's bedroom make you feel? What else do you notice?

15 Does *Lily* remind you of any other picturebooks? If so, which? Have you seen any other books by Satoshi Kitamura? Have you seen *Lily* before or is it new to you? Did you see any other things or patterns in the pictures that remind you of other books by Satoshi Kitamura?

16 What is your favourite picture? Could you show me how you read it?

17 Do you think the pictures are well done? Is Satoshi Kitamura a good artist? Why? Do you think the cover was good for what was going to happen?

18 Did you notice anything special about how Satoshi Kitamura used colour, body language, perspective? What do you notice about the way he draws? How does Satoshi Kitamura make ordinary things look like monsters?

19 Do you find the words or the pictures more interesting? Do they tell the same story in different ways? Would the words still be good without the pictures? Would the pictures still be good without the words?

20 Would you describe *Lily Takes a Walk* as a good book? Why?
21 Which do you like best: cartoons/films/videos/comics/computer games/other? Do any of those things help you with reading pictures in a picturebook?
22 Is there anything else you would like to tell me about the book?

APPENDIX 3

Interview questions for Zoo

1 Does the cover make you want to read the book? Why? What do the black and white wavy lines suggest to you?
2 Why do you think Anthony Browne chose black and white endpapers?
3 Why do you think Anthony Browne showed a hamster before the story begins when it's a book about going to the zoo?
4 What do you think the snail is doing in the first picture?
5 What do you notice about the people in the queue and on the next page? Why do you think Anthony Browne did that?
6 Tell me about the elephant and the people visiting the zoo?
7 Why do you think we are not shown the orang-utan's face? How do you think it is feeling?
8 What do you find interesting about the gorilla picture? Why? What do you think Anthony Browne wanted readers to feel about these animals in the zoo?
9 What do you think the last two pictures are about? What do you think Anthony Browne wants us to feel about zoos?
10 What do you think Anthony Browne wants us to feel about the family visiting the zoo?
11 What is your favourite picture? Could you show me how you read it?
12 Would you describe *Zoo* as a good book? Why?
13 Do you think the pictures are well done? Is Anthony Browne a good artist? Why?
14 Do you like programmes on TV/cartoons/film/video/comics/computer games? Which do you like best?
15 Do any of those things help you with reading pictures?
16 Did you notice anything special about how Anthony Browne used colour, body language, perspective?
17 Do you find the words or the pictures more interesting? Do they tell the same story in different ways? Would the words still be good without the pictures? Would the pictures still be good without the words?
18 Is there anything else you would like to tell me about the book? Does *Zoo* remind you of any other picturebooks? If so, which? Have you seen this book before or is it new to you?

APPENDIX 4

Interview questions for The Tunnel

1 Does the cover make you want to read the book? Why?
2 Tell me about the endpapers.

3 [*spread with sister in bed*] Tell me about this picture.
4 [*spread in junkyard*] Tell me about the differences between the brother and sister. What does this picture tell us about both of them? Why?
5 [*spreads where brother and sister go into tunnel*] Is there anything you want to tell me about these pictures?
6 [*2 spreads of forest*] Is there anything strange about these pictures? What do they make you think of? Can you see any animals in the forest? Why is there an axe? Who do you think has nailed the strips of wood to that tree/lit that fire/lives in that cottage?
7 How does it make you feel when the sister rescues the brother? Why is there a ring of stones around the boy? Why does it disappear and reappear as a ring of daisies?
8 Why are the children smiling at each other on the final page?
9 Tell me more about the football and book on the final endpapers. Is this the same as the front endpaper? Why not?
10 Does *The Tunnel* remind you of any other picturebooks? If so, which? Have you seen any other books by Anthony Browne? Have you seen *The Tunnel* before or is it new to you?
11 What is your favourite picture? Could you show me how you read it?
12 Would you describe *The Tunnel* as a good book? Why?
13 Do you think the pictures are well done? Is Anthony Browne a good artist? Why?
14 Which do you like best: cartoons/films/videos/comics/computer games/other? Do any of those things help you with reading pictures in a picturebook?
15 Did you notice anything special about how Anthony Browne used colour, body language, perspective?
16 Do you find the words or the pictures more interesting? Do they tell the same story in different ways? Would the words still be good without the pictures? Would the pictures still be good without the words?
17 Is there anything else you would like to tell me about the book?

APPENDIX 5

Follow-up interview questions

1 Have you seen this book since we read it last time? Have you seen any other Anthony Browne/Satoshi Kitamura picturebooks? What about any other interesting picturebooks you've seen recently?
2 Do you remember the book or would you like to read it again? Tell me what you remember most about this book.
3 What do you remember most about the way things look?
4 What does Anthony Browne/Satoshi Kitamura want to make the people who read this picturebook think about?
5 Why do you think Anthony Browne/Satoshi Kitamura make us look at things this way in this picture [*Zoo*: gorilla; *The Tunnel*: junkyard; *Lily*: alley with skip]? Does it make you read the book in a different way?

6   What goes on in your head as you look at the pictures? Is it the same as when you watch a programme on TV, a film, or play a computer game? What about a book without pictures?

7   How do you think each artist decides what to write as words and what to draw in the pictures?

Questions for each book

Lily Takes a Walk

1   Tell me about the way Satoshi Kitamura draws lines.

2   Do you remember that Lily and Nicky are always looking in different directions? Now that you've looked at it again, what does that tell us about them?

3   Quite a few people noticed that Satoshi Kitamura drew rubbish in some of the pictures. What do you think he's trying to tell us?

The Tunnel

1   How do the endpapers take you into the story?

2   Why do you think Anthony Browne chose to draw things that remind us of fairy tales?

3   Why does Rose look so happy at the end?

Zoo

1   Partly this book is about an ordinary family's day out. What is Anthony Browne saying about families?

2   What do you think Anthony Browne thinks of cages and prisons?

3   After thinking about this, why do you think he made the cover this way and the endpapers black and white?

4   Everyone mentioned that the humans are turning into animals. What is happening to the animals? What is he trying to tell us about the differences between humans and animals?

APPENDIX 6

Codes for data analysis

Levels of interpretation

- no explanation given
- mis-readings (wrong)
- literal explanation
- implausible/imaginative explanation but not supported by either text or illustrations
- plausible/based on information from narrative

- critical understanding, awareness of significance in relation to whole, including ethical and moral issues
- engaged description
- interrogation: superficial/engaged, anticipation
- imaginative deduction.

Categories of perception

- significant details: including artist's games or 'tricks' and apparent incompleteness/incoherence
- intratextual references
- visual features: appreciation of craft/colours, patterns, etc.
- relationship between text and picture
- empathy: elementary, complex, expectations
- analogy: personal, drawing on own experience
- intertextual references
- artist's intentions
- implied audience
- awareness of own reading/viewing process
- characters: 'inner-standing', motives, relationships, expectations
- atmosphere/mood
- genre awareness
- book/story knowledge, including bibliographic aspects
- world knowledge.

Some of these codes were adapted from Thomson (1987).

APPENDIX 7

PhD Theses 2005–2015

Bagelman, C. (2015) 'Picturing transformative texts: anti-colonial learning and the picture-book', University of Glasgow, at: http://theses.gla.ac.uk/6134/

Diamond, M. S. (2008) 'The impact of text-picture relationships on reader recall and inference making: a study of fourth graders' responses to narrative picturebooks', Temple University, Philadelphia, at: http://digital.library.temple.edu/cdm/ref/collection/p245801coll10/id/6680

Haywood, S. F. (2011) 'Lacunae and potential in the development of talking stories and their use to support literacy in the early years', University of the West of England, Bristol, at: http://ethos.bl.uk/OrderDetails.do?did=3&uin=uk.bl.ethos.573387

McGuire, C. E. (2013) 'Children's writing and talk in a postmodern picturebook study group', University of Pennsylvania, at: http://repository.upenn.edu/dissertations/AAI3594832/

Mourão, S. (2012) 'English picturebook illustrations and language development in early years education', University of Aveiro, Portugal, at: http://ria.ua.pt/handle/10773/9180

Noble, K. (2007) 'Picture thinking: the development of visual literacy in young children', The University of Cambridge, at: https://www.educ.cam.ac.uk/people/doctoralstudents/theses/

Prior, L. A. (2012) 'There is more to the story . . . support for children's construction of meaning from contemporary picturebook read-alouds', The University of Texas, at San Antonio, at: http://gradworks.umi.com/35/08/3508835.html

Rietschlin, A. C. (2012) 'Children's responses to global literature read alouds in a second grade classroom', The Ohio State University, at: https://etd.ohiolink.edu/!etd.send_file?accession=osu1336438346&disposition=inline

Sheu, H. C. (2005) 'Reading stories as digging for treasure: the educational values and challenges of using English picture story books in Taiwan', University of York, at http://ethos.bl.uk/OrderDetails.do?did=6&uin=uk.bl.ethos.425456

Stacey, A. (2011) 'Young children's oral and artistic responses to five picturebooks by Anthony Browne', University of Victoria (Canada), at: http://sunzi.lib.hku.hk/ER/detail/hkul/4846219

Thomas, L. C. (2010) 'Exploring second graders' understanding of the text–illustration relationship in picture storybooks and informational picture books', Kansas State University, at http://krex.k-state.edu/dspace/handle/2097/3679

Tsai, J. P. (2010) 'Journeying: young children's responses to picture books of traumatic and sensitive issues', University of Warwick, at: http://wrap.warwick.ac.uk/34620/

Willson, A.M. (2013) 'Examining children's comprehension of conventional, wordless, and postmodern picturebooks', The University of Texas at San Antonio, at: http://gradworks.umi.com/35/63/3563271.html

Bibliography

Picturebooks and apps

Browne, A. (1979) *Bear Hunt*, London: Hamish Hamilton.

——(1983) *Gorilla*, London: Julia MacRae Books.

——(1987) *Piggybook*, London: Magnet.

——(1989) *The Tunnel*, London: Julia MacRae Books.

——(1992) *Changes*, London: Walker Books.

——(1994) *Zoo*, London: Red Fox (first published by Julia MacRae Books, 1992).

——(1997) *Willy the Dreamer*, London: Walker Books.

——(1999) *Voices in the Park*, London: Picture Corgi.

——(2000) *Willy's Pictures*, London: Walker Books.

——(2001) *My Dad*, London: Picture Corgi.

——(2003) *The Shape Game*, London: Doubleday.

Carter, D. A. (2011) *Spot the Dot* [Mobile App], Ruckus Mobile Media, available from: itunes.apple.com (accessed 24/04/2015).

——(2013) *Spot the Dot*, New York: Scholastic.

Dunbar, P. (2008) *Penguin*, London: Walker.

Harper, M. (2013) *The Animal Alphabet Picture Book for Toddlers (The Essential Kindle Learning Tool for Every Young Child)* [Mobile App], available from: amazon.com (accessed 24/04/2015).

Hutchins, P. (1970) *Rosie's Walk*, London: Bodley Head.

Kitamura, S. (1983) (with H. Oram) *Angry Arthur*, London: Andersen Press.

——(1989) *UFO Diary*, London: Andersen Press.

——(1992) (with H. Oram) *A Boy Wants a Dinosaur*, London: Red Fox.

——(1994) *In the Attic*, London: Andersen Press.

——(1997) *Lily Takes a Walk*, London: Happy Cat Books.

Originator Inc. (2013) *Endless Alphabet* [Mobile App], Version 1.9, available from: itunes.apple.com (accessed 24/04/2015).

Sendak, M. (1993) *We Are All in the Dumps with Jack and Guy*, New York: HarperCollins Publishers.

Smith, L. (2011) *It's a Book*, London: Macmillan.

Stone, J. (1999) *There's a Monster at the End of this Book*, Illus. Michael Smollin, New York: Golden Books.

——(2013) *The Monster at the End of This Book* [Mobile App], Illus. Michael Smollin. Version 5.1, available at: itunes.apple.com (accessed 24/04/2015).

Wiesner, D. (2001) *The Three Pigs*, London: Andersen Press.

Bibliography

Adomat, D. S. (2010) 'Dramatic interpretations: performative responses of young children to picturebook read-alouds', *Children's Literature in Education*, 41(3): 207–221.

Albers, P. (2008) 'Theorizing visual representation in children's literature', *Journal of Literacy Research*, 40(2): 163–200.

Allan, C. (2012) *Playing with Picturebooks: Postmodernism and the Postmodernesque*, New York: Palgrave Macmillan.

Anstey, M. (2002) '"It's not all black and white": postmodern picture books and new literacies', *Journal of Adolescent and Adult Literacy*, 45(6): 444–457.

Anstey, M. and Bull, G. (2000). *Reading the Visual: Written and Illustrated Children's Literature*, Sydney: Harcourt Australia.

——(eds) (2002) *Crossing the Boundaries*, Sydney: Pearson.

——(2009) 'Developing new literacies: responding to picturebooks in multiliterate ways', in Evans, J. (ed.) *Talking Beyond the Page: Reading and Responding to Picturebooks*, London: Routledge, 26–43.

Arizpe, E. (2009) 'Sharing visual experiences of a new culture: immigrant children in Scotland respond to picturebooks and other visual texts', in Evans, J. (ed.) *Talking Beyond the Page: Reading and Responding to Picture Books*, Abingdon: Routledge, 134–151.

——(2010) '"It was all about books": picturebooks, culture and metaliterary awareness' in Colomer, T., Kümmerling-Meibauer, B. and Silva-Díaz, C. (eds) *New Directions in Picturebook Research*. New York: Routledge, 69–82.

——(2013) 'Meaning-making from wordless (or nearly wordless) picturebooks: what educational research expects and what readers have to say', *Cambridge Journal of Education*, 43(2): 163–176.

——(2014) 'Wordless picturebooks: critical and educational perspectives on meaning-making' in Kümmerling-Meibauer, B. (ed.) *Aesthetic and Cognitive Challenges of the Picturebook*, London: Routledge, 91–108.

Arizpe, E., Bagelman, C., Devlin, A. M, Farrell, M. and McAdam, J. E. (2014) 'Visualizing intercultural literacy: engaging critically with diversity and migration in the classroom through an image-based approach', *Language and Intercultural Communication*, 14(3): 304–321.

Arizpe, E. and Blatt, J. (2011) 'How responses to picturebooks reflect and support the emotional development of young bilingual children' in Kümmerling-Meibauer, B. (ed.) *Emergent Literacy: Children's Books from 0 to 3*, Amsterdam: John Benjamins.

Arizpe, E., Colomer, T. and Martínez-Roldán, C. with Bagelman, C., Bellorín, B., Farrell, M., Fittipaldi, M., Grilli, G., Manresa, M., Margallo, A. M., McAdam, J., Real, N. and Terrusi, M. (2014) *Visual Journeys through Wordless Narratives: An International Inquiry with Immigrant Children and 'The Arrival'*, London: Bloomsbury Academic.

Arizpe, E., Farrell, M. and McAdam, J. (eds) (2013) *Picturebooks: Beyond the Borders of Art, Narrative and Culture*, London: Routledge.

Arizpe, E. and McAdam, J. (2011) 'Crossing visual borders and connecting cultures: children's responses to the photographic theme in David Wiesner's *Flotsam*', *New Review of Children's Literature and Librarianship*, 17(2): 227–243.

Arizpe, E. and Styles, M. (2003) *Children Reading Pictures: Interpreting Visual Texts* (1st edn), London: Routledge.

——(2008) 'A critical review of research into children's responses to multimodal texts', in Flood, J., Heath, S. B. and Lapp, D. (eds) *Handbook of Research on Teaching Literacy through the Communicative and Visual Arts*, New York: Lawrence Erlbaum Associates, 363–373.

Arizpe, E. and Styles, M. with Cowan, K., Mallouri, L. and Wolpert, M. A. (2008) 'The voices behind the pictures: children responding to postmodern picturebooks', in Sipe, L.R. and Pantaleo, S. (eds) *Postmodern Picturebooks: Play, Parody and Self-Referentiality*, London: Routledge, 207–222.

Arnheim, R. (1966) *Towards a Psychology of Art*, Berkeley: University of California Press.
——(1970) *Visual Thinking*, London: Faber.
——(1989) *Thoughts on Art Education*, Santa Monica, CA: Getty Center for Education in the Arts.
Australia's National Curriculum (ACARA) (2013) *The Australian Curriculum*, accessed (02/05/2015) at: http://www.australiancurriculum.edu.au/GeneralCapabilities/literacy/organising-elements/visual-knowledge
Avgerinou, M. and Ericson, J. (1997) 'A review of the concept of visual literacy', *British Journal of Educational Technology*, 28(4): 280–291.
Bader, B. (1976) *American Picture Books: From Noah's Ark to the Beast Within*, New York: Macmillan.
Balgazette, C. and Buckingham, D. (2013) 'Literacy, media and multimodality: a critical response', *Literacy*, 47(2): 95–102.
Barrs, M. and Cork, V. (2001) *The Reader in the Writer*, London: Centre for Language in Primary Education.
Bartlett, F. C. (1932) *Remembering: A Study in Experimental and Social Psychology*, Cambridge: Cambridge University Press.
Bearne, E. (2003) 'Rethinking literacy: communication, representation and text', *Reading Literacy and Language*, 37(3): 98–103.
——(2004) 'Multimodal texts: what they are and how children use them', in Evans, J. (ed.) *Literacy Moves On*, London: David Fulton, 16–30.
——(2009) 'Multimodality, literacy and texts: developing a discourse', *Journal of Early Childhood Literacy*, 9(2): 156–187.
Bednall, J., Cranston, L. and Bearne, E. (2008) 'The most wonderful adventure . . . going beyond the literal', *English Four to Eleven*, 32: 19–26.
Benson, C. (1986) 'Art and language in middle childhood: a question of translation', *Word and Image*, 2(2): 123–140.
Biesta, G. (2005) 'What can critical pedagogy learn from postmodernism? Further reflections on the impossible future of critical pedagogy', in Gur-Ze'ev, I. (ed.) *Critical Theory and Critical Pedagogy Today: Toward a New Critical Language in Education*, Haifa, Israel: University of Haifa Press, 143–159.
Bland, J. (2013) *Children's Literature and Learner Empowerment: Children and Teenagers in English Language Education*, London: Bloomsbury Academic.
Botelho, M. and Rudman, M. (2009) *Critical Multicultural Analysis of Children's Literature: Mirrors, Windows and Doors*, New York: Routledge.
Braid, C. and Finch, B. (2015) '"Ah, I know why . . .": children developing understandings through engaging with a picture book', *Literacy*, published online doi: 10.1111/et.12057.
Bromley, H. (2000) '"Never be without a Beano!" Comics, children and literacy', in Anderson, H. and Styles, M. (eds) *Teaching through Texts: Promoting Literacy through Popular and Literary Texts in the Primary Classroom*, London: Routledge, 29–42.
Brooks, W. and Browne, S. (2012) 'Towards a culturally situated reader response theory', *Children's Literature in Education*, 43(1): 74–85.
Bruner, J. S. (1962) *On Knowing: Essays for the Left Hand*, Cambridge, MA: Harvard University Press.
——(1983) *Child's Talk: Learning to Use Language*, Oxford: Oxford University Press.
——(1986) *Actual Minds, Possible Worlds*, London: Harvard University Press.
Bull, G. and Anstey, M. (2010) *Evolving Pedagogies: Reading and Writing in a Multimodal World*, Victoria: Curriculum Press.
Cai, M. (2008) 'Transactional theory and the study of multicultural literature', *Language Arts*, 85(3): 212–220.
Callow, J. (2008) 'Show me: principles for assessing students' visual literacy', *The Reading Teacher*, 61(8): 616–626.

Callow, J. and Zammit, K. (2002) 'Visual literacy: from picturebooks to electronic texts', in Monteith, M. (ed.) *Teaching Primary Literacy with ICT*, Buckingham: Open University Press, 188–201.

Campagnaro, M. (2015) '"These books made me really curious": how visual explorations shape young readers' taste', in Evans. J. (ed.) (2015) *Challenging and Controversial Picturebooks: Creative and Critical Responses to Visual Texts*, London: Routledge.

Carger, C. L. (2004) 'Art and literacy with bilingual children', *Language Arts*, 81(4): 283–292.

Carr, N. (2010) *The Shallows: How the Internet Is Changing the Way We Read, Think and Remember*, New York: Atlantic Books.

Cedeira Serantes, C. (2011) 'Faster than books and more involved than movies: understanding the contemporary reading experience of young adult readers of graphic novels and comic books', in *Proceedings of the Annual Conference of CAIS /Actes du congrès annuel de l'ACSI*, accessed (04/05/2015) at: http://www.cais-acsi.ca/ojs/index.php/cais/issue/view/27

Chambers, A. (1993) *Tell Me: Children, Reading and Talk*, Exeter: Thimble Press.

Chang, A, Tilahun, L. and Breazeal, C. (2014) 'Visualisations of data from the Literacy Tablet Reading Project in Rural Ethiopia', Presentation at Electronic Visualisation and the Arts (EVA 2014), accessed (23/04/2015) at: http://www.bcs.org/upload/pdf/ewic_ev14_s9paper2.pdf

Clark, K. (1960) *Looking at Pictures*, London: John Murray.

Comber, B. (2001) 'Critical literacy: power and pleasure with language in the early years', *The Australian Journal of Language and Literacy*, 24(3): 168–181.

Cox, M. (1992) *Children's Drawings*, London: Penguin.

Crawford, P. A. and Hade, D. (2000) 'Inside the picture, outside the frame: semiotics and the reading of wordless picture books', *Journal of Research in Childhood Education*, 15(1): 66–80.

Cummins, J. (1996) *Negotiating Identities: Education for Empowerment in a Diverse Society*, Ontario: California Association for Bilingual Education.

Cuperman, R. C. (2013) 'Prejudice and stereotypes revealed through reader responses in pre-school students', *New Review of Children's Literature and Librarianship*, 19(2): 119–138.

Davies, J. and Brember, I. (1993) 'Comics or stories? Differences in the reading attitudes and habits of girls and boys in Years 2, 4 and 6', *Gender and Education*, 5(3): 305–320.

Davis, J. (1993) 'Why Sally can draw: an aesthetic perspective', *Educational Horizons*, 71(2): 86–93.

de Kerckhove, D. (1997) *Connected Intelligence: The Arrival of the Web Society*, Toronto: Somerville House Publishing.

Debes, J. (1968) 'Some foundations for visual literacy', *Audiovisual Instruction*, 13: 961–964.

Dewey, J. (1978) *Art as Experience*, New York: Doubleday.

Dondis, D. A. (1973) *A Primer of Visual Literacy*, Cambridge, MA: MIT Press.

Doonan, J. (1991) 'Satoshi Kitamura: aesthetic dimensions', *Children's Literature*, 19: 107–137.

——(1993) *Looking at Pictures in Picture Books*, Exeter: Thimble Press.

——(1999) 'Drawing out ideas: a second decade of Anthony Browne', *The Lion and the Unicorn*, 23(1): 30–56.

Dresang, E. (1999) *Radical Change: Books for Youth in a Digital Age*, New York: The H.W. Wilson Company.

Edwards D. and Mercer, N. (1987) *Common Knowledge*, London: Routledge.

Enever, J. and Schmid-Shonbein, G. (eds) (2006) *Picture Books and Young Learners of English*, Munich: Langenscheidt ELT GmbH.

Erickson, F. (1986) 'Qualitative methods in research on teaching', in Wittrock, M. C. (ed.) *Handbook of Research on Teaching* (3rd edn), New York: Macmillan, 119–161.

Evans, J. (ed.) (1998) 'What's in the picture? Responding to illustrations in picture books', London: Sage.

——(ed.) (2009a) *Talking Beyond the Page: Reading and Responding to Picturebooks*, London: Routledge.

——(2009b) 'Creative and aesthetic responses to picturebooks and fine art', *Education 3–13: International Journal of Primary, Elementary and Early Years Education*, 37(2): 177–190.

——(2011) 'Do you live a life of Riley? Thinking and talking about the purpose of life in picture-book responses', *New Review of Children's Literature and Librarianship*, 17(2): 189–209.

——(ed.) (2015a) *Challenging and Controversial Picturebooks: Creative and Critical Responses to Visual Texts*. London: Routledge.

——(2015b) 'Could this happen to us? Responding to issues of migration in picturebooks', in Evans, J. (ed.) *Challenging and Controversial Picturebooks: Creative and Critical Responses to Visual Texts*, London: Routledge.

Farrell, M., Arizpe, E. and McAdam, J. (2010) 'Journeys across visual borders with *The Arrival* by Shaun Tan: annotated spreads as a method for understanding pupil's creation of meaning through visual images', *Australian Journal of Language and Literacy* 33(3): 198–210.

Fisher, R. (1998) *Teaching Thinking: Philosophical Enquiry in the Classroom*, London: Cassell.

Formby, S. (2014) *Children's Early Literacy Practices at Home and in Early Years Settings: Second Annual Survey of Parents and Practitioners,* London: National Literacy Trust.

Freire, P. (2008) *Education for Critical Consciousness*, London: Continuum.

Gardner, H. (1973) *The Arts and Human Development*, New York: John Wiley & Sons.

——(1980) *Artful Scribbles*, London: Jill Norman Limited.

——(1982) *Developmental Psychology*, Boston, MA: Little Brown and Co.

Gee, J. P. (2005) *An Introduction to Discourse Analysis: Theory and Method* (2nd edn), New York: Routledge.

Ghosh. K. (2015) 'Who's afraid of the big bad wolf: responses to the portrayal of wolves in picturebooks', in Evans, J. (ed.) *Challenging and Controversial Picturebooks: Creative and Critical Responses to Visual Texts*, London: Routledge.

Glaser, B. and Strauss, A. (1967) *The Discovery of Grounded Theory*, Chicago, IL: Aldine Publishing Co.

Goldstone, B. P. (2004) 'The postmodern picture book: a new subgenre', *Language Arts* 81(3): 196–204.

Gombrich, E. H. (1962) *Art and Illusion*, London: Phaidon Press.

Graham, J. (1990) *Pictures on the Page*, Sheffield: NATE.

Gregory, E. (1997) *Making Sense of a New World: Learning To Read in a Second Language*, London: Paul Chapman.

Gregory, E. and Biarnès, J. (1994) 'Tony and Jean-François looking for sense in the strangeness of school', in Dombey, H. and Meek, M. (eds) *First Steps Together*, Stoke-on-Trent: Trentham Books.

Hartman, H. (2013) *What Colors Do You Eat?* Unite for Literacy, accessed (24/04/2015) at: http://uniteforliteracy.com/book?BookId=163

Heath, S. B. (1983) *Ways with Words*, Cambridge: Cambridge University Press.

——(2000) 'Seeing our way into learning', *Cambridge Journal of Education*, 30(1): 121–132.

——(2006) 'Dynamics of completion: gaps, blanks, and improvisation', in Turner, M. (ed.) *The Artful Mind*, New York: Oxford University Press, 133–152.

Heath, S. B., and Wolf, J. L. (2012) 'Brain and behavior: the coherence of teenage response to YA literature', in Hilton, M. and Nikolajeva, M. (eds) *Contemporary Adolescent Literature and Culture: The Emergent Adult*, Farnham: Ashgate, 139–154.

Heath, S. B., and Wolf, S. (2004) *Visual Learning in the Community School*, London: Arts Council England, Creative Partnerships.

Heathcote, D. (1983) *Learning, Knowing and Language in Drama*, Milton Keynes: Open University Press.

Hogan, P. C. (2011) *What Literature Teaches Us about Emotion,* New York: Cambridge University Press.

Hortin, A. J. (1982) 'A need for a theory of visual literacy', *Reading Improvement*, 19(4): 257–267.

Hudelson, S., Smith, K. and Knudsen Hawes, L. (2005) '"Have you ever used this book with children?" Elementary children's responses to "bilingual" picture books', in Cohen, J.,

McAlister, K. T., Rolstad, K. and MacSwan, J. (eds) *ISB4: Proceedings of the 4th International Symposium on Bilingualism*, Somerville, MA: Cascadilla Press, 1053–1061.

International Children's Digital Library, http://en.childrenslibrary.org

Iser, W. (1978) *The Act of Reading: A Theory of Aesthetic Response*. London: Johns Hopkins University Press.

Isaacson, A. (2014) 'Are tablets the way out of child illiteracy?' accessed (24/04/2015) at: http://www.smithsonianmag.com/ist/?next=/innovation/are-tablets-way-out-child-illiteracy-180952826/

Johnston, I. and Bainbridge, J. (eds) (2013) *Reading Diversity through Canadian Picture Books: Preservice Teachers Explore Identity, Ideology and Pedagogy*, Toronto: University of Toronto Press.

Kamler, B. and Comber, B. (1997) 'Critical Literacies: politicising the language classroom', accessed (02/07/12) at: http://www.schools.ash.org.au/litweb/barb1.html

Kellog, R. (1979) *Children's Drawings, Children's Minds*, New York: Avon.

Kiefer, B. (1993) 'Children's responses to picture books: a developmental perspective', in Holland, K. (ed.) *Journeying: Children Responding to Literature*, London: Heinemann, 267–283.

——(1995). *The Potential of Picturebooks: From Visual Literacy to Aesthetic Understanding*, Upper Saddle River, NJ: Prentice-Hall.

Kress, G. (1997) *Before Writing: Rethinking Paths to Literacy*, London: Routledge.

——(2003) *Literacy in the New Media Age*, London: Routledge.

——(2010) *Multimodality: A Social Semiotic Approach to Contemporary Communication*, London: Routledge.

Kress, G. and van Leeuwen, T. (1996) *Reading Images: The Grammar of Visual Design*, London: Routledge.

——(2006) *Reading Images: The Grammer of Visual Design* (2nd edn), London: Routledge.

Kümmerling-Meibauer, B. (1999) 'Metalinguistic awareness and the child's developing concept of irony: the relationship between pictures and text in ironic picture books', *The Lion and the Unicorn*, 23(2): 157–183.

——(ed.) (2014) *Picturebooks: Representation and Narration*, London: Routledge.

Kümmerling-Meibauer, B. and Meibauer, J. (2013) 'Towards a towards a cognitive theory of picturebooks', *International Research in Children's Literature*, 6(2): 143–160.

——(2015) 'Maps in picturebooks: cognitive status and narrative functions', *BFLT Nordic Journal of Childlit Aesthetics*, accessed (24/04/15) at: http://www.childlitaesthetics.net/index.php/blft/article/view/26970%20-%20article

Langer, S. (1942) Philosophy in a New Key: A Study in the Symbolism of Reason, Rite and Art. Cambridge, MA: Harvard University Press.

(1953) *Feeling and Form: A Theory of Art Developed from Philosophy in a New Key*, London: Routledge and Kegan Paul.

——(1990) *Philosophy in a New Key: A Study in the Symbolism of Reason, Rite and Art*, (3rd edn), Cambridge, MA: Harvard University Press.

Leonard, M. A., Lorch, E. P., Milich, R. and Hagans, N. (2009) 'Parent–child joint picturebook reading among children with ADHD', *Journal of Attention Disorders,* 12(4): 361–371.

Lewis, D. (1990) 'The constructedness of texts: picturebooks and the metafictive', *Signal*, 61(3): 131–146.

——(1996) 'Going along with Mr Gumpy: polysystemy and play in the modern picture book', *Signal*, 80: 105–119.

——(2001) *Reading Contemporary Picturebooks*, London: RoutledgeFalmer

Lewis, D. and Greene, J. (1983) *Your Children's Drawings: Their Hidden Meanings*, London: Hutchinson.

Lichtman, M. (2012) *Qualitative Research in Education: A User's Guide* (3rd edn), London: Sage.

Lohfink, G. and Loya, J. (2010) 'The nature of Mexican American third graders' engagement with culturally relevant picture books', *Bilingual Research Journal*, 33(3): 346–363.

Lott, C. (2001) 'Picture books in the high school English classroom', in Ericson, B. (ed.), *Teaching Reading in High School English Classes*. Urbana, IL: National Council of Teachers of English, 139–154.

Luke, A. and Freebody, P. (1997) 'Shaping the social practices of reading', in Muspratt, S., Luke, A. and Freebody, P. (eds) *Constructing Critical Literacies: Teaching and Learning Textual Practice*, Cresskill, NJ: Hampton Press Inc, 185–225.

Lysaker, J. T. (2006) 'Young children's readings of wordless picture books: what's "self" got to do with it?', *Journal of Early Childhood Literacy*, 6(1): 33–55.

Lysaker, J. T. and Miller, A. (2013) 'Engaging social imagination: the developmental work of wordless book reading', *Journal of Early Childhood Literacy*, 13(2): 147–174.

Lysaker, J. and Sedberry, T. (2015) 'Reading difference: picture book retellings as contexts for exploring personal meanings of race and culture', *Literacy*, 49(2): 105–111.

Mackey, M. (2003) '"The most thinking book": attention, performance and the picturebook', in Styles, M. and Bearne, E. (eds) *Art, Narrative and Childhood,* Stoke-on-Trent: Trentham Books.

——(2007) *Literacies across Media: Playing the Text* (2nd edn), London: RoutledgeFalmer.

——(2011) *Narrative Pleasures in Young Adult Novels, Films, and Video Games*, Basingstoke: Palgrave Macmillan.

Madura, S. (1998) 'An artistic element: four transitional readers and writers respond to the picture books of Patricia Polacco and Gerald McDermott', *National Reading Conference Yearbook*, 47: 366–376.

Manguel, A. (1997) *A History of Reading*, London: Flamingo.

Marshall, E. (2015) 'Fear and Strangeness in picturebooks: fractured fairy tales, graphic knowledge and teachers concerns', in Evans, J. (ed.) *Challenging and Controversial Picturebooks: Creative and Critical Responses to Visual Texts,* London: Routledge.

Martin, N. (2009) *Art as an Early Intervention Tool for Children with Autism*, London: Jessica Kingsley Pub.

Martin, T. and Leather, B. (1994) *Readers and Texts in the Primary Years*, Buckingham: Open University Press.

Martínez, M. and Roser, N. L. (2003) 'Children's responses to literature', in Flood, J., Lapp, D., Squire, J. R. and Jensen, J. M. (eds) *Handbook of Research on Teaching the English Language Arts* (2nd edn), Marwah, NJ: Erlbaum, 799–813.

Martínez-Roldán, C. M., and Newcomer, S. (2011) 'Reading between the pictures: immigrant students' interpretations of the arrival', *Language Arts*, 88(3): 188–197.

McAdam, J. E., Arizpe, E., Devlin, A. M., Farrell, M., and Farrar, J. (2014) 'Journeys from images to words', Project Report, Esmée Fairbairn Foundation.

McCarty, T. (1993) 'Language, literacy and the image of the child in American Indian classrooms', *Language Arts*, 70(3): 182–192.

McClay, J. (2000) '"Wait a second . . . ": negotiating complex narratives in *Black and White*', *Children's Literature in Education*, 31(2): 91–106.

McGilp, E. (2014) 'From picturebook to multilingual collage: bringing learners' first language and culture into the pre-school classroom', *Children's Literature in English Language Education*, 2(2): 31–49.

McGonigal, J. and Arizpe, E. (2007) *Learning to Read a New Culture: How Immigrant and Asylum Seeking Children Experience Scottish Identity through Classroom Books*, Report: Edinburgh: Scottish Government, accessed (23/04/2015) at http://www.scotland.gov.uk/Publications/2007/10/31125406/0

McGuire, C., Belfatti, M. and Ghiso, M. (2008) '"It doesn't say how?": third graders' collaborative sense-making from postmodern picturebooks', in Sipe, L. R. and Pantaleo, S. (eds) *Postmodern Picturebooks: Play, Parody and Self-Referentiality,* London: Routledge, 193–206.

Medina, C. (2010) 'Reading across communities in biliteracy practices: examining translocal discourses and cultural flows in literature discussions', *Reading Research Quarterly*, 45(1): 40–60.

Meek, M. (1988) *How Texts Teach What Readers Learn,* Stroud: Thimble Press.

Merchant, G. (2014) 'Young children and interactive story-apps', in Burnett, C. Davies, J. Merchant, G. and Rowsell, J. (eds) *New Literacies around the Globe: Policy and Pedagogy,* New York: Routledge, 121–137.

Mines, H. (2000) 'The relationship between children's cultural literacies and their readings of literary texts', Ph.D. thesis, University of Brighton.

Mitchell, W. J. T. (1986) *Iconology: Image, Text and Ideology,* Chicago, IL: University of Chicago Press.

——(1994) *Picture Theory: Essays on Verbal and Visual Representation,* Chicago, IL: University of Chicago Press.

Moll, L.C., Amanti, C., Neff, D. and Gonzalez, N. (1992) 'Funds of knowledge for teaching: using a qualitative approach to connect homes and classrooms', *Theory Into Practice,* 31(2): 132–141.

——(2005) 'Funds of knowledge for teaching: using a qualitative approach to connect homes and classrooms', in González, N., Moll, L. C. and Amanti, C. (eds) *Funds of Knowledge: Theorizing Practices In Households, Communities, and Classrooms,* Mahwah, NJ: Lawrence Erlbaum, 71–87.

Møller Daugaard, L. and Blok Johansen, M. (2014) 'Multilingual children's interaction with metafiction in a postmodern picture book', *Language and Education,* 28(2): 120–140.

Mourão, S. (2012), 'Response to the "The Lost Thing": notes from a secondary classroom', *Children's Literature in English Language Education,* 1(1): 81–105.

——(2015) 'What's real and what's not: playing with the mind in wordless picturebooks', in Evans. J. (ed.) *Challenging and Controversial Picturebooks: Creative and Critical Responses to Visual Texts,* London: Routledge.

Mroz, M., Smith, F. and Hardman, F. (2000) 'The discourse of the literacy hour', *Cambridge Journal of Education,* 30(3): 379–390.

New London Group (1996) 'A pedagogy of multiliteracies: designing social futures,' *Harvard Educational Review,* 66(1): 60–92.

Nikolajeva, M. (2012) 'Reading other people's minds through word and image', *Children's Literature in Education,* 43(3): 273–291.

——(2013) 'Picturebooks and emotional literacy', *The Reading Teacher,* 67(4): 249–254.

——(2014) *Reading for Learning: Cognitive Approaches to Children's Literature,* Amsterdam: John Benjamins.

Nikolajeva, M. and Scott, C. (2000) 'The dynamics of picturebook communication', *Children's Literature in Education,* 31: 225–239.

—— (2001) *How Picturebooks Work,* London: Garland.

Nikola-Lisa, W. (1994) 'Play, panache, pastiche: postmodern impulses in contemporary picture books', *Children's Literature Association Quarterly,* 19(1): 35–40.

Nodelman, P. (1988) *Words about Pictures: The Narrative Art of Children's Picture Books,* London: University of Georgia Press.

——(2008) *The Hidden Adult: Defining Children's Literature,* Baltimore: Johns Hopkins University Press.

——(2010) 'On the border between implication and actuality: children inside and outside of picture books', *Journal of Children's Literature Studies,* 7(2): 1–21.

O'Brien, J. (1994) 'Critical literacy in an early childhood classroom: a progress report', *The Australian Journal of Language and Literacy,* 17(1): 36–44.

——(2001) '"I knew that already": how children's books limit inquiry' in Boran, S. and Comber, B. (eds) *Critiquing Whole Language and Classroom Inquiry,* Urbana, IL: National Council of Teachers of English, 142–168.

O'Brien, J. and Comber, B. (2001) 'Negotiating critical literacies with young children', in Barratt-Pugh, C. and Rohl, M. (eds) *Literacy Learning in the Early Years,* Buckingham: Open University Press, 152–171.

Oslick, M. E. (2013) 'Children's voices: reactions to a criminal justice issue picture book', *The Reading Teacher*, 66(7): 543–552.

Painter, C., Martin, J. R. and Unsworth, L. (2013) *Reading Visual Narratives*, Sheffield: Equinox.

Paley, V. G. (2005) *A Child's Work: The Importance of Fantasy Play*, Chicago: University of Chicago Press.

Pantaleo, S. (2002) 'Grade 1 children meet David Wiesner's three pigs', *Journal of Children's Literature*, 28(2): 72–84.

——(2004a) 'Young children and radical change characteristics in picturebooks', *The Reading Teacher*, 58(2): 178–187.

——(2004b) 'Young children interpret the metafictive in Anthony Browne's *Voices in the Park*', *Journal of Early Childhood Literacy*, 4(2): 211–233.

——(2005) 'Young children engage with the metafictive in picture books', *Australian Journal of Language and Literacy*, 28(1): 19–37.

——(2008) *Exploring Student Response to Contemporary Picturebooks*, Toronto: University of Toronto Press.

——(2009a) 'Exploring children's responses to the postmodern picturebook, *Who's Afraid of the Big Bad Book?*' in Evans, J. (ed.) *Talking Beyond the Page: Reading and Responding to Picturebooks*, London: Routledge, 44–61.

——(2009b) 'The influence of postmodern picturebooks on three boys' narrative competence', *Australian Journal of Language and Literacy*, 32(3): 191–210.

——(2010) 'Developing narrative competence through reading and writing metafictive texts', *Literacy Research and Instruction*, 49(3): 264–281.

——(2011a) 'Grade 7 students reading graphic novels: "You need to do a lot of thinking"', *English in Education*, 45(2): 113–131.

——(2011b) 'Middle years students' collaborative talk about *The Red Tree*: "A book that really works your mind"', *Australian Journal of Language and Literacy*, 34(3): 260–278.

——(2011c) 'Warning: a grade 7 student disrupts narrative boundaries', *Journal of Literacy Research*, 43(1): 39–67.

——(2012a) 'Exploring the intertextualities in a grade 7 student's graphic narrative', *L1-Educational Studies in Education and Literature,* 12(1): 23–55.

——(2012b) 'Meaning-making with colour in multimodal texts: one 11-year-old student's purposeful "doing"', *Literacy*, 46(3): 147–155.

——(2012c) 'Middle-school students reading and creating multimodal texts: a case study', *Education 3–13: International Journal of Primary, Elementary and Early Years Education,* 40(3): 295–314.

——(2012d) 'Middle years students thinking with and about typography in multimodal texts', *Literacy Learning: The Middle Years*, 20(1): 37–50.

——(2013) 'Paneling "matters" in elementary students' graphic narratives', *Literacy Research and Instruction*, 52(2): 150–171.

——(2014) 'Reading images in graphic novels: taking students to a "greater thinking level"', *English in Australia*, 49(1): 38–51.

——(2015) 'Filling the gaps: exploring the writerly metaphors in Shaun Tan's *The Red Tree*', in Evans, J. (ed.) *Challenging and Controversial Picturebooks: Creative and Critical Responses to Visual Texts*, London: Routledge.

Pantaleo, S. and Bomphray, A. (2011) 'Exploring grade 7 students' written responses to Shaun Tan's *The Arrival*', *Changing English: Studies in Culture and Education*, 18(2): 173–185.

Paris, A. H. and Paris, S. G. (2001) 'Children's comprehension of narrative picture books: CIERA Report 3–012', accessed (24/04/2015) at: http://www.ciera.org/library/reports/inquiry-3/3-012/3-012.html

Parsons, M. J. (1987) *How We Understand Art*, Cambridge: Cambridge University Press.

Perkins, D. (1994) *The Intelligent Eye: Learning to Think by Looking at Art*, Cambridge, MA: Harvard Graduate School of Education.

Piaget, J. (1997) *The Origin of Intelligence in the Child*, London: Routledge.

Prior, L., Willson, A. and Martínez, M. (2012) 'Picture this: visual literacy as a pathway to character understanding', *The Reading Teacher*, 66(3): 195–206.

Quenqua, D. (2014) 'Is E-reading to your toddler story time, or simply screen time?' accessed (24/04/2015) at: http://www.nytimes.com/2014/10/12/us/is-e-reading-to-your-toddler-story-time-or-simply-screen-time.html

Ramos, A. M. and Ramos, R. (2012) 'Ecoliteracy through imagery: a close reading of two wordless picture books,' *Children's Literature in Education*, 42(4): 325–349.

Raney, K. (1998) 'A matter of survival: on being visually literate', *The English and Media Magazine*, 39: 37–42.

Reifel, S. (2007) 'Hermeneutic text analysis of play: exploring meaningful early childhood classroom events', in Amos Hatch, J. (ed.) *Early Childhood Qualitative Research*, London: Routledge, 25–42.

Rogoff, B. (1990) *Apprenticeship in Thinking: Cognitive Development in Social Context*, New York: Oxford University Press.

Rosen, B. (1989) *And None of It Was Nonsense*, London: Mary Glasgow Publications.

Rosenblatt, L. M. (1978) *The Reader, The Text, The Poem: The Transactional Theory of the Literary Work*, Carbondale, IL: Southern Illinois University Press.

——(1982) 'The literary transaction: evocation and response', *Theory into Practice*, 21: 268–277.

——(1986) 'The aesthetic transaction', *Journal of Aesthetic Education*, 20(4): 122–128.

Salisbury, M. (2007) *Play Pen: New Children's Book Illustration*, London: Lawrence King Publishing.

Salisbury, M. and Styles, M. (2012) *Children's Picturebooks: The Art of Visual Storytelling*, London: Laurence King.

Sedgwick, D. and Sedgwick, F. (1993) *Drawing to Learn*, London: Hodder & Stoughton.

Sendak, M. (1988) Caldecott and Co: Notes a Books and Pictures. London: Reinhardt Books.

——(1994a) *Caldecott and Co: Notes on Books and Pictures*, London: Reinhardt Books.

——(1994b). *Preface. I Dream of Peace: Images of War*, New York: UNICEF HarperCollins.

Serafini, F. (2002) 'A journey with the Wild Things: a reader response perspective in practice', *Journal of Children's Literature*, 28(1): 73–79.

——(2005) 'Voices in the park, voices in the classroom: readers responding to postmodern picture books', *Literacy Research and Instruction*, 44(3): 47–64.

——(2009) 'Understanding visual images in picturebooks', in Evans, J. (ed.) *Talking Beyond the Page: Reading and Responding to Picturebooks*, Abingdon: Routledge, 10–25.

——(2014) *Reading the Visual: An Introduction to Teaching Multimodal Literacy*, New York: Teachers College Press.

Serafini, F. and Ladd, S. M. (2008) 'The challenge of moving beyond the literal in literature discussions', *Journal of Language and Literacy Education*, 4(2): 6–20.

Short, K. (2004) 'Building teachers' understandings of art as meaning-making in picture books', *International Reading Association Journal of Children's Literature and Reading: The Dragon Lode*, 22(2): 12–18.

Short, K. G. and Thomas, L. (2011) 'Developing intercultural understandings through global children's literature', in Meyer, R. J. and Whitmore, K. F. (eds) *Reclaiming Reading: Teachers, Students, and Researchers Regaining Spaces for Thinking and Action*, New York: Routledge, 149–162.

Siegler, R. S. (2000) 'The rebirth of children's learning', *Child Development Journal*, 71(1): 26–35.

Sinatra, R. (1986) *Visual Literacy Connections to Thinking, Reading and Writing*, Springfield, IL: Charles C. Thomas.

Sipe, L. R. (1996) 'First and second graders construct literary understanding during readalouds of picture storybooks', Unpublished doctoral dissertation, The Ohio State University.

——(1998) 'How picture books work: a semiotically framed theory of text–picture relationships', *Children's Literature in Education*, 29(2): 97–108.

——(1999) 'Children's response to literature: author, text, reader, context', *Theory into Practice*, 38(3): 120–129.

——(2000) '"Those 2 gingerbread boys could be brothers": how children use intertextual connections during storybook readalouds', *Children's Literature in Education*, 31(2): 73–88.

——(2001) 'A palimpsest of stories: young children's construction of intertextual links among fairytale variants', *Reading Research and Instruction*, 40(4): 335–352.

——(2008a) *Storytime: Young Children's Literary Understanding in the Classroom*, New York: Teachers College Press.

——(2008b) 'Young children's visual meaning making in response to picturebooks', in Flood, J., Heath, S. B. and Lapp, D. (eds) *Handbook on Research in Teaching Literacy through the Communicative and Visual Arts*, London: Lawrence Erlbaum, 381–391.

——(2011) 'Young children's responses to picture storybooks: five types of literary understanding', Seminar, Universitat Autònoma, Barcelona, accessed (18/04/2015) at: http://literatura.gretel.cat/sites/default/files/barcelona_lecture.pdf

Sipe, L. R., and Brightman, A. (2005) 'Young children's visual meaning-making during readalouds of picture storybooks', *National Reading Conference Yearbook*, 54: 349–361.

——(2009) 'Young children's interpretations of page breaks in contemporary picture storybooks', *Journal of Literacy Research*, 41(1): 68–103.

Sipe, L. R., and Ghiso, M. P. (2005) 'Looking closely at characters: how illustrations support children's understandings of character through picturebook illustrations', in Roser, N. and Martínez, M. (eds) *What a Character! Character Study as a Guide to Literary Meaning Making in Grades K-8*, Newark: International Reading Association, 134–153.

Sipe, L. R. and McGuire, C. E. (2006a) 'Picturebook endpapers: resources for literary and aesthetic preparation', in *Children's Literature in Education*, 37(4): 291–304.

——(2006b) 'Young children's resistance to stories', *The Reading Teacher*, 60(1): 6–13.

Sipe, L. R. and Pantaleo, S. (eds) (2008) *Postmodern Picturebooks: Play, Parody and Self-Referentiality*, London: Routledge.

——(2012) 'Diverse narrative structures in contemporary picturebooks: opportunities for children's meaning-making', *Journal of Children's Literature*, 38(1): 6–15.

Smith, V. (2000) 'Developing critical reading: how interactions between children, teachers and text support the process of becoming a reader', Ph.D. thesis, University College, Worcester.

——(2005) *Making Reading Mean*, Herts: United Kingdom Literacy Association.

——(2009) 'Making and breaking frames: crossing the borders of expectation in picturebooks', in Evans, J. (ed.) *Talking Beyond the Page: Reading and Responding to Picturebooks*, Routledge: London, 81–97.

Strauss, A. J. (1987) *Qualitative Analysis for Social Scientists*, Cambridge: Cambridge University Press.

Strauss, A. and Corbin, J. (1998) *Basics of Qualitative Research: Techniques and Procedures for Developing Grounded Theory* (2nd edn), Thousand Oaks, CA: Sage.

Street, B. (1984) *Literacy in Theory and Practice*, Cambridge: Cambridge University Press.

Styles, M. (1996) 'Inside the tunnel: a radical kind of reading – picture books, pupils and post-modernism', in Watson, V. and Styles, M. (eds) *Talking Pictures*, London: Hodder & Stoughton.

Styles, M. and Bearne, E. (eds) (2003) *Art, Narrative and Childhood*, Stoke-on-Trent: Trentham Books.

Suhor, C. and Little, D. (1988) 'Visual literacy and print literacy: theoretical considerations and points of contact', *Reading Psychology*, 9(4): 469–481.

Swaggerty, E. (2009) '"That just really knocks me out": fourth grade students navigate post-modern picture books', *Journal of Language and Literacy Education*, 5(1): 9–31.

Thomson, J. (1987) *Understanding Teenagers' Reading*, Melbourne: Methuen.

Tucker, N. (1974) 'Looking at pictures', *Children's Literature in Education*, 14: 37–51.

Unite for Literacy, http://uniteforliteracy.com

Unsworth, L. and Wheeler, J. (2002) 'Re-valuing the role of images in reviewing picture books', *Reading Literacy and Language*, 36(2): 68–74.

Unsworth, L., Thomas, T., Simpson, A. and Asha, J. (2005) *Children's Literature and Computer Based Teaching*, Berkshire: Open University Press.

van der Pol, C. (2012) 'Reading picturebooks as literature: four-to-six-year-old children and the development of literary competence', *Children's Literature in Education*, 43(1): 93–106.

van Renen, C. (2011) 'Having their say: engaging with contemporary picture books at work and at play', *Journal of Literary Studies*, 27(2): 1–25.

Vermeule, B. (2010) *Why Do We Care about Literary Characters?* Baltimore: Johns Hopkins University Press.

Vygotsky, L. (1978) *Mind in Society*, M. Cole, V. John-Steiner, S. Scribner and E. Suberman (eds) Cambridge, MA: Harvard University Press.

——(1986) *Thought and Language*, A. Kozulin (ed.) Cambridge, MA: MIT Press.

Walsh, M. (2003) '"Reading" pictures: what do they reveal? Young children's reading of visual texts', *Reading Literacy and Language*, 37(3): 123–130.

——(2006) 'The "textual shift": examining the reading process with print, visual and multimodal texts', *Australian Journal of Language and Literacy*, 29(1): 24–37.

Walsh, M., Cranitch, M. and Maras, K. (2012) 'Into the deep end: the experience with Flotsam in Australia', *TESOL in Context. Special Edition S3*, accessed (24/04/2015) at: http://www.tesol.org.au/Publications/Special-Editions

Watson, V. (1993) 'Multi-layered texts and multi-layered readers', *Cambridge Journal of Education*, 23(1): 15–24.

——(1996) 'The left-handed reader: linear sentences and unmapped pictures', in Watson, V. and Styles, M. (eds) *Talking Pictures*, London: Hodder & Stoughton, 145–163.

Watson, V. and Styles, M. (eds) (1996) *Talking Pictures: Pictorial Texts and Young Readers*, London: Hodder and Stoughton.

Wells, G. (1986) *The Meaning Makers*, London: Hodder & Stoughton.

Williams, C. and McLean, M. (1997) 'Young deaf children's responses to picturebook reading in a pre-school setting', *Research in the Teaching of English*, 31(3): 337–366.

Wolf, M. (2007) *Proust and the Squid: The Story of Science and the Reading Brain*, New York: HarperCollins.

Wolf, M., Gottwald, S., Galyean, T., Morris, R. and Breazeal, C. (2014) 'The reading brain, global literacy, and the eradication of poverty', *Bread and Brain, Education and Poverty*, accessed (24/04/2015) at: http://www.casinapioiv.va/content/dam/accademia/pdf/sv125/sv125-wolf.pdf

Wolfberg, P. J. (1999) *Play and Imagination in Children with Autism*, New York: Teachers' College Press.

Yannicopoulou, A. (2004) 'Visual aspects of written texts: preschoolers view comics', *L1–Educational Studies in Language and Literature*, 4(2–3): 169–181.

Youngs, S. and Serafini, F. (2013) 'Discussing picturebooks across perceptual, structural and ideological perspectives', *Journal of Language and Literacy Education*, 9(1): 185–200.

Zickuhr, C. (2013) 'In a digital age, parents value printed books for their kids', Pew Research Center, accessed (04/05/2015) at: http://www.pewresearch.org/fact-tank/2013/05/28/in-a-digital-age-parents-value-printed-books-for-their-kids/

Index